Jackson County, Tennessee Chancery Court Minutes Volume A November 1840- February 1851

Pat Spurlock

Jackson County, Tennessee Chancery Court Minutes Volume A November 1840-February 1851.

Copyright © 2012 Pat Spurlock.

ISBN-13: 978-1480101500

ISBN-10: 1480101508

INTRODUCTION

There are few early Jackson County records due to the August 1872 courthouse fire so these abstracts are important to the genealogist and historian looking for official information prior to that time.

This work is an abstraction of records on microfilm at the Tennessee State Library and Archives. No pertinent information was omitted, only redundant legalese which is indicated by an ellipsis. In many cases, the entire record is given. Front material has been updated as of 2012 but the transcriptions are just as found in the original volume published in 1999. Original page numbers are the first item listed at each abstract with subsequent page numbers given in parentheses throughout the abstract. Spelling and grammatical errors were retained. Comments are footnoted with names and places fully indexed and set in boldface by this transcriber.

Researchers should request a copy of the actual document as proof. To obtain copies write the Tennessee State Library and Archives requesting a "County Records Form." They provide one form at a time at no cost to you. When you fill out the form, make a notation that the record is found on Jackson County Microfilm Reel 1, County Court Minutes, Volume A, and give the page number of the original record. Return the completed form and you will receive a reply in a few weeks. The archives will inform you of their copy fees after locating the record. Their address is: Tennessee State Library and Archives, Public Services Section, 403 Seventh Avenue North, Nashville, Tennessee 37219-5041.

I hope you enjoy using this book and it makes it easier for you to work with your Jackson County families.

Pat Spurlock

JACKSON COUNTY, TENNESSEE CHANCERY COURT MINUTES
VOLUME A NOVEMBER 1840-FEBRUARY 1851

Page 1: District of Jackson County, **4 November 1840**. **Bromfield Ridley**, Chancellor, 4th Division appeared in the Court House in Gainesborough. **George M. McWhorter** appointed Clerk & Master of the Chancery Court ... George M. McWhorter, **Nathaniel G. Jackson, Watson M. Cooke, Richard P. Brooks, Amos J. Chapman** and **James G. Quarles** (Page 2) all of Jackson County are bound to **James K. Polk** Governor of Tennessee ... George M. McWhorter appointed for six years. /S/ George M. McWhorter, Watson M. Cook, A. J. Chapman, Nathaniel G. Jackson, Rich'd P. Brooks, Jas. G. Quarles and B. L. Ridley.

Page 3: ... **George M. McWhorter, Nathaniel G. Jackson, Watson M. Cooke, Richard P. Brooks, Amos J. Chapman** and **James G. Quarles** all of (Jackson County) are held and firmly bound unto **William Fose** Trustee for said county in the sum of $5500.00 ... James G. Quarles, **John A. Minnis**, (Page 4) **Samuel Turney** ... admitted as Solicitors of said court. **David G. Shepherd** and **James M. Shepherd** petition for the sale of land for **Augustus Shepherd** et al ... notice has been published in the <u>Republican Banner</u> a newspaper printed at **Nashville** ... it would be in the interest of said heirs that lands be sold for the purpose of division.

Page 4: **George D. Allen** Vs **Hugh P. Allen** Administrator. Final Decree ... upon the word of **Alexander Montgomery** to whom this cause was referred by the parties to wit: It appears from schedule marked A that **Michael Henry** has received of the joint funds over and above what George Allen had recd $101.15 and (Page 5) there yet remains an undivided $155.101/2 out of which George Allen would be entitled to $101.151/2 ... that George D. Allen surrender to Hugh P. Allen Admin. of M. Henry all the notes debts or property of whatever description belonging to the partnership. /S/ Hugh P. Allen and George D. Allen, both by X-mark ... that complainant deliver to (the) administrator of Michael Henry all the notes debts or property of whatsoever description belonging to said partnership and ... defendant pay to the complainant forty two dollars and sixty nine and a half cents and the costs herein.

Page 5: **Chisms Heirs**. Exparte ... On petition of **Nancy Trigg Chism** and **Priscilla Francis Chism** by their Guardian **Mounce Gore** and **Ann Frances Chism** the former minor heirs of **James Chism**, dec'd and the latter his relict it appeared to the court that said James Chism died seized in fee simple of a tract of land in Jackson County on a branch of **Doe Creek** the boundaries of which are particularly set forth in the petition including the tan yard and Burk Mill & also two town lots in **Gainesborough** Nos. 55 & 56 on which **Tollivar Kirkpatrick** now lives and that said Chism died intestate ... referred to the Master to report whether the widow relinquishes her dower and if not what is (Page 6) her dower.

Page 6: **Richard F. Cooke** Vs **Nicholas Cheek**. Motion ... the defendant by his counsel ... as relates to the injunction on his real estate be over ruled ... injunction remain in full force.

Page 6: **Avery (?) M. Hicklin** Vs **Adonis C. Hamilton**. Motion ... came the defendant by his counsel and moved the court that the complainant be ruled to security for the said defendant if it shall appear that he has wrongfully sued out his writ of attachment.

Page 6: **John Williams** Vs **Thomas L. Clements** et al. Motion to file Cross Bill ... came **Jesse McClellen** by his counsel ... time is given him till Monday the 9th Novr [sic] 1840 to file his cross bill.

Page 7: **David G. Shepherd** and **James M. Shepherd** Vs **Augustine Shepherd** et al. Final Decree ... **Sarah Baker Shepherd** died seized of 5 tracts of land in Jackson County worth as follows-to wit-one tract containing 80 acres $7.50 per acre ... one tract containing 15 acres worth $6.75 per acre-one tract containing 150 acres worth 62 1/2 cents per acre one tract containing 30 acres in which the widow of **John Shepherd** dec'd age 27 years has dower, worth $5.50 per acre-one tract containing 4 1/2 acres well improved in which the widow also has dower worth $115 per acre-one improved town lot worth $250 & unimproved town lots in **Granville** worth $27 each-one other unimproved town lot worth $15-that said land lies principally on the waters of **Cumberland River** and **Martin's Creek** and there are no springs on any of it save one on the lower tract which contains 80 acres ... that it would be to the advantage and interest of the heirs of said **Sarah Baker** decd that said lands should be sold and the proceeds distributed among them ... and decreed by the court that the Master sell the lands ... at public auction upon the premises ... (Page 8) ....

Page 8: **Settle's Heirs** and Executor. Exparte ... **Joel L. Settle** died in the County of Jackson having first bequeathed the whole of real & personal property to his wife **Jane Settle** during her lifetime in widowhood and on the happening of either event the same to be equally divided amongst his children and that said **Jane** has departed this life leaving complainants **Lafayette**, **Sydney**, **Tecumseh**, **Sewell**, **Tipton** and **Joel** their children surviving. It also appeared to the court that the land and negroes particularly described in the petition are not susceptible of division or partition, and it being suggested to the court here that it is obviously to the advantage of all parties interested that the land and negroes be sold....

Page 9: **Settles Heirs** and Executor Exparte to Final Decree ... examined **Joshua R. Stone** and **William Gipson** touching the matters in said interlocutory decree ... the land and negroes be sold with a view to a division and the Master reports the minimum cash value of the two tracts is $2000. To be sold at public auction in Gainesborough after advertising at three or more of the most public places in the county and in some one of the newspapers published in Nashville....

Page 10: **Chisms Heirs** and Widow. Exparte. Final Decree ... examined **James G. Quarles** and **Richard P. Brooks** ... it is obvious to the interest of all parties that the town lots and land be sold ... with equitable division ... The Master further reports that widows dower is worth and that the minimum value of the lots and land is as follows-to wit-the house and lots are worth $200. The tan yard and Burk mill is worth $500 and the widow's dower $250 ... respectively submitted-**Geo. M. McWhorter** ... land including tan yard and the house and lots to be sold at public auction upon a credit until the first day of February next ... and report to the next term (Page 11). The court adjourned. /S/ **Bronfield [sic] Ridley**.

Page 11: **May Term 1841**. Held at the court house in Gainesboro on the first Monday being the 3rd day of May, **Bromfield L. Ridley** Chancellor.

Page 11: **Nicholas Cheek** Vs **Richard F. Cooke** ... continued ... to the next term ... defendant permitted to take the depositions of **William Billingsley**, **William Fose**, **Thomas Murry** and **Henry Richmond** touching the general character and credit of **William Shaden** and cross examine **William H.? Hughes**....

Page 11: **William Johnson** Vs **Enoch Carter** et al. O.B.[1] ... defendant is allowed to take the depositions of **William Q. Hughes**, **Eli Jackson** and **Sady Middleton** to be read in said case.

Page 11: **Settles Heirs.** Exparte ... (Page 12) ... (Page 13) Report of sale pursuant to decree made in this case at the November Term. One tract of land containing 565 acres ... purchased

---
[1] The term "O.B." is used throughout the original minute book. It stands for "Original Bill."

by **Perry Mahaney** for $2400 due in one and two years with **Thomas L. Bransford** and **Sam E. Hare** security. One tract containing 110 acres purchased by **Joel Lynn** for $810 with **Thomas L. Bransford** and Sam E. Hare security. One negro man **Willie** purchased by **Joseph Eaton** for $702 with **Russell M. Kinnaird** and **Merlin Young** security. One negro woman **Maria** and child purchased by **Joel Lynn** for $780 with Thomas L. Bransford and Sam E. Hare security. One negro girl **Harriett** purchased by **Joseph J. Walker** for $652 with **John B. Haile** and **Nicholas Haile** securities. One negro girl **Rachel** purchased by **Richard P. Brooks** for $300 with **Sam E. Hare** and **James W. Lock** security ... two negro boys **Randal** and **Anderson** purchased by **Andrew Whitley** for the following prices: **Randal** for $405. Fifty dollars of which was paid in cash and **Anderson** for $406 for which negroes the Master reports that he took the note of Merlin Young for $271.95–one 12 months after date with Joseph Eaton and **Andrew Whitley** security and the note of **Alexander Montgomery** and **Andrew Whitley** security ... and that the title to the following described tract ... Beginning on a maple tree standing on the bank of **Cumberland River Edwin F. McKinney's** south west corner, running east with McKinney's south boundary line (Page 14) his South East corner in all 540 poles to a stake in the North East corner of the original survey. Thence South with the East boundary line of said original tract 200 poles to a stake. Thence West with **Pharris'** North boundary line 254 poles to a beach tree the beginning corner of the part of said tract purchased by Joel Lynn. Thence with the line of said **Lynn's** tract North 45 1/2 º West 46 poles to a stake on the top of a high ridge thence North 42º West with the ... dividing line between **Raccoon** and **Coonskin** branches 44 poles to two beech trees thence West 24 poles to a beech thence North 67º East 8 poles to a stake in the middle of **Hurricane branch** thence South 29º West 28 poles to a stake in the middle of said branch. Thence South 75º West 24 poles to a box elder thence South 77º West 48 poles to a stake thence South 55º West 16 poles to a beech tree marked M.G. thence North 86º West 8 poles to a stake on the bank of Cumberland River thence North 10º West up said river with its various meanders to the beginning. Containing 565 acres more or less to be divested out of **LaFayette Settle, Sidney Settle, Tecumse Settle, Sewell Settle, Tipton Settle** and **Joel Settle** heirs and distributed of **Joel L. Settle** decd and vested in said Perry Mahanay and his heirs and that a lien be retained upon said land until the purchase money is paid. That the title to the following ... land ... Beginning at a beech tree standing in the North boundary line of **Nathan Pharris'** tract of land running thence North 451/2º West with the various coles(?) on Perry Mahanay's line to Cumberland river–thence down said river with its various meanders 88 poles to a small forked lynn sapling standing on the bank of said river it being the North West corner of **Nathan Pharris'** tract of land on which he now lives. Thence East with Pharris North boundary line 248 poles to the beginning. Containing 110 acres, more or less, be divested out of said heirs and distributed of said Joel L. Settle deceased and vested in said Joel Lynn and his heirs containing a lien upon the land for the purchase money–that the right in the said negro man **Willie** aged about 30 years be divested out of the heirs and distributed of said Joel L. Settle deceased and vested in said **Joseph Eaton** and his heirs. That the right in the negro woman **Maria** aged about 28 years and her child be divested out of said heirs and distributed of said Joel L. Settle deceased and vested in (Page 15) **Joel Lynn** and his heirs and that the title to the negro girl **Harriet** be divested out of the heirs and distributed of said Joel L. Settle dec'd and vested in **Joseph L. Walker** and his heirs. That the right of property in the negro girl **Rachel** be divested out of the heirs and distributed of said **Joel L. Settle** deceased and vested in **Richard P. Brooks** ... the right of property in the two negro boys **Randal** and **Anderson** be divested out of the said heirs and distributed of said Joel L. Settle deceased and vested in **Anderson Whitley** and his heirs and that a lien be retained on all of said negroes until the purchase money is paid ... **James T. Quarles** is allowed $35 as a fee for attending to the interest of the minors as a solicitor and the same be paid him by the administrator of **Jane Settle** decd ... that **Mounce Gore**, Administrator of Jane Settle dec'd pay the costs of this suit ....

Page 15: Tuesday morning **4 May 1841**. **David G. Shepherd** and **James M. Shepherd** vs **Augustin Shepherd**, **Thomas Baker** guardian of the children of **Sarah Baker** formerly **Sarah Shepherd**, **Jesse George Shepherd**, **Joseph S. Perkins** and his wife **Nancy** formerly **Nancy Shepherd**, **Garland Farrar** and his wife **Mary L.** formerly **Mary L. Shepherd**, **Martin B. Shepherd**, **Thomas Shepherd**, **Benjamin A. Shepherd** and **Joseph H. Shepherd**. Decree ... David G. & James M. Shepherd vs (Page 16) Augustin Shepherd et al. Report of sale pursuant to a decree made in this case at the November Term 1840 Court for Jackson County. On the 5 December a public sale was held upon the premises all the property mentioned was purchased as follows: 84 acre tract, the 15 acre tract, the 4 1/2 acre tract, the 30 acre tract and the improved town lot were purchased by **David G.** & **James M. Shepherd** for $1804 due in one and two years with **John Hughes** security. The four unimproved town lots were bought by **Mark H. Morrow** for $125 due in one and two years with **James M. Shepherd** security and that the 150 acre tract was purchased by **Leonard Huff** for $190. $50 of which was paid in cash and the ballance falling in one and two years with **William Huff** security ....

Page 16: **Christopher Sharr**[2] vs **Avery K. Lancaster**. O.B. (Page 17) ... on the 4th day of August 1839 the complainant and defendant entered into partnership in the grocery business for the term of two years ... the parties have not fully settled all their accounts growing out of said partnership. Ordered that the Master take an accounting of all the partnership accounts not already settled.

Page 17: **Ridley Roberts** et al. Exparte Petition. It appearing ... Ridley Roberts and **George W. C. Shaw** were joint owners of a tract of 100 acres in Jackson County and that George W. C. Shaw departed this life intestate leaving **Martha Shaw** his Widow and **Burchet Shaw**, **Matilda Shaw** and **Rebecca Shaw** his heirs at law all are minors and Martha Shaw their guardian. Court orders the land to be sold ....

Page 18: **Martha Shaw** et al vs **Christopher Sharr** and **Rollins Hogin**. O.B. Ordered that an account of all the partnership and transactions between Christopher Sharr **Samuel Shaw** and **George W. C. Shaw** be taken. And the defendant Christopher Sharr file a cross bill on or before the 1st Monday in June next.

Page 18: **David Herbert** vs **James McBroom** et al. O.B. On affidavit of defendant McBroom this cause is continued to the next term and said McBroom is allowed to take the depositions of **Hezekiah Dean**, **Matthew Cowan** and **Thaxton Carter** to be read as evidence in this cause.

Page 18: **Chisms Heirs** and Widow. Exparte Petition ... Report of sale (Page 19) pursuant to a decree made at the Nov. Term 1840 for Jackson County. From the sale at the court house door in Gainesboro all the land and town lots were purchased by **Tollivar Kirkpatrick** for $800 for which he gave two notes due 1st Feb. 1841 to-wit: One on said Tollivar and **Thomas D. Cassetty** with **Sampson W. Cassetty** security and one on said Tollivar and Thomas D. Cassetty with **Russel M. Kinnaird** security for $275. A lien is retained upon said land and town lots for the further security of the purchase money ... Said land is in Jackson County on **Doe Creek** bounded as follows–beginning at a stake in the North boundary line of the town of Gainesborough one foot west of the house opposite to the tan yard running thence eastwardly with the north boundary line of said town 194 feet to a stake in said line thence North ten degrees west to a stake thence South eighty degrees west 174 feet to a stake thence South ten degrees east 99 feet to the beginning containing nineteen thousand two hundred and six square feet including the tan yard and bark(?) mill. And town lots 55 and 56. All divested out of said

---

[2] The surname appears to be SHARR but it may be SHAW. Both Shaw and Shares/Sharer are found in local records.

Nancy Trigg Chism and **Priscilla Frances Chism** heirs of said **James Chism** decd. The right of dower in said lands is divested out of said **Ann F. Chism** widow of said decd. And that the title to said land including the tan yard aforesaid and town lots be vested in Tolivar Kirkpatrick and his (Page 20) heirs ....

Page 20: **Settles Heirs.** Exparte Petition ... **Joel Settle** decd died seized and possessed of a lot adjoining the town of Gainesboro on the West and North of the road leading from said town to Fort Blount containing not more than half an acre with dwelling house and other improvements on the same and the petitioners are his heirs at law. Ordered the same to be sold for the purpose of division among said devisees ... Court adjourned.

Page 22: November Term, 1841. Held at the court house in Gainesboro for the District of Jackson County in the 4th Chancery Division on the first Monday it being 1 November 1841. **Bromfield L. Ridley** Chancellor.

Page 22: **David Herbert** vs **James McBroom** et al ... continued to next term. Defendant to be allowed to take the depositions of **Henry L. Tucker** and **Mark Cameron**, **Ridley Roberts**, **Thomas Johnson**, **Hugh Stewart**, **Matthew Cowan**, **Samuel Enocs**, **Adderson Mattocks** and **Champ Stanton** touching the general character of **Hezekiah Dunn**. Defendant to pay the cost of continuance, the costs of the depositions ....

Page 22: **Martha Shaw** et al vs **Christopher Sharr** and **Rollins Hogin**. Motion. An account ordered and the Master to report to the next term of court.

Page 23: **Nicholas Cheek** vs **Richard F. Cooke**. Motion. Continued to next term so said complainant may take the depositions of **David Mansell**, **Samuel Mansell**, **Jesse Mansell**, **John Trapp** and **Benjamin Brown** touching the character of **William Shadden**, **David Patton** and **Elijah Car**.

Page 23: **Elijah Terry** vs **Augustine Shepherd** and **George M. McWhirter** ... referred to the Clerk and Master to take an account and report to the present Term.

Page 23: **James Young** et ux vs **James Draper** et al. Motion. In this cause all the defendants except **Brice M. Draper** are permitted to have time till the First Monday of December next to file their answers.

Page 23: **Avra M. Hicklin** vs **Adam C. Hamilton** ... ordered ... that this cause be consolidated with the cause of Adam C. Hamilton et al vs said **Avery M. Hicklin.**

Page 23: **John Williams** vs **Thomas L. Clements** et al. It is ordered by the court that this cause be consolidated with that of **Jesse McClendan** (Page 24) against the said **Thomas L. Clements** and others.

Page 24: **Siles F. Maddux** by his next friend[3] vs **Isaac E. Ferrell** et al ... ordered that defendants motion to dissolve the injunction be overruled ... further ordered that Defendant Isaac E. hand over to the Master ... the note on Defendants **Hughes**, **Smith** and **Roberts** and that the said Master ... proceed to collect the same. Court adjourned till tomorrow morning 8 o'clock. /S/ **Bromfield Ridley**.

---

[3] The term "Next Friend" was given to a trusted person who stood in for a claimant in a court case. They were usually chosen by the person and not the court.

Page 24: Tuesday Morning November 2, 1841. **John M. Richmond** vs **Pinckney McCarver** ... Continued until next Term ... defendant permitted to take the deposition of **Jackson Woods** paying the cost of deposition.

Page 24: **William Johnson** vs **Enock Carter** et al. Continued until next Term ... defendant permitted to take depositions of **William H. Hughes** and **Mark Cameron** touching confessions of payment and (Page 25) the deposition of **Nancy Henderson** touching said payment.

Page 25: **Ridley Roberts**, **Martha Shaw** & **Burchet Shaw Matilda Shaw** and **Rebecca C. Shaw** by their guardian Martha Shaw. Exparte Decree ... Property value fixed at $100 and said land should be sold at the court house door in Gainesboro. That Burchet Shaw, Matilda Shaw and Rebecca Shaw are all the minor heirs at law of **G. W. C. Shaw** decd. Submitted to **Geo. M. McWhirter** C & M ....

Page 26: **Samuel E. Stone** & Co. vs **Matthew M. Bland** et al. Motion. Ordered ... this cause be remanded to the Rules and that the same be consolidated with the case of Matthew M. Bland vs the said Samuel E. Stone et al. The defendants Stone and **Settle** shall have time till the December Rules to file their answers.

Page 26: **Squire Hunter** vs **Pinckney McCarver**. Order. In this case the deposition of **Samuel R. Hays** is excepted to ... complainant has two months to take said depositions over.

Page 26: **John N. Gates**, **William H. Wilson**, **James T. Wilson**, **George Martin** and **Mary F.** his wife, **Robert K.(?) Chism** and **Nancy H.** his wife, & **Samuel T. Wilson Elizabeth B. Wilson**, **Narcissa J. Wilson** and **John A. Wilson** by their guardian **William H. Wilson** and **James T. Galder(?)** and **Sarah C** his wife vs **Wilson McCalgin**. (Page 27) ... in the presence of counsel on both sides ... the land in the filings ... are so situated that partition of the share of said defendant may be made without prejudicing the sales of the ballance of the lands ... that the ballance of said lands be sold after laying off to said defendant his share ... that **Bailey Butler**, **Nancy Andrews**, **Denton Plumlee**, **William Plumlee** and **Samuel B. M. Fowler** ... are appointed commissioners to lay off and set apart to defendant Wilson McCalgin his share ... to the 330 acres ... also to the 439 acres in the pleadings mentioned the share of said defendant being one tenth of said lands and by consent ... in laying off the share of said defendant in the 330 acres said commissioners shall begin at **Welcome Butler's** corner on McCalgins line running with said line to the river, thence down the river, thence North to Butler's line ... so as to give one tenth of said 330 acres ... In laying off the share of said defendant in the 439 acres, said commissioners shall lay off as is set apart one tenth thereof ....

Page 28: **James Young** and wife vs **Brice M. Draper** et al. Motion ... of Defendant ... to dissolve the injunction be [sic] and the same is hereby overruled.

Page 28: **Bird Cannon** and wife vs **Garret Sadler** et al. Motion ... defendants **Abisha Cannon** and wife permitted to have till the first Monday in December next to file their answers ....

Page 28: **Robert Patterson** & Co. vs **M. L. Armstrong** et al ... Defendant **Fowler** is permitted to take the deposition of his co-defendant **Micajah L. Armstrong** ....

Page 28: **William Scanland** Administrator of the estate of **William Lock** Decd vs **John Burris** ... (Page 29) ... the complainants as Administrator of **William Locke** deceased, had attained a judgement in the Jackson County Circuit Court against the defendant for $344.06 besides the cost of suit. Judgement was entered July 26, 1838 and directed to the Sheriff of White County.

Sheriff levied the same upon a horse in the possession of Defendant Burris and said same for $286 to the complainant being the highest bidder ... said Sheriff entered a credit for $286. Burris had no title to said horse ... he belonged to a man by the name of **McGee** who sued and recovered the price of said horse from the Sheriff—and the complainant gave an indemnity bond to the Sheriff ... the Court being satisfied the horse was the property of Burris ... ordered that the credit on said execution of $286 be vacated and for nothing taken and returned ... that the complainant be entitled to his execution upon said judgment and the Defendant be enjoined from setting up and investing on said credit ....

Page 29: **Bailey Butler jr** et al vs **Lucy Ursery** et al ... it is suggested ... that Defendants Lucy Ursery and **Joel Rich** have died since the commencement of this suit.

Page 30: **Russel M. Kinnaird** and **Thomas L. Bransford** vs **Dice Hawkins** and **John Hawkins**, **James Alexander Hawkins**, **Robert Hawkins**, **Louisiana Hawkins**, **Martha D. Hawkins Cleveland Winchester Hawkins** and **Elizabeth Jane Hawkins** minor heirs of **Nelson Hawkins** decd by there guardian Dice Hawkins ... defend-ants were indebted to complainants in the sums mentioned in the pleadings ... in order to secure the payment of the same, the defendant executed the mortgage designation as exhibit B for 805(?) acres of land lying in Jackson County ... there is a ballance upon said debts of $197.11 down to this date and which sum remains unpaid ... unless defendants pay unto the Officer of the Clerk and Master... $197.11 and all costs in this cause within thirty days from this instant the said Master ... shall proceed to sell said land upon a credit of six and twelve months at the Court House door in Gainesboro ... And a lien is taken upon the land until it is paid ....

Page 30: **Elijah Toney** vs **Augustin Shepherd** and **George M. McWhirter** (Page 31) ... Augustin Shepherd is justly indebted to Toney for $212.63. Complainant is to recover from Shepherd the $212.63 ... Shepherd has an interest in the estate of **Sarah Baker Shepherd** decd of $188.09 1/11 cents which consists in notes now in the hands of McWhirter—one half of said amount will fall due 5 December 1841 and the other half on 5 December 1842. Court decrees that McWhirter proceed to collect said notes when they fall due and with the proceeds first pay the costs and fees that Shepherd is liable and pay on account of processing the sale of the estate of **Sarah Baker Shepherd** Decd.

Page 31: It is ordered the master proceed to collect the notes now in his hands belonging to the Heirs of **Joel L. Settle** decd, the heirs & distributees of **Sarah Baker Shepherd** decd and **Chisms Heirs** and Widow ....

Page 32: **Christopher Sharr** vs **Avra F.(?) Lancaster**. Order. The defendants exceptions to the report to the Master are allowed.

Page 32: Heirs of **Joel L. Settle** decd. Exparte Decree ... A report of the sale pursuant to an interlocutory decree made at the May Term 1841 of this Court. That on the 7th of June after giving notice ... the house with all the land mentioned in complainants petition which was knocked down to **William Putty** ... at the price of $145 for which the master reports he took the note of said William Putty with **John M. Gipson** and **Merlin Young** security, payable 12 months after date. (Page 33) Court adjourned till tomorrow morning.

Page 33: Wednesday Morning Nov 9 1841. **Nicholas Cheek** vs **Richard F. Cooke**. Ordered that the parties take the depositions they are permitted to take in the time of four months from this day.

Page 33: **Christopher Sharr** vs **Avra K. Lancaster**. Decree. Heard on the 3d [*sic*] day of November 1841. The exception to which had heretofore been disallowed from which report it appears that the partnership transaction was not finally settled and there is a balance due from Defendant to Complainant of $10.20. Defendant ordered to pay the balance.

Page 33: **George D. Allen** vs **Hugh P. Allen** Admr &c ... (Page 34) on motion of complainant it is ordered ... that Scri Facias issue ~~directed to Polly Henry guardian ad lite of~~[4] against the heirs of **Michael Henry** decd to show cause &c.

Page 34: **A. M. Hicklin** Exr. of **Hugh Hicklin** D<u>ec</u> vs **A. C. Hamilton** ... Hugh Hicklin made & published his will on 13 Octr 1831[5] and shortly then after departed this life in (Jackson County) ... there is a bequest in said will emancipating his negro woman **Sukey** ... complainants in the Cross-Bill **Alvira** and **Turner** are the children of Sukey born after the death of the Testator ... Sukey on the (blank) day of 1840 was regularly emancipated by the County Court of Jackson that being the place of residence of said Hugh Hicklin at the time of his death. The bill and cross bill are dismissed and the said **Alvira** & **Turner Hicklin** being entitled to their freedom .... (Page 35) Court adjourned. /S/ **Bromfield Ridley**.

Page 36: **May Term 1842**. Chancery Court began and held at the Court House in Gainesboro for the Chancery District composed of the County of Jackson on the first Monday, it being 2 May 1842. **Bromfield Ridley** Chancellor, presiding.

Page 36: Tuesday Morning **3 May 1842**. **Silas F. Maddusk** By &c. vs **Jefferson Ferrell** et al. Time given defendants to take any testimony they think proper.

Page 36: **William Johnson** vs **Enoch Carter** et al. On motion of Defendants counsel it is ordered that the rule made at the last Term ... requiring the Complainant to justify his security for the (Page 37) suit dismissed.

Page 37: **Daniel Herbert** vs **James McBroom Jr.** et al. Continued until next term and complainant permitted to take the deposition of **John Roland** and defendant McBroom permitted to retake the deposition of **Henry L. Tucker** and
Cassy Shaw.

Page 37: **David Griffith** Admr &c. vs **William Johnson**. On motion of complainants counsel this cause is remanded to the Rules with leave for complt. to make the heirs of **Nathan Price** defendants.

Page 37: **Squire Hunter** vs **Pinckney McCarver** and **Hiram J. Nettles**. Decree Final ... the sale of the horse in the pleadings was absolute and no wise conditioned on a mortgage ....

Page 38: **Russel M. Kinnaird** and **Thomas L. Bransford** vs **Dice Hawkins**, **John Hawkins**, **James Alexander Hawkins**, **Robert Hawkins**, **Louisiana Hawkins**, **Martha D. Hawkins**, **Cle<u>a</u>veland Winchester Hawkins** and **Jane Hawkins**. The sale of said land in pleadings is here reported. On 15 January 1842 after giving notice as required all land was sold at the Court House door in Gainesboro to Kinnaird & Bransford for $220. The Master reports he took the notes of Kinnaird & Bransford due in 6 & 12 months with **Joel W. Settle** Security and a lien was retained upon the land for the purchase money. **Geo. M. McWhirter** C & M, reports that this

---

[4] This strikeout line is shown exactly as written.

[5] The year may be 1837 instead of 1831.

title be passed to the following described tract in Jackson County -Beginning at a beech and running South 55 poles (Page 39) to ... the bank of **Roaring River**—thence up said river as it meanders S. 37º E. 17 poles to a dogwood thence East 26 poles to a sugar tree—thence North 69 poles to a Hickory and Dogwood—thence West 35 poles to the Beginning containing by estimate 15 acres ... one other tract in said County on the Waters of Roaring River bounded as follows: Beginning on ... the North bank of said Roaring River near what is called the Dirt Cave and running up said river with its meanders to the mouth of the **Horse Point Branch**-thence a North West course... to the Beginning containing by estimate 800 acres being Entry No. 1874 entered in the name of **Nelson Hawkins** and to include all the lands contained in said boundary not otherwise appropriated or owned ... one other tract of land Entry No. 646 entered in the name of **Curry Lee** lying on the North side of Roaring River and bounded as follows: Beginning at ... the North corner of said Lees land and running West or near a West course down said river to **John Chapman's** line-thence with said line to where the **Widow Chapman** lives ... for compliment-containing 100 acres. With a reservation out of the two last described tracts of one hundred acres of land which was sold by Nelson Hawkins to **Benjamin Chapman** as will appear by deed from Hawkins to said Chapman. Be and the same is hereby divested out of the said Dice Hawkins, John Hawkins James Alexander Hawkins, Robert Hawkins, Louisiana Hawkins, Martha D. Hawkins, Cleveland Winchester Hawkins and **Elizabeth Jane Hawkins** ... and vested in the said Russel M. Kinnaird and Thomas L. Bransford ... (Page 40) ....

Page 40: **Samuel E. Stone** and **Leroy B. Settle** vs **Henry F. Burke** and his wife **Elizabeth** and **Matthew M. Bland** and Matthew M. Bland vs **Samuel E. Stone** and Leroy B. Settle and Henry F. Burke. Cross Bill ... Henry F. Burke is a distributee of the estate of **Sally Bland** Decd in place of his wife **Elizabeth Burke**, formerly **Elizabeth Bland** daughter of Sally Bland ... complainants Stone and Settle hold several notes on **Henry F. Burke** and there remains yet a balance due them on said notes ... Henry F. Burke is indebted to the **Matthew M. Bland**. It is ordered by the Court that the Master take an account showing the amount of the distributive share of the Henry F. Burke in place of his said wife as distributee of the estate of said **Sally Bland** ... and report to the (Page 41) Court the next term.

Page 41: **Matthew Duke** et al vs **Willis Mullins** et uxor. Interlocutory Order ... the Master take proof touching the susceptibility of division of the land in the bill and make a report.

Page 41: **Harrison Howard** et al vs **Christopher Clemmons** et al. In this case the death of the Defendant **John Clemmons** was suggested and the complainant on motion enters a nolle prosequi as to him ... and Christopher Clemmons Executor of John Clemmons Decd have leave to file a cross bill.

Page 41: **Hezekiah Crowell** vs **Joseph Jarod, Elizabeth Presley, Coosa M. Presley Millennicum(?) B. Presley, Arena H. Presley, Dionysus B. Presley, Sarah J. Presley, Ruth E. Presley** and **John P. Presley**. Decree final. (Page 42) ... on 24 November 1837 the complainant purchased of **Sanders Presley** the following land: Situated on the waters of **Indian Creek** of **Caney Fork** containing 140 acres for which complainant took the title bond of said Presley and ... the said Presley purchased the same tract from the Defendant Jarod and that he also took the title bond of Jarod. It further appears Presley paid the consideration to Jarod and that complainant has also paid the consideration to Presley ... that Presley departed this life and the Defendants are the heirs at law of Presley except the Defendant Jarod and Elizabeth and they are minors under the age of 21 years and have no regular guardian and their mother Elizabeth Presley has been appointed their guardian ad litem against whom judgement for confessed has also been taken. Court orders all right and title of the defendants be divested out of them and the same be vested in the complainant ... Court adjourned ... /S/ **Bromfield Ridley**.

Page 43: **Pinckney McCarver** vs **John Eakle** et al ...The above cause came to be heard upon the motion to dissolve the injunction upon the Bill and Answer of the Defendant John Eakle ... and should be so decreed ....

Page 43: **James Young** et ux vs **Brice M. Draper** et al. The death of the Defendant **Stephen Holladay** is suggested and admitted and by consent the cause is revived against **Brice M. Draper** and **Henrietta Holladay** Executors of said Stephen Holladay Decd.

Page 43: **John N. Gales** vs **David Biggerstaff** . . . upon Motion of Defendant to dissolve this Injunction ... Deft. denies all the equity of Complainant's Bill and there is money due in the amount of (Page 44) $269.20 including the interest and the cost $8.68 ... **Merlin Young Wilenne Butler** and **Bailey B. Kendall** are the securities for the injunction ... the injunction be dissolved and complainants and his said securities pay to the defendants $269.20.

Page 44: **James Young** and **Betsy** his wife vs **James Draper**, **Obediah Evans** and **Sally** his wife, **Stephen Holliday** and **Henrietta** his wife **John Rogers** and **Ann** his wife. **Edward B. Draper Brice M. Draper Milton Draper Thomas L. Draper Thomas Huddleston** & **Susanna** his wife and **Sarah Draper** – **Edward P. Pate** and **Lucy** his wife and **Lawrence Draper.** Decree ... take and state an account as to how much of the estate of **Thomas Draper** decd has come to the hands of Complainants **James Young** & Defendant **Brice M. Draper** as Administrators of the estate of said **Thomas Draper** decd each. How much each Administrator has paid out in discharging debts and costs relative to said account and whether the costs paid by each were necessary costs and how much each administrator has paid over to the legatees respectively and that said Master ascertain how much each of the legatees of the estate of Thomas has received (Page 45) from the Testator or Administrators regarding the award filed with the papers in the cause ... the Master ascertains whether the note executed by **James Draper** to Thomas Draper for $135.39 has been paid or whether the same was given him by way of advancements ... it is further agreed by the parties that the award of **Silas C. Cornwell**, **Cornelius Carver** and **John A. Stone(?)** filed in this cause may be set up and so far as it does not conflict with the above may govern the distribution and settlement of the estate of Thomas Draper deceased and the valuation of the slaves of said estate as fixed by said Administrators shall remain undisturbed ... there is some difficulty between said distributees as to the intention of the testator in devising $500 to Thomas Draper and some doubt exists in their minds as to whether said testator intended to devise to Thomas said sum of $500 over the amount devised to the balance of his heirs. It is agreed that the same be submitted to the Court ... who is of opinion the intention of the testator was not that the devise of $500 to Thomas should not have the sum over and above an equal distribution ... (Page 46) report to be made at the next term ....

Page 46: **Robert Patterson**, **William C. Patterson** and **James E. Nequs(?)** vs **Micajah L. Armstrong**, **Samuel B. M. Fowler** and **(blank) Abbott** and **(blank) Wood** ... in the presence of Solicitors of the parties ... complainants at the March Term 1839 of the Circuit Court of Jackson County recovered a judgement against the Defendant Armstrong for about the sum of $1751.84 besides costs ... an execution was returned by the Sheriff and no property to be found except weigh [sic] to make $23 ... said Defendant Armstrong did on 25 June 1839 give to the defendants Wood & Abbott a note made by said defendant Fowler in favor of said Armstrong for $1200.00 with a credit of $200.00 on same for the purpose of securing the payment of $691.02 which said Armstrong and Howard owed to them which sum with interest up to this time is $982.75 ....

Page 47: **John N. Gates** vs **Stephen Langford**. Decree ... upon Bill answer and the motion of Defendants Solicitor ... dissolve the injunction ....

Page 47: **Eliza McKinley** et al vs **Matthew C. McKinley** Admr &c ... motion to dissolve the injunction heretofore granted (Page 48) ... McKinley permitted to proceed with his executions at law in the collection of judgement heretofore enjoined ... he is permitted to collect the notes on Eliza in his favor ....

Page 48: **John Williams** vs **Jesse McClendan** et al. Bill & Cross Bill. By consent parties shall have till June Rules 1842 to file their Bills.

Page 48: **William Johnson** vs **Enoch Carter** et al ... complainant departed this life previous to the making ... of a rule to dismiss the same ... order rescinded ....

Page 48: **Matthue [sic] Duke** et al vs **Willis Mullins** & Wife ... Pursuant to (Page 49) an interlocutory order herein pronounced at the present Term ... the Master has examined **James Young** and **William Moreland** touching the susceptibility of division of the land described in the Bill ... it would be ... to the interest & advantage of all parties concerned that said land should be sold as it cannot be divided without injury to the heirs ... minimum price of the same should be $642.00 ....

Page 49: **Bryson Hood** vs **Sarah Rector** and **David M. Rector** ... David M. shall have till the July Term of the Circuit Court of Jackson County to file his answer.

Page 49: **Nicholas Cheek** vs **Richard F. Cooke**. Bill & Cross Bill. Decree ... (Page 50) ... the matters set up in complainants original Bill for a recission of the contract of the sale of the land in the pleadings mentioned are devised by Defendants answer and the same are not sustained proof upon the part of complainant. Ordered ... that the original Bill be dismissed and because it appears ... the complainant Cheek and his security **Thomas Cassetty** are insolvent that the Defendant pay the costs of suit in the first instance and have judgement over against complainant and said Thomas Cassetty for the same ... the Cross Bill be dismissed–and the complainant therein pay the costs of same from which the complainant prays an appeal to the Supreme Court at Nashville which is granted to him ....

Page 50: **Wilson C. Canter** et al vs **Levi Canter** et al ... [It] is ordered the Master examine testimony touching the value of the land and the susceptibilities of the division of said land among the heirs ... also the notice of the widows dower.

Page 51: **William C. Canter** et al vs **James Canter** et al. Decree ... In obedience to an interlocutory order pronounced in this cause at the present term the undersigned reports he examined **William Moreland** and **Alfred W. Ross** on oath ... they are acquainted with the land in the Bill and the heirs of **Zachariah Canter** and said land is not susceptible of partition among the heirs entitled without injury. Ordered to be sold and is worth $3.00 an acre The widows dower is worth a childs part or one fourth part of said land. /S/ **G. M. McWhirter** ....

Page 51: **Geo. D. Allen** & **Hugh P. Allen** Admr. Scri facias. Dismissed.

Page 52: **Letty Roberts** Executrix of **Jas Roberts** decd. Exparte ... debts due from the estate of Petitioner's testator exceed the assets ... except slaves ... the Master take an account of the assets and the amount said estate is indebted and also the cash valuation of the negroes.

Page 52: **Letty Roberts** Executrix of **Jas. Roberts** decd. Exparte ... Report of the Master ... outstanding debts against the estate of **James Roberts** decd amount to $320.859 [*sic*] and the assets in the hands of petitioner amount to $1863.34 leaving an excess of debts $1345.25. Cash valuation of the negroes amount in Tennessee Bank notes to $1850. Disel[6] is valued at $450 which being deducted leaves $1400 valuation in Bank notes. It also appears that Tennessee Bank notes are now at a discount of 13 to 14 percent (Page 53) which would make the negroes in the Bill amount to $1600. /S/ **G.M. McWhirter** C.M. The slaves are ordered to be sold at the Court House in Gainesboro at public auction ... giving 20 days notice of the time and place of sale by advertisement on the Court House door at Granville, Dixon's Springs in Smith County and Sparta in White county and that he have power to send the Sheriff of Jackson County to take and deliver him immediate possession of the negro man **Old Handy** so as to have him present at said sale and that he report to the next Term ....

Page 53: **John M. Richmond** vs **Pinckney McCarver** ... on 23 December 1836 complainant sold to **Jackson Wood** a part of lot no 1 in Gainesboro and executed a bond to said Wood conditioned to make to him a title to said lot the same when the consideration money should be paid ... on 18 March 1837 Jackson Wood assigned and transferred to defendant title bond ... a part of the consideration money ... is still due ... (Page 54) It also appeared that Jackson Wood has left this state and is insolvent ... report to be made at next court.

Page 54: **Ridley Roberts** et al. Exparte ... no sale has been effected of the land in the Decree pronounced at last Term ... said land cannot be sold for the minimum price ... order is rescinded and it ordered the Master to sell land to the highest bidder at public auction ....

Page 55: **Cook** vs **Cheek**. Cause taken to the Supreme Court.

Page 55: **Wilson** et al vs **McCalgin** [*sic*]. Cause continued until next term for reason of the loss of a portion of the file papers.

Page 56: Blank page.

Page 57: November Term 1842, 7 November. Chancery Court began at the Court House in Gainesboro for the Chancery District composed of the Counties of Jackson and Putnam. **Bromfield L. Ridley** Chancellor, presiding.

Page 57: **Ridley Roberts, Martha Shaw, Burchet Shaw, Matilda Shaw** and **Rebecca C. Shaw**. Exparte Decree. **Ridley Roberts** and Shaws widow and heirs–Exparte report. On 18 July 1842 at the Court House in Gainesboro, the land in the petition was sold to **Thackston Carter** ... (for) $30 which the Master took Carter's notes payable 12 months after date with **Henry Richmond** and **John H. Ballew** security ... (Page 58) land lying in **Putnam County** which was formerly Jackson County ... on the ridge in the **Walters** road near Shaws old stand containing by estimation 100 acres ....

Page 58: **George S. Bugg**, Esqr ... admitted ... as a practicing Solicitor of this Court.

Page 58: **Pinckney McCarver** vs **John Eakle**, et al . . . by affidavit of Complts Solicitor the

---

[6] This is nearly illegible. It may be "Disel" or "Diset." It is likely the name of a Negro who is to be kept for the widow since the amount is deducted from the total valuation. Please check the original document if this information is critical to your research.

deposition of **Harrison McCarver** who is a material witness in the cause was but partially taken ....

Page 59: **Miranda Swearingen** vs **William Swearingen**. Bill dismissed by the Court.

Page 59: **Henry Crowder** vs **Reece & Morrell** et al. Bill dismissed by the Court.

Page 59: **Thomas L. Bransford** et al vs **John Stafford** et al. Bill dismissed by Complainants.

Page 59: **William Amonet** et al vs **Joshua P. Hale** et al. Bill dismissed by Complainants.

Page 59: **Alexander Montgomery** vs **E.J. Wilson** et al ... it appearing that two terms of the Court have elapsed since the filing of the Bill and that no steps have been taken in the prosecution of the same ... that the suit be abated.

Page 60: **Thomas D. Hutchinson** vs **William A. Gailbreath** et al. Complainant dismisses the Bill.

Page 60: **Thomas L. Bransford** et al vs **James Hutchinson** et al. Complainants dismiss the Bill.

Page 60: **William Johnson** vs **Enoch Carter** et al ... it appearing two terms of this court have elapsed since the death of the Complt and that steps have been taken to revive the same. Suit abated at the cost of the Complts for which Executors may issue. Court adjourned till tomorrow morning. /S/ **Bromfield Ridley**.

Page 60: Tuesday morning 8 o'clock. **William R. Kenner** et al vs **Burton Marchbanks** et al. On motion of the Defendants, they are allowed till January Rules to file their answer. (Page 61) The Defendants **Carr Terry**, **Elijah Carr**, **Herald D. Marchbanks** and **Richard F. Cooke** by their counsel came into court and agree ....

Page 61: **William R. Kenner, Thomas L. Bransford, Russel M. Kinnaird, Benjamin E. Williams, Sampson W. Cassetty, Samuel E. Stone, Joseph Eaton, William Gipson, Amos J. Chapman, Merlin Young, James W. Lock, Jacob G. Blankenship, Nathaniel G. Jackson, Joshua R. Stone, William Putty, Thomas D. Cassetty, Tollivar Kirkpatrick** and **Achilles Hare** vs **Isaac Burk, Burton Marchbanks, Richard F. Cooke. Carr Terry, Elijah Carr, Herald D. Marchbanks, Henry L. McDaniel, Craven Maddux** and **Lawson Clark**, Commissioners of **Putnam County** ... on petition of Complainants by their counsel it is allowed and deemed by the Court that **Leroy H. Cage** of **Smith County** and **Mounce Gore** of Jackson County be appointed surveyors for the purpose of surveying the said Counties of Putnam and Jackson ....

Page 62: **Sarah McKinley, Jane McKinley, Mary McKinley, Elizabeth McKinley, Martha McKinley** minors by their guardian **Eliza McKinley, Robert G.(?) Hughes** and his wife **Mariana**, and Elizabeth McKinley in her own right and **Simon Hogin** vs **Matthew McKinley** Administrator of the Estate of **James McKinley** Decd. Decree ... the Master is ordered to take an accounting between the parties of this suit and report the first day of January next.

Page 62: **Brison Hood** vs **Sarah Rector** and **David M. Rector**. In this cause on motion and affidavit of the Defendant David M. Rector, the rule taking the Bill for confessed as to said David M. is set aside (Page 63) and he is now permitted to file his answer and a Cross Bill.

Page 63: **James Young** and **Betsey Young** his wife vs **Brice M. Draper, James Draper, Lawson**

H. Draper, **Thomas L. Draper**, **Milton Draper**, **Edward B. Draper**, **Obadiah Evans** and **Sally** his wife, **Henrietta Holliday**, **John Rogers** and **Anna** his wife, **Thomas Huddleston** and **Susannah** his wife **Edward Pate** and **Lucy** his wife and **Sarah Draper**. Decree Final ... upon interlocutory decree and the report of the Master ... James Young and wife vs James Draper and others. Report. In pursuance to an interlocutory Decree made at the May Term 1842(?) of this Court in this cause requiring the Clerk and Master to take and state an accounting and report how much of the estate of **Thomas Draper** Decd has come into the hands of each of his Administrators. How much of said Estate was paid out in discharge of Debts of said Decd and of Debts and costs relative to said Estate. How much such Administrator has paid to the legatees of said Estate respectively. How much of said Estate has each legatee recd either from the Decd or his Admr. or both ... whether the Admrs or either of them have hired out any of the negroes of the Estate, if so, for how much, is the same collected & to whom (Page 64) was the slave awarded and in whose hands is the hire ....

James Young is chargeable to Admr		$3925.70
From that sum deduct amt paid of debt of Decd	$99.951/2	
Amount paid of Debt relative to Estate	133.891/2	
Necessary fees and costs paid	375.80	
Amt of Debts either bad or not collected	394.21	803.81
Leaving a balance in **Young's** hands of		$3121.89
Amt chargeable to **Brice M. Draper** as Admr		$801.00
Deduct amt paid of Debts of Decd	$7.50	
Amt of debts relative to Estate paid	11.25	18.75
Leaving a balance in **Draper's** hands of		$782.2?
James Young has paid to Legatees as follows		
To **Sarah Draper** Oct. 9, 1860	$201.00	
" " Oct. 10, 1841	30.00	
" " Oct 19, 1841	217.871/2	
" " Decr 28, 1840	49.69	
To **E.P. Pate** for Mar. 29, 1841	7.69	$506.2?
To **James Draper** Sept. 13, 1840	31.92	
To **E.P. Pate** for Mar. 28, 1841	7.69	39.61
To **Obadiah Evans** June 22, 1841	126.85	
" " May 2, 1842	117.48	
To **E.P. Pate** for Mar. 29, 1841	7.69	252.??
To **Stephen Holladay** Dec 28, 1841	4.85	
To **E.P. Pate** for Mar. 29, 1841	7.69	252.00
To **Thomas L. Draper** Dec. 28, 1841	46.561/4	
To **E.P. Pate** for Mar. 29, 1841	7.69	54.251/2
To **John Rogers** June 22, 1841	246.23	
" " July 18, 1842	50.00	
(Page 65) " " Oct. 1, 1841	$30.50	
" " Dec. 28, 1841	34.183/4	
To **E.P. Pate** for Mar 29, 1841	7.69	$328.601/4
To **Thomas Huddleston** Jan 9, 1841	198.94	
" Mar. 11, 1841	297.91	
" Apl 24, 1841	20.00	
" Oct. 4, 1841	100.00	
" Apl 8, 1842	125.00	721.85
To **Edward P. Pate**, Oct 1, 1841	56.75	
" Dec. 28, 1841	11.571/2	68.321/2
To **Edward B. Draper** pd **Pate** for Mar. 28, 1841	7.69	7.69

To **Brice M. Draper** Sep 10, 1840	76.62	
" pd **Pate** for Mar 29, 1841	7.69	
" Sep. 10, 1840	96.12/12	
" Sep. 10, 1840	587.50	
" Oct. 1, 1841	33.681/?	
" Sep. 10, 1840	133.81	
" Oct. 1, 1841	33.151/4	
" Sep. 10, 1840	51.44	
" Dec. 28, 1841	40.811/4	
" Sep 10, 1840	42.92	1099.753/4
Whole acct paid by **Young** to Legatees	3090.703/4	3090.703/4
Leaving a balance in **Young's** hands of		31.18
Brice M. Draper has paid out to Legatees to wit:		
To **Stephen Holladay** Aug 6, 1841	$96.00	$96.00
To **James Draper** July 13, 1841	274.00	274.00
To **Obadiah Evans** June 1, 1841	60.00	
" Oct. 16, 1841	70.00	130.00
To **Thomas L. Draper** July 15, 1841	36.00	36.00
To **Lawson H. Draper** Nov 26, 1841	50.00	
" Mar 21 1841	25.00	
(Page 66) To **Sarah Draper** Oct 19, 1841	482.121/2	482.121/2
To **Edward B. Draper** Dec 28, 1841	28.93	28.93
To **John Rogers** Aug 30, 1841	115.00	115.00
Whole Amt paid by **Brice M. Draper** to Legatees		1238.2?
Draper has paid out to the Legatees more than came into his hands as Admr	456.031/4	456.0?
Sarah Draper has recd from the Estate exclusive of her Dower in lands as follows:		
From Arbitrators 1 negro valued at	750.00	
From **James Young** as Admr	506.251/2	
From **Brice M. Draper** as Admr	482.121/2	1738.0?
James Young and wife have recd		
From Decd in his lifetime	683.42	
From Arbitrators 2 negroes valued at	725.00	
From Estate since testators death	7.69	
From Amt due from Admr	31.18	1447.??
James Draper has recd		
From testator in his lifetime	946.00	
From Arbitrators negro valued at	600.00	
From **James Young** as Admr	39.61	
From **Brice M. Draper** as Admr	274.00	1859.??
Obadiah Evans and wife have recd		
From testator in his lifetime	125.00	
From Arbitrators 1 negro worth	725.00	
From **James Young** Admr	252.02	
From **Brice M. Draper** as Admr	130.00	1832.02
Stephen Holladay and wife have recd		
From testator in his lifetime	805.00	
From Arbitrators 2 negroes valued at	800.00	
From **James Young** as Admr	12.54	
(Page 67) From **Brice M. Draper** as Admr	96.00	1713.54

John Rogers and wife have recd
From testator in his lifetime	520.62	
By exchange of negroes with **Huddleston**	850.00	
From **James Young** as Admr	328.60/12	
From **Brice M. Draper** as Admr	118.00	1814.223/4

Lawson H. Draper has recd From testator in his lifetime   900.00
From Arbitrators 2 negroes valued at	160.00	
From **Brice M. Draper** as Admr	76.25	1736.25

Edward B. Draper has recd
From testator in his lifetime	875.00	
From Arbitrators 1 negro worth	750.00	
From **James Young** as Admr	7.69	
From **Brice M. Draper** as Admr	28.95	1661.62

Milton Draper has recd
From testator in his lifetime	1484.12	
From Arbitrators 1 negro worth	500.00	2284.12

Thomas L. Draper has recd
From testator in his lifetime	1700.00	
From **James Young** as Admr	54.291/4	
From **Brice M. Draper** as Admr	36.00	1790.251/4

Edward P. Pate and wife have recd
From testator in his lifetime	1125.00	
From Arbitrators 2 negroes valued at	600.00	
From **James Young** as Admr	68.321/2	

Thomas Huddleston and wife have recd
From testator in his lifetime	650.00	
By exchange of negroes with **Rogers**	450.0	
From **James Young** as Admr	731.88	1821.85

Brice M. Draper has recd
From testator in his lifetime	1525.00	
(Page 68) From Arbitrators 2 negroes valued at	750.00	
From **James Young** as Admr	1099.553/4	3379.7?
From this amt deduct the sum overpaid by **Brice Draper** as Admr	456.031/4	
... the examination of **James Draper**, **Obadiah Evans** and others of the legatees that there was an argument among the legatees to acquit **Brice M. Draper** of one half the interest in all the notes set off by Young up to the death of the testator which argument reduced the amount paid him by Young $101.241/4 and reduces the Acct chargeable to Young as Admr $101.241/4 and also the amt paid out ...	101.241/4	557.??
Estate at the present time		2817.49

It is further reported ... there is no proof of a positive nature to the note of $135.39 given by **James Draper** & **Thomas Draper** Decd ... that by reference heard to the examination of **Alexander Montgomery** Clerk of the County Court of Jackson County ... $200 would be a reasonable allowance to the Administrators ... that **James Young** hired out to **Brice M. Draper** the negro girl **Mary** awarded to **Milton Draper** ... **Young** had no right to hire out said negro ... (Page 69) ... that the whole amount of the Estate of **Thomas Draper** Decd is as follows:

Amt in the hands of **James Young** Admr &c	3121.83/4	
Deduct amt of interest given **B.M. Draper**	101.241/4	
Deduct Amt of hire of **Milton Drapers** negro	36.061/9	
Balance left in the hands of **Young**	2995.581/4	
Amt chargeable to **Brice Draper** as Admr	782.271/9	
Amt Given off by Testator in his lifetime	11939.16	
Amt Valuation of negroes that are distributed	8560.00	
Whole Amt of Estate divided & undivided		24272.011/2
From which deduct amt allowed Administrators		200.00
Leaves a balance to be divided of		24072.011/2
There being 13 heirs of this amt each is entitled to		1851.691/2
Sarah Draper has recd	1738.38	
Which is less than her share		113.311/2
James Young and wife have recd	1447.29	
Which is less than equal share		404.401/2
Amt allowed **James Young** as Admr		120.00
Amt of allowance increased by the Court		30.00
Whole amt that they are minus		554.401/2
James Draper has recd	1859.61	
Which is more than an equal share		7.911/2
Obadiah Evans and wife have recd	1832.02	
Which is less than an equal share		18.679
Stephen Holladay and wife have recd	1713.54	
Which is less than an equal share		138.151/2
(Page 70) **John Rogers** and wife have recd	1814.221/4	
Which is less than an equal share		37.4?[7]
Lawson H. Draper has recd	1736.25	
Which is less than an equal share		115.4?
Edward B. Draper had recd	1661.62	
Which is less than an equal share		193.0?
Milton Draper has recd	2284.12	
Which is more than an equal share		432.4?
Thomas L. Draper has recd	1790.281/4	
Which is less than an equal share		61.4?
Edward P. Pate and wife have recd	1793.321/2	
Which is less than an equal share		58.39
Thomas Huddleston and wife have recd	1821.25	
Which is less than an equal share		29.8?
Brice M. Draper has recd	2819.481/4	
From which deduct Amt allowed him as Admr	80.00	
Amt [sic] Hire of negro girl **Mary**	360.061/4	
Leaving his receipts	3701.42	
Which is more than an equal share		849.74?
Amt of allowance reduced by Court		30.00
Which makes the Amt recd		879.72?

It is observed that in the foregoing estimate the note for $135.39 in **James Draper** is left entirely out of consideration neither is any notice taken of misc bad and uncollected debts in

---

[7] The book binding is tight in many places. Numerals hidden in the binding in the Draper settlement are listed as "?."

Young's hands or of the negro valued at $500 and given to **Thomas L. Draper** by deed from the legatees .... /S/ **G. M. McWhirter** Clerk & Master.

Page 71: **James Young** and wife vs **Brice M. Draper** and others. Exceptions. Complainants come by their Solicitors and except as follows ... note made by James Draper to **Thomas Draper** for $135.39 should be charged to said James or allowed him as an advancement ... the proof shows James Young rendered more than three fourths of the services that were rendered in attending to said administration .... /S/ **McClain** & **Nelson** & **Goodall**, Solrs.

Page 71: **James Young** and wife vs **Brice M. Draper** and others. Exceptions to report ... the note dated 21 March 1821 for $135.39 is presumed to have been paid or that same formed part of the sum of $800 mentioned in the will of **Thomas Draper** as being advance to him ... The Defendants all except to that part of item in complainants account of $275.80 which consists of $75 paid Messrs. **Nelson** & **Goodall** ... /S/ **A. Cullum(?)** Solr. Whereupon the Court disallowed the first exception taken by Complainants Solicitors and adjudges the note of $135.39 dated 21 March 1821 upon **James Draper** payable to Thomas Draper Decd form a part of the sum of $800 charged to the said James Draper ... And as to the second exception, the same was allowed by (Page 72) Court and ordered the same to be so altered as to allow James Young the sum of $150 for his services as Administrator and to Brice M. Draper $50 for his services as Administrator ... the Complainants first exception to the Master report And the second exception of the Defendants is disallowed ... it is further decreed that the Complainant Young deliver over to **Milton Draper** the note of $36.06 1/4 upon Brice M. Draper being the note taken for the hire of a negro awarded to said **Milton Draper** ... We whose names are hereto subscribed having been chosen by the heirs and legatees of **Thomas Draper** Decd to take an account of all that has heretofore been advanced by the parent to each of his children in his lifetime ... also to lay off any value of the land and negroes which have not been valued in the will, and to do all other things which a Court of Equity will or could do ... have met at the late residence of the decd in presence of **James Young**, **James Draper**, **Stephen Holladay**, **Obadiah Evans**, **John Rogers**, **Thomas L. Draper**, **Edward Pate**, **Thomas Huddleston**, **Edward B. Draper Brice M. Draper** and Milton Draper ... (Page 73) we find the different legatees charged with the following ...

James Young and wife have received		683.42
James Draper has received	811.50	
1 negro girl worth	135.00	946.50
Obadiah Evans and wife recd	500.00	
1 negro girl worth	325.	725.00
Stephen Holladay and wife recd	530.	
1 negro girl	275.	805.00
John Rogers and wife recd	100.	
1 negro girl worth–sundries 20.62	420.62	520.62
Lawson H. Draper recd	500.	
1 negro boy worth	400.	400.
Edward B. Draper recd	500.	
1/2 [sic] negro boy **Charles**	300.	
Cash not inventoried	75.	895.00
Brice M. Draper received	100.	
1/2 negro boy **Charles**	300.	
Cash not inventoried	75.	
150 acres of land	1050.	1525.
Milton Draper received	61.12	
150 acres land	1050.	

Cash	500.	
Credit by 1 years work, sow & shoats	1611.12	1486.12
	127.	
Thomas L. Draper, Recd	250.	
For land	700.	
1 negro boy **Dan**	450.	
1 negro boy **Booker**	300.	1700.
Edward P.ate recd and wife	100.	
1 negro girl worth	325.	
100 acres land	700.	1125.
Thomas Huddleston & Wife recd	100.	
one negro girl	150.	
(Page 74) 100 acres of land	400.	650.
Whole account chargeable to all the legatees		119.39

Given under our hands and seals 2 December 1840. /S/ **John A. Sloan, Silas C. Cornwell, Cornelius Carver**.

Page 75: **Christopher Clemons** vs **Harman Howard** et al ... on motion of the Defts Solicitor the rule taking the Bill for confessed as to all the Defts is by order of the court set aside so far as the same relates to the Defts. Harman Howard and wife and **Thomas Howard** and wife..

Page 75: **Letty Roberts** Exec. &c Exparte petition for sale of slaves ... on motion and of the consent of Complts Solr. the order made at the last Term of this court ... is extended ... let the said report come in at the next Term of this court.

Page 75: **John N. Gates** vs **David Biggerstaff** ... the Defendants Answer met fully with and completely defeated all of the Complainants Equity ... case dismissed.

Page 75: **John N. Gates** vs **Stephen Langford**. (Page 76) ... Defendants Answer met fully with and completely defeated all of the Complainants Equity ... case dismissed.

Page 76: **Bird Cannon** and wife vs **Garrett Sadler** et al ... cause remanded to the rules ... opened for the parties to take what depositions they might think proper.

Page 76: **Lyman E. Bill** vs **Thomas Gentry** ... complainant and defendant made an agreement about the profits of certain saw mills and grist mills in Jackson County and their partnership accounts are unsettled ... Clerk & Master to take an account between the parties in said partnership transactions ... to completely report what damages defendant (Page 77) has sustained if any ....

Page 77: **William Jarod** vs **Hugh W. Carlin**. Decree ... that about 60 barrels of corn had been received belonging to the Defendant ... that Defendant acted in disobedience by resisting said recovery forcibly ... the court doth order ... **David H. Nichol** sell said corn upon the premises at public sale to the highest bidder ....

Page 77: **Martha Shaw** and **Rollins Hogin** vs **Christopher Shaw**. Decree ... (Page 78) ... **David G. Shepherd, John Hughes** and **Henry Sadler** divided the land in the pleadings into three equal parts in quantity and value did set apart to the heirs at law of **George C. Shaw**, Christopher Shaw and the heirs at law of **Samuel Shaw** Decd their respective shares. It is further agreed by the parties that Christopher Shaw pay to complainant Martha Shaw who is the widow of the said Geo. W.C. Shaw three years rent preceding the present year ... and she have a lien upon the land of Christopher for said rents ... further agreed Christopher Shaw pay a note to **James Shepherd** Admr of **John Shepherd** of $157 made by Deft and George W. C. Shaw and Samuel Shaw $122 and complainant Martha pay the balance ....

Page 78: **John M. Richmond** vs **Pinckney McCarver**. Decree ... in presence of counsel on both sides ... which report is as follows ... an interlocutory Decree pronounced in this cause at the last Term of this court directing the Master to report the residue of the consideration money for the horses and lot in the pleadings which is due the complainant and yet remains unpaid ... (Page 79) $433.93 ... /S/ **G. M. McWhirter** C & M ... ordered by the Court that the Master sell the horses and part of lot ... first giving 20 days notice of the terms of sale by advertisement at Gainesboro, **Granville**, **Celina** and **White Plains** ....

Page 79: **Pinckney McCarver** vs **John Eakel** et al ... Complainant have leave to amend his Bill so as to make **Isaac Crawford** a Defendant and bring him before the Court.

Page 79: **David Herbert** vs **James McBroom** et al. Decree ... in the presence of Counsel on both sides where it appeared ... that complainant was seized and possessed of a tract of land in Jackson County described in the pleadings and conveyed the same to **Samuel Shaw** by deed absolute upon its face but conditional by parol [*sic*] to secure $17 loaned by said Shaw to him ... (Page 80) ordered by the Court that the Master take and state an account between the parties showing the sum loaned and the legal interest on the same ... of said land whilst in McBroom's possession and also the permanent improvements made on the land by said McBroom and report to the next Term ....

Page 80: **Heirs of Joel L. Settle** Decd ... On motion of petitioners solicitor ... the costs and solicitor's fee in this suit be paid by **Mounce Gore** Administrator of **Jane Settle** Dec ... the widow of said Joel L. Settle Decd ... it also appearing there are no assets in the hands of said administrator to pay the fees ... costs are to be paid out of the fund in hands of the Clerk of this Court arising from the sale of the lands ....

Page 80: **John N. Gates** vs **Benjamin D. Holmes** et al. Decree ... (Page 81) Defendant Holmes receive against complainant and **Merlin Young**, **E. L. Langford** and **Z. H. Mayfield** his securities ... $95.21 being the amount of the judgement .... stopped here

Page 81: **John N. Gates**, **William H. Wilson**, **James S. Wilson**, **George Martin** and **Mary L.** his wife, **Robert F.(?) Chism** & **Nancy H.** his wife, **Samuel T. Wilson**, **Elizabeth B. Wilson**, **Narcissa J. Wilson** and **John A. Wilson** the last four by their guardian William H. Wilson, **James T. Goldes(?)** and **Sarah C.** his wife of ~~Green County State of Kentucky~~ Complainants vs **Wilson McColgin** Defendant. Decree final ... Commissioners ... set apart to Wilson McColgin his undivided interest in the 330 acre tract and also in the 439 acre tract in the pleadings ... filed their report showing they had laid off for said Wilson McColgin 26 acres two roads and 20 poles, part of said 330 acre tract ... bounded as follows, beginning at a stake corner of **Welcome Butler's** survey running thence South 20 east 112 poles to three beeches in the bank of **Cumberland River**, (corner of said Wilson McColgin) thence west 37 1/4 poles to a forked elm thence north 20 West to a beech in Butlers line, thence East with Butlers line to the beginning ... (Page 82) Commissioners had laid off and set apart to said Wilson McColgin 43 acres part of said 439 acre tract bounded as follows. Beginning at a white oak in the North boundary line of an 18 acre survey of said McColgins running thence north 19º West 100 poles to a white oak, thence South 71º West 68 1/2 poles to a stake thence South 72 poles to a stake thence West to the beginning ... by consent of the parties by their solicitors ordered by the court that all the right and title both legal and equitable of the said William H. Wilson, John N. Gates, James S. Wilson, George Martin and Mary L. his wife Robert N.(?) Chism and Nancy H. his wife, Samuel T. Wilson, Elizabeth Wilson, Narcissa J. Wilson and John Wilson and James T. Goldes and Sarah his wife ... be divested out of said Pltfs ... and vested in the said Wilson McColgin ... on 25 December 1841 when John N. Gates ... became the purchaser of all the balance of the land in the pleadings mentioned ... (Page 83) Wilson McColgin pay the cost of the partition ....

Page 84: **Williams & Clark** Admrs &c vs **Thos. L. Clements** et al. Original Bill. And **Jesse McClendon** vs **Thomas L. Clements** et al. Cross Bill. Came the parties by their solicitors where it appearing ... that the death of **John Williams** one of the Defendants in the Cross Bill has been suggested ... and admitted and a Bill of reverse has been filed against **Joseph R. Williams** and **Peter Clarke(?)** Administrators &c of said Decd ... set for hearing Exparte to Defendant **J. L. Dillard, Green B. Lowe, L. L. Clements** and **G. W. McClendon** and Thos. L. Clements that the balance due on the judgement of Complainants against Adm amounts to the $425.70 ... with interest amounts to $539.85 and it also appearing ... that said Complainants have liens on the lands in the pleadings ... (Page 85) ordered that the Master proceed to sell the tract of land ... giving 40 days notice and advertisement at the Court House in Gainesboro at **Highland**, at **Granville** and at **Bagdad** ....

Page 86: **Silas F. Maddux** by his next friend **Cravin Maddux** vs **Jefferson Ferrell, Matthew C. Ferrell, Ridley Roberts, Thomas Smith, William Q. Hughes** and **Isaac E. Ferrell**. Decree final ... the complainant had not taken out execution upon his judgement at case against defendant Jefferson Ferrell and had the same returned no property found ....

Page 86: **Wilson C. Carter, William P. Holliman** & **Elizabeth** his wife & **William W.ade Holliman Margaret Holliman** and **John P. Holliman** the three last minors by their guardian or next friend **Devore Brown** vs **Levi Carter** and **Mary Carter** and **James Carter** ... upon the Petition of William P. Holliman and his wife Elizabeth Holliman ... Elizabeth was made a party complainant in this cause without her consent neither had she been properly (Page 87) examined touching her consent to having the lands mentioned in the pleadings in this cause sold ... Petitioners claim some portion of said land in severalty ... ordered that the reports be set aside. That said petitioners be stricken from this Bill as complainants ....

Page 87: **Heirs of Joel L. Settle** Decd. Exparte ... ordered that the Master pay over to **Peter J. Cox** guardian for Joel L. Settle and **Suel Settle** out of the monies in his hands of their estate of Joel L. Settle Decd ... for the use and benefit of said wards.

Page 87: **Matthew Duke** et al vs **Willis Mullins** and wife. ... upon report of the Master the lands described in complainants Bill ... were sold to **Micajah Duke** for $642 for which the Master took his notes in 1 & 2 years with security ....

Page 88: Court adjourned.

Page 89: Chancery Court began for the Chancery District composed of the Counties of Jackson and Putnam in the 4th Chancery Division at the Court House in Gainesborough on the First Monday in **May** it being the 1st day of the month 1843. Present the Honorable **Bromfield L. Ridley** Chancellor &c presiding.

Page 89: **Aaron Biggerstaff** et al vs **James Nevins** et al. Defendants permitted till June Rules to file their answers to Complainants Bill.

Page 89: **David Griffith** Admr &c vs **William Henson** . . . on motion of Complain-ants Solicitor Complainant is permitted to amend his Bill so as to make the heirs of **Nathan Price** Decd defendants to this Bill.

Page 89: **James Young** & wife vs **Brice M. Draper** et al. The order made at the last Term of this Court directing the Clerk and Master to make settlement &c in this cause be reversed and that the Clerk and Master report to the next Term &c.

Page 90: **Lyman E. Bill** vs **Thomas Gentry** ... order made at the last Term directing the Master to take an account be reversed ... Master report to the next Term &c.

Page 90: **Eliza McKinley** et al vs **Matthew C. Mckinley**. Case dismissed.

Page 90: **William McClain**, Esqr. **Alva Cullum** Esqr. **William B. Campbell** Esqr. **John L. Goodall** Esqr. **John B. McCormack** Esqr. and **William B. Richardson** Esqr.... placed upon the roll as practising [sic] solictors [sic] of this court.

Page 90: Tuesday, **May 2, 1843**, 8 o'clock. **Bromfield Ridley** presiding. **George M. McWhirter** Clerk and Master tendered his resignation ... (Page 91) George M. McWhirter is reappointed to fill that office for the Term of Six years ... George M. McWhirter then presented to the Chancellor the three following bonds ... we George M. McWhirter, **James T. Quarles**, **Thomas L. Bransford**, **Samuel B. M. Fowler**, **Russel M. Kinnaird** and **Merlin Young**, all of Jackson County are held and firmly bound unto **James C. Jones**, Governor of the State of Tennessee and his successors in office in the penal sum of $5000.00 ....

Pages 92 –93: (Contains copies of individual bonds for the above named securities. No genealogical nor historical information is given.)

Page 93: **William Jarod** vs **Hugh W. Carlin** ... Defendant is discharged from the attachment against him ....

Page 93: **Heirs of Joel L. Settle** Decd. Exparte. On motion and petition of the guardian of the heirs ... ordered that the Master apportion among said heirs the funds in his hands arising from the sales of the land and negro sold by order of this court ... (Page 94) ....

Page 94: **George S. Bugg**, Esqr & **William H. Richardson** Esqr. ... placed upon the roll as practising [sic] solicitors of this Court.

Page 94: **Samuel E. Hare** & **Watson M. Cook** vs **David Richie** and **William C. Burke**. Complainants Bill dismissed and they pay the costs of same.

Page 94: **John N. Gates** vs **Benjamin D. Homes** & wife and others. Complainants Bill dismissed and he pay all costs of same.

Page 95: **Brison Hood** vs **Sarah Rector** and **David M. Rector**. Injunction Bill. And David M. Rector vs Brison Hood. Cross Bill. Came the parties by their solicitors. Brison Hood and Sarah Rector and David M. Rector have agreed to compromise their Chancery suits pending in the Chancery Court at Gainesborough and all matters in dispute between them as follows–said Hood is to have the Negro boy **Charles** and said Sarah and David M. to pay said Hood $200. Sarah and David M. Rector to have the negroes **Cinda**, **Reuben**, **Eliza** & **Lou** ... Sarah and David M. to pay all the costs of ... suits pending between them and each party to pay their own lawyers fees ... Sarah also releases and discharges Brison from ... every obligation that he is under to support and entertain her. /S/ 25 March 1843 by Brison Hood, David M. Rector and **R. P. Brooks** Agent for Sarah Rector. It is agreed that Sarah Rector shall hold the within named negroes Cinda, Reuben, Eliza and Lou with their increase during her natural life, with remainder in (Page 96) said slaves and their increase to said David M. Rector and that a decree be accordingly entered vesting the title pursuant to this agreement 1 May 1843. /S/ Sarah Rector by X-Mark and David M. Rector. Test: **Hart**, Sol. And the said Sarah & David M. also filed the following receipt of said Brison Hood to wit: Received of Sarah Rector $200 in full of the sum agreed to be paid by her to me according to an agreement entered into this day 25 March 1843. /S/ Bryson Hood. Test: **Jas F. Quarles** ....

Page 97: **Letty Roberts** ... Master reports in pursuance to a decree pronounced at the May Term 1842 of this court he on 6 June 1842 ... proceeded to sell at public sale at the Court House in Gainesboro ... for cash in hand all the negroes mentioned in the petition ... as follows: **Handy**, **Sally** and **Harriett** by **John Hughes** $545.00. **Jim** purchased by **Samuel Sullivan** $361.00 and **Dick** purchased by **Reece C. Stewart** $367.00 ... /S/ **G. M. McWhirter** C & M ... the title to the negroes ... be divested of said **James Roberts** and vested in John Hughes ... Samuel Sullivan ... **Reece C. Stewart** ... that **John Scanland** Sheriff of Jackson County be allowed $5.00 for attaching Handy & Jim ... into his possession.

Page 97: **Asa Lynn, Joseph Greene** and **Mounce Gore** vs **Joseph J. Walker**. (Page 98) ... upon Bill and Answer and Motion to dissolve Complainants injunction ... the Answer of the Defendant devised all the Equity set up in Complainants Bill ... Complainants injunction ... be dissolved ... Defendant is permitted to proceed with the collection of his judgement ....

Page 98: **John N. Gates** vs **Samuel B. M. Fowler** and others ... the Answers of the Defendants devised all the Equity set up in Complainants Bill ... decreed by the Court that said Complainants injunction in this cause be dissolved ....

Page 98: **John M. Richmond** vs **Pinckney McCarver** ... report ... in pursuance to interlocutory decree at last term of this court he on the 17th day (Page 99) of December 1842 ... proceeded at the court house in Gainsboro [sic] to sell the horses and part of lot No. 1 in said town ... property was purchased by **Robert Richmond** at the price of $160 for which sum the Master took his three several notes with **Kinnaird** and **Bransford** his security ... a lien was retained upon said property for the purchase money ... /S/ **G M McWhirter** C & M.

Page 99: **William R. __ver, Thomas L. Bransford, William Gipson, A. J. Chapman, Benj. E. Williams, S. W. Cassetty, S. E. Stone, Joseph Eaton, Merlin Young, J. W. Lock, J. G. Backinstoe(?), N. G. Jackson, J. N. Stone, William Putty, Thomas D. Cassetty, L. F. R. Kirkpatrick** and **Z. Hare** vs **Isaac Buck, Richard F. Cooke, Carr Terry, Elijah Carr, H. D. Marchbanks, H. L. McDaniel, Burton Marchbanks, Carven Maddux** and **Larson Clark** ... (Page 100) ... Complainants dismiss their Bill ... defendants pay ... complainants the sum of $135.00 and the cost of the suit ....

Page 100: **Martha Shaw & Rollins Hogin** vs **Christopher Shaw** ... in the presence of Solicitors on both sides ... We the Commissioners appointed by the Chancery Court of Jackson County at its November Term to divide and appropriate the lands mentioned in the order ... have allotted and appropriated to the widow and heirs of **G. W. C. Shaw** decd a portion of said land called lot No. 1 and bounded as follows beginning at a beech about 2 poles above the Spring Branch on the Bank of **Cumberland River** near the mouth of a lane leading from **Smyrna Meeting House** to said river-running N 87º E. 9 1/2 poles to a stake thence N. 86º E. 32 poles thence S. 78º E. 28 poles thence S. 75º E. 21 1/2 poles thence South 168 poles to a white oak in **Sadler's** formerly **Col. J. W. Smiths** line thence East with the ridge 18 poles to a stake thence__ 60º E. 75 poles to a white oak thence (Page 101) N. 61 poles to a Beech thence Nor. 47º W. with the ridge 46 poles thence N. 18º W. 60 poles thence North 25 poles to a stake & two sugar tree pointers in **Rollins Hogins** West boundary line thence N. 80º West 78 poles to a stake in the road near the dwelling house on said lot–thence S. 78 1/2 W. leaving a smoke house on lot No. 2 near the line 64 poles to a double or forked maple on the bank of Cumberland River–thence down said river with its meanders South 40 poles to the Beginning including the dwelling house barn. stables &c. containing by estimation 106 acres. Lot No. 2 allotted to the heirs at law of **Samuel Shaw** decd Beginning at a maple on the bank of river corner of Lot No. 3 running thence East leaving a maple tree standing inside of the field about one pole to the South in all 160 poles to a rock in **Holloman's** west boundary and 2 iron woods for pointers–thence south with Holloman's line passing his corner in all 70 poles to the corner of lot No. 1.–thence North 80 degrees west with the line of lot No. 1. 78 poles to a stake in the road thence South 78 1/2 degrees West with the line of lot No. 1 64 poles to a maple on the bank of the river the North west corner of lot no. 1–thence up said river with its meanders 65 poles to the beginning containing 67 1/2 acres. Lot no. 3 allotted to Christopher Shaw. Beginning at a beech and sugar tree on the bank of Cumberland River the North East corner of the tract and the South West corner of a tract belonging to **Shepherd** running thence East with Shepherd's south boundary line in all 160 poles to a locust and elm on the top of a ridge the North East corner of Lot no. 3 and of the tract thence South with the West boundary line of Holloman's 58 1/2 poles to the North East corner of (Page 102) Lot No. 2–thence West with the line No. 2 165 poles to a maple on the bank of Cumberland River corner of lot No. 2 thence up said river with its meanders North to the beginning. Containing 58 1/2 acres. Your commissioner ... applied the rents of said tract of land for the years 1839.40 [sic] & 41 for $75 for each of the above named years for the total sum of $225.00 ... submitted 27 Jan 1843. /S/ **David G. Shepherd**, **John Hughes** and **Henry W. Sadler** ... the land in the report divest out of the heirs of **George W. C. Shaw**, the heirs at law of Samuel Shaw and Christopher Shaw and the same be vested in the said parties as partitioned ....

Page 102: **Kinnaird** and **Bransford** vs **Henry Eakle** et al. (Page 103) In this cause it appearing Henry Eakle, Sen. has interest in the matter in controversy in this suit, and said Eakle not being before the court. It is therefore ordered by the court that Eakle be permitted to file his Bill in the nature of a Cross Bill to protect his interest.

Page 103: **James W. Locke** vs **Robert White**, **Patrick N. Dudney** & **Sidney S. Dudney** ... Defendants to answer the Complainants Bill ....

Page 103: **John Williams** vs **Jesse McClellan** et al. And Jesse McClellan vs John

Williams et al. Bill & Cross Bill. In this case the Clerk and Master is allowed to have time till the next Term of this court to make his report.

Page 104: **Bird Cannon** & wife vs **Garret Sadler** and others ... continued until the next term ... defendants to take the deposition of a defendant **Henry Sadler**.

Page 104: **William Jarod** vs **Hugh W. Carlin** ... the matters in the Defendants Demurrer are sufficient to sustain it ... because it appears ... the Complainant has equity in his Bill it is ... ordered ... the Complainant be allowed to amend his Bill ....

Page 104: **Samuel E. Stone** & **Leroy B. Settle** vs **Matthew M. Bland** and **Henry F. Burke.** And Matthew M. Bland vs Henry F. Burke, Saml E Stone & L B Settle. Bill and Cross Bill. (Page 105) ...

in the presence of the solicitors on both sides ... Defendant Henry F. Burke is indebted to Complainants ... in the sum of $168.07 and to the Complainant in the Cross Bill in the sum of $434.64 3/4 and also Matthew M. Bland has in his hands as Administrator of **Sally Bland** decd a fund of $446.09 12 which the said Burke and wife are entitled to as distributees of said Sally Bland decd ... the funds in the hands of said Matthew M. Bland Administrator of said Sally Bland decd belonging to Henry F. Burke and wife be applied to the payment of said $434.64 1/2 [*sic*] ... Bland pay the costs of the Cross Bill and Samuel E. Stone and Leroy B Settle pay the costs of the Bill in the first instance ....

Page 105: **Harman Howard** and others vs **Christopher Clemons** and others. And Christopher Clemons et al vs Harman Howard et al. Bill and Cross Bill. (Page 106) ... in the presence of the solicitors of both sides ... it appeared ... **John Clemons** departed this life in Jackson County having first made and published his last will and testament which has been proved and recorded in the County Court of said County in which ... it is directed that the negro woman **Jin** and her child **Sarah Ann** be set at liberty and the three yellow children **Mary, (F?)armer** and **James** be bound out until the age of 21 years and then be set at liberty, and be taught to read the New Testament ... Christopher Clemons is security of said will ... that since the death of said decedent the negro woman Jin had another child named **Lina** and that she is dead and that all of said negroes are under the age of 21 years ... the Complainants in the Bill are not entitled to hire for said negroes and are not entitled to have said negroes distributed and that complainants bill be dismissed ... complainants in the Cross Bill are not entitled to the relief sought not having brought themselves within the provision of the act of 1829 ... complainants in the original Bill pray an appeal from the decision of the Chancellor to the next Term of the Supreme Court of the state of Tennessee at Nashville in said State on the First Monday December next, which is granted them ... (Page 107) where-upon came Harman Howard and **Stewart Watson** unto court and executed bond ....

Page 107: **David Herbert** vs **James McBroom** ... in the presence of Solicitors on both sides ... report of the Master which ... Pursuant to an interlocutory decree pronounced at the last term directing the Clerk to take and State an account of the rents and profits of the land in litigation ... from the proof in the cause he finds McBroom has been in possession of said land from July 1837 till the present time 5 years and 10 months ... (Page 108) land lying in Jackson, now **Putnam County** on **Shaws Branch** of **Martins Creek** granted to Complainant Herbert by the state of Tennessee beginning at a berch [*sic*] sugar tree and hickory in the east boundary line of James McBroom's 50 acre tract and about 8 poles north of his South east corner running thence North with said line and passing his corner and crossing Shaws Branch at 159 poles in all 177 7/10's of a pole to a sugar tree and ash near **Dry Branch** thence East 90 poles to a sugar tree near the top of a ridge thence South crossing a branch at 77 poles and **Hurricane Branch** at 121 poles in all 177 7/10's of a pole to a mulberry, Elm, Hornbeam and two ashes in the West side of a ridge thence West crossing Shaws Branch at 20 poles a small branch at 26 poles in all 90 poles to the beginning containing 100 acres ... a writ of possession is awarded complainant ... said defendant prays an appeal in the cause to the Supreme Court of the State of Tennessee to be held at **Nashville** on the 1st Monday of December next which to him is granted upon his giving bond and security according to law. Whereupon said deft. M'Broom [*sic*] with **Samuel Turney** his surety came into court and executed bond in the sum of $500 ....

Page 108: **Merlin Young** ... appointed deputy Clerk of this Court ... (Page 109) ....

Page 109: **Kinnaird** & **Bransford** vs **Henry Eakle** et al ... complainants dismiss this bill as to Defendant **Gates** ... Court adjourned.

Page 110: (Blank page except for a doodle, "Many men of many minds marry [many] kinds of Mary.")

Page 111: November Term 1843. Held at the court house in Gainesboro for the Counties of Jackson and Putnam in the 4th Chancery Division ... 6 November 1843 in the presence of **Thomas L. Williams** Chancellor presiding by interchange with **Bromfield L. Ridley**.

Page 111: **John Scanland** vs **Isaac Hogin** et al. Leave given both parties to take proof generally for five months from this date.

Page 111: **James Young** et ux vs **Brice M. Draper** et al. Orders made in this cause at the last term be revived ... the Master is directed to report to the next Term ....

Page 111: **John Williams** vs **Thos. L. Clemens** et al. And **Jesse McClendon** vs John Williams & others. Bill & Cross Bill. (Page 112) ... Master reports in pursuance to an interlocutory decree pronounced at November term 1842 he on 22 December 1842 after giving notice to sell the lands mentioned ... the same were purchased by Jesse McClendon ... at the following prices: 50 acres tract at $170. 5 acres tract at $39 and the mills and one acre of ground in which they are situated at $71 ... for which he took the notes of Jesse McClendon payable at time required by said decree together with **Merlin Young** and **Amon Hale** his securities and a lien retained upon the land for the purchase money ....

Page 111: **William Gipson** vs **William Poston** ... complainant this day filed his affidavit setting forth that defendant is committing great waste upon the lands in the pleadings by cutting destroying and selling the timber thereof ... said land is valuable more on account of its timber than for any thing else (Page 113) and that fear is entertained by the complainant that if the waste is permitted to be continued he will not be able to make the balance of his purchase money out of the same. It is ordered ... all persons be enjoined from committing waste upon the timber of said land ... except such as may be necessary for firewood.

Page 113: **William Gipson** vs **William Poston**. Decree ... complainant sold to defendant by title bond 88 acres of land in Jackson county several years ago and that part of the purchase money for said land is due and unpaid ....

Page 113: **John Myers** vs **Josiah Copeland**. Decree ... on 24 January 184? the (Page 114) defendant executed his note to **David W. Martin** for $152.73 1/2 payable on or before the first day of April then next and that said note had become the rightful property of the complainant by a regular assignment for a valuable consideration that yet remains due ... defendant is and was at the time of filing the bill a resident Citizen of **New Orleans** ... **Louisiana** and ... is the legal and rightful owner and is seized of a tract of Land lying in (Jackson County) ... bounded and described as follows: beginning at a beech the north East corner of **John Griffiths** old tract and running west with the Griffith tract 333 poles to a poplar and beech thence north 160 poles to a hickory thence East 80 poles to a beech South one pole to a stake thence East to a beech standing on the west bank of **Jennings Creek** it being the corner of the **William Morrell** tract thence down the bank of said creek to a beech the other corner of the Morrell tract crossing the creek to a small sugar tree at the foot of a hill on the west bank of a small branch thence up said branch with its meanders on the line of said Morrell tract five poles to a stake thence north to a buckeye and then sugar trees in the line of said Morrale [sic] tract thence East 38 poles to a large beech in the line of said Morrell tract thence south 75 poles to a double linn thence west 73 poles to a stake in the east boundary line of **James Young** old boundary line thence south to the beginning containing 363 acres and that said tract of land was attached by the Sheriff of

Jackson county on 28 February 1843 ... ordered to be sold (Page 115) at the court house in Gainesboro after advertising ....

Page 115: **Samuel E. Hare** and **Watson M. Cook** vs **Christopher Shaw** ... Christopher Shaw on 9 March 1842 morgaged [*sic*] by deed of that date to the complainants the land in the pleadings ... it further appearing said C. Shaw is not a resident of Tennessee and publication has been made in the Carthage Republican (Carthage, TN) ... the Master after advertising the same at least five public places one of which to be at the court house door in Gainesboro and one at **Granville** ....

Page 116: **John N. Gates** vs **Benjamin D. Holmes** et al. Ordered by the court that complainants Bill be dismissed and that he pay the costs of same.

Page 116: **David Griffith** vs **William Henson** et al ... cause remanded to the rules.

Page 116: **Lyman E. Bill** vs **Thomas Gentry** ... complainant has availed himself of the Bankrupt Law ... ordered the pleadings be amended as to make the General Assignee in Bankruptcy for the Middle district of ... Tennessee a party complainant to this suit ....
Page 116: **William Jarod** vs **Hugh W. Carlin** ... cause remanded to the rules and each of the parties permitted to take what testimony they think proper if taken within five months from this date.

Page 117: **Sam E. Hare** vs **H** & **John W. Richmond** ... continued ....

Page 117: **John Rodgers** vs **Eliza McKinley** ... continued ....

Page 117: **James W. Locke** vs **Robert White** et al ... continued ... parties permit-ted to take what proof they may think necessary touching the general character of **Mary Cornwell** and **John Cummings** if taken within five months from this date.

Page 117: **Asa Lynn** et al vs **Joseph J. Walker**. Cause remanded to the rules ... parties permitted to take what proof they may think proper if taken within five months from this date.

Page 117: **Russel M Kinnaird** & **Thomas L. Bransford** vs **Josiah Copeland** ... (Page 118) ... Defendant is indebted to the Complainants in the sum of $199.05 and Deft. is a non resident and now resides in the city of **New Orleans** ... **Louisiana** and he is seized of the lands in the pleadings and he owns no personal property in this state ... Clerk to sell the lands ... and the proceeds of the sale be applied to the payment and the costs herein ....

Page 118: **Joel Lynn** vs **Josiah Copeland** & **Leroy B. Settle** ... Copeland is indebted to the Complainant in the sum of $264.06 ... Copeland is a non resident of this State and is the owner of 363 acres in Jackson County ... Copeland conveyed by deed of mortgage to Defendant Settle on 28 September 1835 other lands in the County of Jackson to secure said Settle in the payment of money due of said Copeland to said Settle ... (Page 119) decreed ... the 363 acres be sold ....

Page 119: **Matthew C. McKinley** and **Elizabeth Moore** &c vs **Robert Burton** and **William Q. Hughes**. Decree ... **James and Josiah McKinley** on 19 March 1838 by deed of that date conveyed to Matthew C. in trust for said Elizabeth (and) her children Negro slave **Barbary** and her increase ... said negroes are not liable for the satisfaction of the judgements obtained by the Defendants against **Richard Moore** ... defendants are perpetually enjoined from selling said Negroes ... by virtue of execution on said judgements against Richard Moore ....

Page 120: **William Canter, Margaret Holloman, William W.ade Holloman** by their next friend **Dixon Brown** vs **Levi Canter, Nancy Canter, James Canter, William P. Holloman** and his wife **Elizabeth** ... it appeared to the Court that **Zachariah Canter** departed this life and at his death he claimed title to 80 acres in Jackson County on the North side of **Cumberland River** on the same in **Brooks Bend** joining the lands of **Micajah Duke** on the West of **Matthew Duke's** on the North & East of **Thomas Burton** and **Johnath** [sic] **Dixon** the East ... William P. Holloman and his wife Elizabeth claim title to 40 acres of said tract in severalty. Clerk to report upon the title of same that they may have acquired by conveyance or by the Statue of Limitations and report next Term. Court adjourned ....

Page 120: Tuesday morning 7 Nov 1843 9 o'clock. Hon. **Thomas L. Williams** presiding.

Page 121: **Solomon S. Leonard** vs **Alva Graves** et al ... continued ....

Page 121: **Andrew McClellan** & **Beverly Graves** vs **Alva Graves** et al ... continued ...

Page 121: **Daniel Lee** Admr &c vs Creditors of **Abraham Lee** Decd. Ordered ... the Creditors of Abraham Lee Decd appear and make themselves Defendants in this suit and file their claims against said Decd on or before the next Term ....

Page 121: **Harrison J. Hughes** vs **George W. Webb**. By complainant dismissed.

Page 121: **Nancy Pharris** by &c vs **Absalom Pharris**. Plaintiff dismisses her Bill.

Page 122: **Matthew C. McKineley** [sic] & **Elizabeth Moore** by &c vs **William Q. Hughes** & **Robert G. Burton**. Cause for the present remanded to the rules for proof to be taken within five months from this date.

Page 122: **Bird S. Cannon** et ux. vs **Abisha Cannon** et al ... for reasons appearing by affidavit of the agent of Cmplts ... the Clerk issue writs of injunction restraining the Defendants **Henry & Garret Sadler** or either of them from hiring, sending or permitting any of the negroes in litigation in this suit from leaving this Chancery District until the final hearing of this cause.

Page 122: **Thompson Cason** vs **Sterling Harris** ... this court has not jurisdiction of any of the matters alleged in said Bill ... Complts Bill be dismissed ....

Page 123: **William G. Darwin** vs **John G. Burke**. Deft. Burke has leave to take the negro attached into his possession by his first giving bond and security for the forth coming of said negro at the next term of this court. Sheriff of Jackson County take said negro into possession and hire him out until the next term of this court taking bond and security for the hire and also for the forthcoming of the negro at the next term of this court and make report ....

Page 123: **Cannon** et al vs Cannon et al. On affidavit of Deft. **Garret Sadler** this bill is continued ... time is given both parties to take general proof as to identity of Complt **Lucinda** ....

Page 123: **Sam E. Stone** & **Leroy B. Settle** vs **Henry F. Burke** et al ... Henry F. is indebted to Complainant (but the amount is uncertain) and said defendant is not an inhabitant of this state and has no (Page 124) personal property except what is in the hands of his co defendants **Wm C. Burke** and **Richd P. Brooks** as Administrators of the Estate of **John Burke** Decd. Clerk ordered to take an accounting of the indebtedness of Henry F. to Complts and state an account of the distributive share of said Henry F. Burke of the Estate of said John Burke, decd within the hands of said Wm Burke & Richd P. Brooks as Admrs ....

Page 124: **Russel M. Kinnaird** & **Thomas. L. Bransford** vs **Henry Eakle Jr.**, **George Kinnaird**, et al ... Eakle is indebted to complainant for $126.77 1/4 and said defend-ant has no property real or personal in this State and is not an inhabitant of this State and George Kinnaird is indebted to the co-defendant in the sum of $146.46 due by note ... ordered that George Kinnaird pay said complainants $126.77 [sic] due complaints by said Henry and execution issue therefore and Henry Eakle be perpetually enjoined from collecting said $126.77 1/4 and the injunction be dis-solved for the ballance [sic] of the debt due by said George to his codefendant ....

Page 125: **Christopher Clemons** vs **Harmon Howard** et al ... continued ... leave given complainant to take the depositions of **Boon Pennington James Gully** and **John R. Welch** ... **David Griffith Temperance Stone Henry Eakle Sr Abraham Hughes Locke Hale Henry Ritter Alfred Pursel Phillip Robertson**, **Alexander Hardin** and **John Right** ... defendants permitted to take rebutting testimony.

Page 125: **Lewis R. Vance** vs **James L. Hughes**. Continued ....

Page 125: **John Myers** vs **Josiah Copeland** ... on (blank) the defendant executed to **David Johnson** by note for $138.62 1/2 and it fell due 25 April 1842 and complain-ant purchased note from Johnson ... the same was transpired to complainant about the last of March 1842 by delivery ... (Page 126) Defendant is and was at the time of the filing a resident of the city of **New Orleans** ... and was seized and possessed of a certain tract of land in Jackson County containing 363 acres bounded as follows: Beginning at the beech the N. E. corner of **John Griffiths** old tract running thence West with the Griffith tract 333 poles to a poplar & beech thence North 160 po. [sic] to a hickory thence East 80 po. [sic] to a beech thence South 1 po. [sic] to a stake thence East to a beech standing on the West bank of **Jennings Creek** it being a corner of **William Morrele** tract thence down the bank of said creek to a beech on the corner of the Morrele tract thence South 61 3/4º E. with a line of the said Morrele tract crossing the creek to a small sugartree at the foot of a hill and on the West bank of a small branch thence up said branch with its meanders & with the line of the Morrele tract thence East 38 po. [sic] to a large beech in the line of the said Morrele tract thence South 75 po. [sic] to a double lynn thence West 75 po. [sic] to a stake in the East boundary line of **James Young's** old tract thence South to the Beginning ... said land was levied by the Sheriff of Jackson County 4 February 1843 by virtue of an attachment issued in this cause. Tract ordered to be sold at the Court House door in Gainesboro (Page 127) ....

Page 127: **Daniel Lee** Admr vs the Creditors of **Abraham Lee.** For reasons appearing by affidavit ... ordered to pay complainant out of the moneys in his hands of the estate of Abraham Lee decd $3.24 being the amount of taxes on the said estate for the years 1842 & 1843 paid by said complainant.

Page 127: **Pinckney McCarver** vs **John Eakle** et al ... upon Bill that Complainant McCarver had purchased of Deft **Cross** a lot in Gainesboro marked in platt [sic] of said town as Lot No. 1 ... that he had paid the purchase money of same. It also appearing that Cross purchased the same of Deft **Richmond** when in part payment he gave a note of $200 on Deft. Eakle. That Eakle had been sued on said note and execution returned nothing and Richmond had filed his Bill against said Complt McCarver to subject (Page 128) said town lot to sale for the purchase money ... the lot has been sold under decree of this Court ... said judgement be perpetually enjoined annulled and for nothing taken ... decreed that the complainant pay the cost of this suit & that he have decree over Defts **Isaac ___ford** for the suit.

Page 128: **Harrison J. Hughes** vs **George W. Webb**. Complainant by his solicitor dismisses his Bill. Court adjourned.

Page 129: **May Term 1844**. Chancery Court held at Gainesboro for the counties of Jackson and Putnam and 4th Chancery Division on the first Monday it being 6 May 1844, **Bromfield L. Ridley** Chancellor presiding ....

Page 129: **Lyman E. Bill** vs **Thomas Gentry** Motion. The order made herein at the last term be modified so as to make the General assignee in Bankruptcy for the Middle District of Tennessee a Defendant to this suit ....

Page 129: **Christopher Clemons** vs **Harmon Howard** et al ... this cause had been set for trial before the Bill had been taken for confessed against **Sampson** and **Margaret Allen** ... said cause set for hearing exparte as to them.

Page 129: **Asa Lynn** et al vs **Joseph J. Walker**. (Page 130) ... continued ....

Page 130: **Wilson C. Canter** et al vs **James Canter** et al ... sale heretofore made of the land in the pleadings was at a former term of this court set aside ... ordered the notes executed by **Richard Duke** the purchaser be delivered to him by the Clerk & Master.

Page 130: **Sophia** et al [sic] vs **Henry & Robert Richmond**. Leave was given the complainants at last term of the Court to take the depositions of **William Scanland**, **Jonathan Rogers** & **Nancy Anderson** and to retake the deposition of **Sampson W. Cassetty** and that the order was omitted to be entered of record. It is now ordered ... cause continued ....

Page 130: **Rice Maxey** Esq ... permitted to practice as a Solicitor in this Court.

Page 130: **James T. Hughs** for &c vs **Henry Cheek** et al. This cause was irregularly set for hearing (Page 131) ... the same remanded to the rules for further steps.

Page 131: **Martha Shaw** et al vs **Christopher Shaw**. Clerk & Master allowed $2 for his services as receiver in this cause. Court adjourned until tomorrow.

Page 131: Tuesday morning. **May 7th 1844**. 8 O'clock. **Bromfield L. Ridley** Chancellor.

Page 131: **William Gipson** vs **William Poston** ... In pursuance to an interlocutory decree in the last term of this court ... there remains due and unpaid $246.04 the balance of the consideration money given for the lands in the pleadings and 75 cents cost. /S/ **G. M. McWhirter** C & M. (Page 132) ... land is to be sold ....

Page 132: **Samuel E. Hare** & **Wilson M. Cooke** vs **Christopher Shaw** ... upon report of the Clerk & Master pursuance [sic] of an interlocutory decree made at the last term ... sold on 28 December 1843 said land ... on a credit of six months when **John Hughs** became the purchaser for $475.00 ... land bounded as follows: Beginning at a beech **Hiram Sadler's** upper corner on the bank of the river about two poles above the mouth of the **Spring Branch** and running N 87º and a half poles (Page 133) thence 86º East 26 poles thence North 82º East 32 poles thence South 78º East 38 poles thence south 75º East 21 1/2 poles to an elm, oak and ash in **Hogin's** line thence South with said line 160 poles to ... the top of a ridge in **Col. Smith's** line thence

Eastward with said line the meanders of the top of said ridge 26 poles to an oak marked as a corner of a division line between said Hogin thence northward with said line 40 poles to a beech thence with said division line with the top of the ridge 170 poles to an iron wood in **Mark Holliman's** corner thence with his line on the top of a ridge northward 109 poles to a locust elm and honeybeam, **Shepherds** corner thence West with his line 160 poles to ... the bank of river thence down the river with its meanderings to the beginning. Containing by estimation 230 acres ... be divested out of said Christopher Shaw ... and vested in said John Hughs ... subject ... to the special lien for the purchase money .... [page 133][8]

Page 133: **William Jarod** vs **Hugh W. Carlin** ... Defendant indebted to complainant by note for $83.66 for rent of certain land ... Defendant being tenant of complain-ant for the year 1842 and it further appearing ... the Defendant was guilty of the charges (Page 134) ... plaintiff to recover $83.66 plus interest accrued ....

Page 134: **Lyman E. Bill** vs **Thomas Gentry** ... ordered the complainant give new security for prosecution on or before the first rule day after this term or said cause will be dismissed.

Page 134: **E. M. Patterson** et al vs **Letty Roberts** Extrx &c. Came the parties by their solicitors and the complainants dismiss their suit ....

Page 134: **Bird Cannon** et ux vs **Garret Sadler** et al ... continued ... upon Defend-ants paying all costs that have accrued (Page 135) ... ordered the cause be opened for proof generally as to the identity of complainant **Lucinda Cannon** ....

Page 135: **James Young** and wife vs **Brice M. Draper** et al ... complainants James and ~~Elizabeth~~ Young refused to comply with the order of this court made ... at a former Term directing Complainants and Defendants to execute quit claim deeds to each other for the respective lots of land awarded to them ... James and ~~Elizabeth are~~ is in contempt of this court by ~~their~~ reason of his refusal to execute such quit claim deed ... ordered that an attachment issue to attach the bod<u>yes</u> of James Young and ~~Elizabeth Young~~ to answer said charge of contempt &c.

Page 135: **Samuel E. Stone** & Co vs **Henry F. Burke** et al. The order made last term is to be revised and the Clerk and master report to the next Term ....

Page 135: **Merlin Young** vs **William Patterson** et al. (Page 136) Complainant by his solicitor dismissed his suit ....

Page 136: **Matthew Duke** et al vs **Willis Mullins** et al ... the Clerk proceed to collect the monies owing upon the sale of the lands sold in this cause and when collected pay the same over to those entitle to receive the same ....

Page 136: **John Scanland** vs **Isaac Hogin** et al. Cause remanded to the rules and leave given the complainant to file an amended Bill.

Page 136: **N. G. Jackson** vs **Benjamin E. Williams**. Clerk appointed receiver in this cause and proceed to collect the notes and accounts and other debts to the firm of **Jackson & Williams**.

Page 136: **Harmon Howard** et al vs **Christopher Clemons** et al. And Christopher Clemons vs

---

[8] This entry is marked through with the word "Rescinded" on both pages of the document.

Harman Howard et al. Bill & Cross Bill. (Page 137) ... a copy of the Will of **John Clemons** Decd was used upon the hearing of this cause ... solicitors on both sides agreed the same was correctly set forth in the answer ... the will was sent to the Court of Errors ... the Clerk and Master is to procure a copy of said will from the office of the Clerk of the County Court of Jackson County and send the same together with a copy of this order to the next Term of the Supreme Court of the State of Tennessee to be held at Nashville on the First Monday of December next.

Page 137: **James W. Lock** vs **Robert White** et al ... at the time of taking the deposition of **Mary Cornwell** to be read in this cause she was the wife of the Security for the prosecution of this suit and therefore an incompetent witness ... (Page 138)[9] Court adjourned until tomorrow.

Page 138: Wednesday morning **May 8 1844**, **Bromfield L. Ridley** presiding.

Page 138: **Perry Mahanay** vs **Edwin F. McKinney** et al ... complainant had here-tofore became the accommodation endorser of Defendant E. F. McKinney for near the sum of $300.00, that as such endorser he had been sued & judgment obtained for about $318.00 and such judgement has been since settled ... Defendant E. F. McKinley [sic] is not now a Citizen of this State but of the State of **Missouri** ... McKinley before he left this State placed in the hands of defendant **Tolbert** three writings obligatory on Defendant **Van Hooser** amounting to about $450.00, the two first due, the other due in 1845 that he placed in his hands some other small claims and (Page 139) that McKinney took the receipt of Tolbert for same which is outstanding, it further appearing that McKinny [sic] was indebted to Tolbert in the sum of about $70 besides interest which was to be paid out of said claims and also McKinny is indebted to **George M McWhirter** by note ... it further appearing McKinney is the owner of the land in the pleadings mentioned lying in Jackson County which has been attached to satisfy complainant demand ... Clerk ordered to take an accounting and report to the next Term and sell said land at public sale in Gainesboro on a credit of 6 & 12 months ....

Page 140: **Christopher Clemmons** vs **Harmon Howard** et al. And Harmon Howard et al vs Christopher Clemens [sic] et al. Bill and Cross Bill ... in the presence of coun-sel upon both sides it appeared that **John Clemens** his lifetime now deceased on 30 September 1837 conveyed to ... Christopher Clements [sic] a tract of land con-taining 400 acres lying in Jackson County on **line [sic] creek** that said deed though absolute upon its face was only intended as a mortgage the Complainant executed to him a defeasance bond to reconvey said land upon the payment of all such sums of money as he may owe to him that said John was intemperate or prodigal in his affairs ... that on 31 January 1840 John and Christopher Clemmons came to a settlement the said John then being sober and of sound mind when John sold to Christopher that portion of said land which lies in the forks of said creek for $640.00 and after paying for the land so sold John was still indebted to Christopher for money loaned and paid for him to the amount of $291.32 ... and such other sums as Christopher might pay for the said John in settling his debts until the 1st of May 1841 ... complainant and defendants are the heirs at law of the said John and the land (Page 141) mentioned be divested out of the Defts and vested in the complainant ... Clerk to take an accounting of the amount due the complainant and also an account of the assets ... further decreed the Cross Bill be dismissed ... remainder of land to be sold at public sale after advertising ... and said Harmon Howard & his wife, complainants in the cross Bill pay the cost thereof ....

Page 141: **William G. Darwin** vs **John G. Burke** . . . upon report of the Clerk ... complt Darwin

---

[9] The word "Rescinded" is written over the copy of this Entry.

had the possession & use of the negro boy **Hall** for 6 months (Page 142) and 13 days and the labor of said boy **Hal** [*sic*] was worth $3 per month ....

Page 142: **Thomas Hicklin, Avery Hicklin, Benjamin Biggerstaff, Elizabeth** his wife, **James Parish** & **Polly**, his wife, **Nelson Nunly** & **Letty**, his wife, and **Aaron Biggerstaff** vs **James Nevins** & **Polly**, his wife, **George W. Atterberry** & **Hannah**, his wife, **Joseph Olive** and **Samuel Olive, James Nevins** & **G. W. Atterberry** Administrators of **Perry Hicklin** Decd. ... Perry Hicklin departed this life in Jackson County several years ago leaving complainants and defendants his heirs at law. That he did possess of an estate real and personal that the land whereof he died seized had been sold for distribution by a decree of the Circuit Court of Jackson County ... that Benjamin Biggerstaff & wife and **Avery M. Hicklin** had transferred their share in said estate to complainant Aaron Biggerstaff that ... James Nevins and George W. Atterberry had administered upon said estate and had took into their possession the assets ... ordered and decreed ... that the Clerk take and state an account charging them with all the assets and effects of the said Perry Hicklin which came to the hands of the said Administrators ... (Page 143) ....

Page 143: **John Myers** vs **Josiah Copeland.** And **John Myers** vs **Josiah Copeland** & **Russell M. Kinnaird** & **Thomas L. Bransford** vs **Josiah Copeland** ... the land in said cases was sold by the master of this court for $850 to Thomas L. Bransford he being the highest bidder ... that the two Bills of John Myers against Josiah Copeland were filed before the Bill of Kinnaird & Bransford and therefore have priority of lien ... which land is butted and bounded as follows ... Beginning at a beach the N.E. corner of **John Griffiths** old tract and running thence West with the Griffith tract 333 poles to a poplar & Beech thence North 160 poles to a hic<u>kry</u> thence E. 80 poles to a beech thence South 1 pole to a stake thence East to ... the west bank of **Jennings Creek** it being a corner (Page 144) of the **William Morrell** tract. Thence down the bank of said creek to a ... corner in the Morrell tract, thence S. 61 3/4º E with the line of said Morel tract crossing the creek ... at the foot of a hill & on the West Bank of a small branch. thence up said branch with its meanders and with the line of the Morrell tract five poles to a stake thence North to ... the line of the said Morrell tract thence E. 38 poles to ...a large beech in the line of the said Morrell tract thence S 75 poles to a double lynn thence W. 73 poles ... to the East boundary line of **James Young's** old tract thence S. to the Beginning containing 360 acres ... decreed the above causes be consolidated ....

Page 144: **Letty Roberts** Executrix of **James Roberts** decd vs **James G. Holliman** ... motion to dissolve the injunction granted (Page 145) ... the equity of complain-ants Bill is fully answered and met by Defendants answer ... the defendant have his execution at law ... upon first entering into bond and security ....

Page 145: **John W. Jewett** Admr &c vs **William W. Woodfolk**. Leave is given the defendant until July rules to file his answer.

Page 145: **Nathaniel G. Jackson** vs **Benjamin E. Williams**. By agreement of the Parties ... the receiver in this cause pay out of the partnership funds which may come to his hands such of the debts due from the firm as the parties shall agree on and time is given the Defendant until June rules next to file his answer ....

Page 145: **Samuel B. M. Fowler** & his wife, **Adaline Fowler** vs **Polly Butler, Thomas H. Butler, Franklin W. Butler Lucetta Butler Erasmus Denton S S Butler Marium Butler, Susanna Butler, John S.(?) Butler Martha Butler** & **Bailey Butler** ... on 20 September 1842 one Bailey Butler made and published his last will & testament in (Jackson County) and shortly thereafter died leaving complainants and defendants his heirs and distributees except (Page 146) said Denton who is guardian for Defendant Lucetta ... in the bequests of said testator to complainants and defendants Lucetta Thomas H. & Franklin W. Butler there is ambiguity and it further appearing that Defendant Thomas H. is the executor of sd will that the testator in his lifetime became liable and was bound as the Security of the Defendant Franklin W. and because it is the opinion of the Court that it was the intention of the Testator to pay all his liabilities of the said Franklin W… that it was the intention of the testator that cmplts should have the tract of land on which they now live it being the same occupied by **William Kendall** at the date of said Will … that Defendant Thomas H. have the lot of land in the will mentioned lying in the lower end of **Turkey Creek** bottom … Defendant Lucetta should have the lot of land in the lower end of the bottom and … that the intention of the parties to this Bill is an amicable settlement of the difficulties arising out of the ambiguous character of parts of the Will and that $20 is a reasonable fee to **Nelson** & **Goodall** in the cause and that the same has been paid by complainant Fowler and ought to have been paid out of the estate … that **Mounce Gore** be appointed to go upon the lands of the estate and survey, lay off, mark & set apart to said Thomas H & Lucetta the tracts of land above … and report to the next term of this court ….

Page 147: **Eliza McKinly** & other of the heirs of **James M.cKinly** decd vs **Matthew C. McKinly** & others … parties consent to a decree that the complainants, who were a portion of the heirs and distributees of James McKinly decd shall have the negro boy **Dick** in the pleadings at the sum of $600 as so much of the distributive share of said Estate that may be coming to them … but because it appears that a portion of said Complainants are infants and appear by guardian and because it does not appear whether such decree would be to their interest … the Clerk ordered to take an accounting to see whether their interest would be better promoted by selling said negro for distribution.

Page 147: **Lewis R. Vance** vs **James T. Hughs**. Cause continued until next term.

Page 147: **Bird Cannon** & wife vs **Garret Sadler** et al … the order made in this cause on yesterday of this term be altered so to permit defendants to take what testimony they think proper touching the identity of complainant **Lucinda** ….

Page 148: **James W. Locke** vs **Robert White** et al … at the time of taking the deposition of **Mary Cornwell** to be read upon the hearing of this cause She was an incompetent witness. On motion said deposition is rejected by the court … cause continued until next term.

Page 148: **John Rogers** vs **Eliza McKinly** et al … there was no equity in complts Bill which was not fully met and answered by the Defendant Eliza … Bill be dismissed.

Page 148: **Aaron Biggerstaff** et al vs **James Nevins** et al. Leave is given the Defendant **George W. Atterberry** until September rules to file his answer ….

Page 148: **Nathan Montgomery** vs **Thomas L. Bransford** et al. Leave given Defen-dants Thomas L. Bransford & **Russell M Kinnaird** to file their answers (Page 149) ….

Page 149: **James Young** & wife vs **Brice M Draper** et al. Order revived and the Master is directed to report to the next term.

Page 149: **Samuel E. Hare** & **Watson M. Cooke** vs **Christopher Shaw** … upon the reports of the Master … He on 28 December 1843 sold the land mentioned … (it was) purchased by **John Hughs** at the price of $475.00 for which sum the master reports he took the note of said Hughs payable 6 months after date together with **Simon Hogin** and **Rawlins Hogin** security and a lien retained upon the land for the purchase money …. /S/ **G. M. McWhirter** C & M.

Page 150: **Samuel E. Hare** & **Watson M. Cooke** vs **Benjamin Monroe** et al ... by agreement of the parties by their counsel ... the Clerk shall take and state an account to the next term of this court of the amount of indebtedness of Defendant Benjamin Monroe to complainants, of the indebtedness of said Monroe to the Defendants **Montgomery** & **McWhirter**, how said debtedness [sic] was created and of the indebtedness of the said Monroe to the firm of Montgomery & Monroe ... ordered that **William Davidson** be appointed receiver ....

Page 150: **James Young** & wife vs **John Scanland Benjamin Scanland Absalom Johnson Nelson Sadler David Johnson** & **Joseph B. Fitzgerald**. At the November 1842 term a decree was rendered in favor of the complainants and against **Brice M Draper** for $879.72 with costs ... on 6 March 1843 an execution issued from the Office of Clerk on said judgement directed to the Sheriff of Jackson County (Page 151) which execution came to the hands of **John Scanland** as Sheriff ... Scanland as Sheriff has failed to return said execution according to law ... that Scanland as Sheriff and said Benjamin Scanland Absalom Johnson Nelson Sadler David Johnson & Joseph B. Fitzgerald as his securities on 7 March 1842 entered into bond in the sum of $12,500.00 payable to **James C. Jones** Governor of the State of Tennessee ... that at the time the said execution was placed in the hands of John Scanland as Sheriff there were three several credits endorsed upon the back of the same amounting in all to $608.93 and there remained due upon said execution at the time the same was placed in the hands of John Scanland a balance of $270.89 1/2 (Page 152) principal and the sum of $18.42 cost ... ordered the complainants recover against sd defendants the sum of $289.31 1/2 and $24.30 interest ... and $39.20 it being the 12 1/2 per cent damages on the same ....

Page 152: **David Griffith** Admr &c vs **William Hinson** et al. Decree ... **Nathan Price** on 4 February 1837 sold to William Hinson the lands in the pleadings for $345.78 for which Hinson executed his Bill single and Nathan executed to Hinson his bond conditioned to make Hinson a title to lands with general warranty ... that Nathan Price departed this life intestate ... that complainant David Griffith is administrator and the defendants **Campbell B. Price Susan Price Thomas K. Price. Patrick Kernel** and **Elizabeth Kernel** & **Nancy Price** are the heirs at law of said Nathan decd. that said notes not being paid at maturity, complainant as Administrator &c recovered judgement against William Hinson in the Circuit Court of Jackson County on said notes at July Term 1840 for $91.03 for debts and damages and $7.90 costs of suit that before filing this Bill a writ of Sci Facies issued from said court to the Sheriff of Jackson County against William Hinson and was returned (Page 153) nothing found It was decreed by the court that the Clerk sell the lands at public sale ....

Page 153: **Solomon L. Leonard** vs **Alvey Graves** ... Defendant is indebted to Complainant for $77.34 debt and interest and $1.34 costs before Justice of the Peace and Defendant is not a resident of this State but is the owner of a negro now in this county named **Aletha** ... that the Master of this court sell said negro girl at the court house in Gainesboro ... the proceeds of sale be applied to the payment of complainants debt ....

Page 153: **Joel Lynn** vs **Josiah Copeland** & **L B Settle** ... (Page 154) Clerk and Master sold the lands in the pleadings to **Thomas L. Bransford** for $850 and the amounts due **John Myers** and **Kinnaird** & Bransford are $766.10 1/2 with accruing interest and cost has priority over complainants debt of $291.98 recovered at last Term of this court and that title has been decreed to said Thomas Bransford in the two cases of Myers against Copeland and the case of Kinnaird & Bransford against said Copeland . . . there is now due from Deft Copeland and his co-defendant Settle $566.96. It is ordered by the Court that report be in all things confirmed and that the proceeds of said sale when collected by the Clerk & Master after satisfying the debts and costs of Myers & Kinnaird & Bransford be appropriated to the payment of complainants debt ... and the mortgage be foreclosed ....

Page 154: **Andrew MClellan** & **Beverly Graves** vs **Alvy Graves, Parmelia Graves** et al ... (Page 155) complainants are bound as securities for the Defendant Alvey in a bond to **Richard P. Brooks** and **William C Burke** Administrators of **John Burke** decd in the sum of $356 and interest from the time said note fell due the price of a negro girl named **Aletha** and the title to said Aletha is vested in Defendant Alvey ... Alvey is not a resident of this state but that negro **Aletha** is in Jackson County ... Defendant Parmelia wife of Defendant **Alvey Graves** is one of the distributees of John Burke Decd and as such is entitled to a share ... ordered that the Clerk & Master sell the negro Aletha at the court house in Gainesboro and the proceeds of said sale after paying the debt and cost in the case of **Solomon Leonard** against Alvey Graves in which an interlocutory decree was provisioned in this court ... and the Clerk & Master inform the Defendant Parmelia by letter that her share of the assets of the estate of John Burke is enjoined in the hands of said Admrs ....

Page 156: **Matthew McKinley** & **Elizabeth Moore** vs **William L. Hughes** & **Robert G. Burton**. Decree ... appeared to the court that the negro woman **Barbara** and her son **Wade** and other increase in the pleadings are the property of **Richard Moore** husband of complainant Elizabeth by gift from **Robert McKinley** to said Elizabeth ... this cause be dissolved ....

Page 156: **Wilson C. Canter** et al vs **William P. Holliman** & wife et al. Decree ... William P. Holliman & his wife **Elizabeth** have no title in severalty to any of the lands in the pleadings neither by gift, the statute of limitations or otherwise ... Clerk and Master ordered to sell the lands in the pleadings at public sale on the premises after advertising in (Page 157) Jackson County one of which shall be at **Granville** & report to next term.

Page 157: **Daniel Lee** Administrator &C vs the Creditors of **Abraham Lee** Decd. Ordered that the Master sell the lands in the pleadings at public sale subject to the widow's dower ....

Page 157: **Silas C. Cornwell** and **Pleasant F. Cornwell** vs **Andrew McClellan** and **William B. Nickens** ... it appeared to the satisfaction of the court that complainants recovered judgement at law against Wm B Nickens for the sum mentioned in the Bill of Complaint ... no property of Defendant Nickins to be found wherefore to levy ... that the Defendant McClellan purchased the negro slave **Cynthia** and her child **Margaret** from his codefendant Nickins prior to the execution of said judgement and for a full and fair consideration and without (Page 158) fraud ... that Defendant Nickins purchased from his codefendant McClellan a certain tract ... containing 200 acres at the price of $4 per acre ... $400 of the purchase money for said land has been paid by the sale of said negroes and the balance remains unpaid but what that balance is does not satisfactorily appear to the Court ... Clerk & Master ordered to ascertain and report upon the title of Defendant McClellan to said land–whether any part of said land is held by a superior adverse title and if so how much and the value thereof ... Court adjourned.

Page 159: **Asa Lynn**, **Joseph Green** & **Mounce Gore** vs **Joseph H. Walker** (Case marked out.)

Page 160: Blank page
Page 161: November Term 1844 of the Chancery Court at Gainesborough. **Bromfield L. Ridley**, Chancellor, presiding. Monday, 11 Nov. 1844, 1 o'clock.

Page 161: **Samuel E. Stone** et al vs **Henry F. Burke** et al. Clerk & Master ordered to take and account and report to the next term of this court.

Page 161: **Hicklin's Heirs** vs Hicklins Admr. Clerk & Master to take an account ... (Page 162) and report to the next term. Court adjourned ....

Page 162: Tuesday morning 12 Nov 1844 8 o'clock.

Page 162: **Eliza McKinley** et al vs **Matthew C. McKinley** et al ... it appearing from the report that it would be to the advantage of the complainants Eliza McKinley, **Sarah McKinley Jane McKinley Mary McKinley Elizabeth McKinley James McKinley Martha McKinley** and **Robert B. McKinley** the last named seven minor children of James McKinley Decd that the negro boy **Dick** should not be sold but should be reserved amongst them and taken by them as a part of their distributive shares at the price of $600.00 ... the cost of this suit be paid out of the funds arising from the sale of the other slaves in the hands of Deft. McKinley Admr of **James McKinley** Decd and that the Administrator pay out of said fund to **Samuel Turney** Complainants (Page 163) solicitor the sum of $50 for his services ....

Page 163: **Perry Mahanay** vs **Edwin F. McKinney** et al. Decree ... the Master as receiver has now in his hands the sum of $571.82 and that McKinney is indebted to said receiver in the sum of $69.95 including interest to 12 Nov. 1844 ... he is also indebted to Defendant **John H. Tolbert** for $87.54 including interest to 12 Nov. 1844 and the complainant as the accommodation endorser of defendant McKinney had paid to the Branch Bank of Tennessee at **Sparta** including cost and interest to 12 Nov. 1844 the sum of $352.41 ... Master to retain out of said (Page 164) fund the cost of this suit ... 2ndly the amount of $69.95 the sum due him by McKinney–Thirdly that he pay over to Defendant Tolbert said sum of $87.54 and that he pay over the balance to complainants ... that the Clerk and Master in obedience to said interlocutory decree had proceeded to sell said land in the pleadings and that **Caloway Sizemore** became the purchaser of the same for $150.00 ... all right & title and interest of Defendant Edwin F. McKinney to the tract of land in the pleadings mentioned be divested and that the title to the same bounded as follows: Beginning at a stake on the top of a ridge lying between said McKinney and **Daniel Morgan** on the south boundary line of the said tract of land running East to the corner as deeded from **Bradley** & **Crenshaw** to said McKinney thence North 113 poles to two stakes–thence west to said beginning ridge to a stake–thence with the meanders of said ridge to the beginning being a part of the tract of land purchased by said McKinney from **John Bradley** and **John Crenshaw** be vested in said Calaway Sizemore ... subject nevertheless to a special lien for the purchase money ... that Defendant **James Carlisle** had contracted with McKinney for said land and that he had executed his notes to McKinney for the (Page 165) sum of $500.00 ... for the same it is therefore ordered that McKinney and all other persons from collecting said notes ... and be perpetually enjoined and in future the same be for nothing taken ... that Defendant John H. Tolbert had executed to Defendant McKinney his receipt for the notes and other claims placed in his hands and which have been attached in this cause and which has been handed over to said receiver ... that McKinney be perpetually enjoined from ever in any way disturbing said Tolbert upon said receipts and that the same in the future be null and void ... it does not appear how much will be left of said $471.82 to be applied to the payment of complainants demand ... It is ordered that the Master be continued as receiver that he make and state an account as to any other funds that may come into his hands ... and report to the next term of this Court.

Page 166: **Samuel M. Fite** Esq. Placed upon the Roll as a practicing Solicitor in this Court.

Page 166: **Lewis R. Vance** vs **James T. Hughes**. By consent ... cause continued ....

Page 166: **John Scanland** vs **Isaac Hogin** et al. Complainant appears by his Solicitor and dismisses his suit as to the Defendant **John Hughes**.

Page 166: **Christopher Clemmons** vs **Harmon Howard** et al ... the account taken in this cause by the Clerk & Master be left open for proof on both sides as to the motion(?) on **Birdwell** & **Gates** but as to no other point ... Court adjourned ....

Page 167: Wednesday Morning 13 Nov 1844. 8 o'clock. **B. L. Ridley** Chancellor presiding.

Page 167: **Solomon L. Leonard** vs **Alvey Graves** ... the Clerk and master sold the negro girl **Aletha** in pursuance of an order of last Term to **Joseph Carver** for $356.00 ....

Page 167: **Andrew McClellan** & **Beverly Graves** vs **Alvey Graves** et al ... the Clerk & Master sold the negro girl **Aletha** in the pleadings pursuant to a decree order at last term for $356 to **Joseph Carver** ... ordered the Clerk and (Page 168) Master take an account of amount due Defendants Alvey & wife in the hands of **Richard P. Brooks** & **William C. Burke** Administrators of the Estate of **John Burke** deceased and report to next Term ....

Page 168: **David Griffith** Admr &c vs **William Henson** et al ... it appears that the Master sold the land in the pleadings pursuant to an interlocutory order made at last Term to **Hiram Crabtree** for $178.00 upon credit of 12 months ... and a special lien upon the same for the purchase money ....

Page 168: **Samuel E. Hare** & **Watson M. Cooke** vs **Christopher Sharr (Shaw?)** ... upon the report of the Clerk and Master made in pursuance to an interlocutory decree made in this court at a former term ... (Page 169) the Clerk & Master in obedience to said decree had provided to sell the land in the pleadings ... **John Hughes** became the purchaser of the same for $475 ... that since the filing of this Bill & prior to the said sale partition had been made of said land and the portion of said Shaw/Sharr set apart to itself ... ordered ... that the Clerk execute to purchaser John Hughes a deed for said land by metes & bounds as set apart by said partition and it appearing there is now due complainants from defendant Shaw/ Sharr with interest to this time the sum of $604.83. It is therefore further decreed that the Clerk pay over to complainants said sum of $475.00 and its is further directed that Defendant Christopher Shaw/Sharr pay to complainants the sum of $129.83 ....

Page 170: **James T. Hughes** for use &c vs **Henry Cheek** et al ... this cause had been improperly set for hearing ... the same be taken from the Docket.

Page 170: **Lyman E. Bill** vs **Thomas Gentry**. Final Order ... complainants Bill be dismissed and he pay the costs of same ....

Page 170: **William Gipson** vs **William Poston**. Decree ... on 8 June 1844 after advertising the land in the pleadings as required by the interlocutory decree of this court pronounced at a former term the Clerk and Master sold the same when the complainant William Gipson became the purchaser at the price of $100 and executed note for the purchase money with **Watson M. Cooke** and **Samuel E. Stone** as securities ... all title claim and interest of ... said William Poston in ... said tract of land divest and the same be vested in the said William Gipson his heirs and assigns (Page 171) ... that the complainant have his writ of possession directed to the Sheriff of Jackson County directing the said Sheriff to displace the said Defendant and put the Complainant into possession of the premises.

Page 171: **Hicklin's Heirs** vs Hicklins Admr. . . . proceed to collect the money upon a note given by **Aaron Biggerstaff** to **Merlin Young** for the land sold by order of the Circuit Court and which belonged to the estate of **Perry Hicklin** decd which note was by said Young ... Court adjourned till tomorrow.

Page 172: Thursday morning. Nov. 14th 1844. 8 o'clock. **B. L. Ridley** Chancellor presiding.

Page 172: **Asa Lynn, Joseph Green** & **Mounce Gore**, complts. vs **Joseph J. Walker** ... on 5 February 1842 Complainants executed to Def. Walker their covenant for $600 payable in current Tennessee Bank notes due & payable1 May 1842 ... said covenant was executed in consideration of a boat load of corn sold by Defendant Walker to Complainant Lynn & Green who were co-partners in the purchase ... which corn said Defendant at the time of the sale represented to Complainant Lynn to be good and sound ... that a portion of the corn at the time of sale was wet and by reason thereof the said boat load of corn became greatly spoiled & injured and that Complainants Lynn & Green have sustained damage by reason thereof $100 and it further appearing that judgement has been recovered by Defendant Walker against Complainant upon said covenant in the Circuit court of Jackson County and that the amount thereof has been paid off & it further appearing that said **Joseph Green** is dead ....

Page 172: **James W. Locke** vs **Robert White Patrick N Dudney** & **Sidney S. Dudney** ... (Page 173) complainant has not established his title at law to the satisfaction of the court, and this court has no jurisdiction of the cause ... complainants bill is hereby dismissed ....

Page 173: **Silas C. Cornwell** & Son vs **Andrew McClellan** & **Wm B Nickens** ... the parties by their solicitors having filed exceptions to the report of the Clerk & Master ... ordered that the exceptions filed by defendants be overruled and ... the exceptions filed by complainant be sustained ... there remains due on the note from Nickens to McClellin of $400 ... that McClellin has not a good title to 100 acres of the land sold to wit, the 75 acres claimed by **Draper & Graham** and the 25 acres claimed by **Pharis** ... ordered that a deduction for said 100 acres at the rate of $2.84 1/2 be deducted from the purchase money due from said Nickens to McClellan ... the Clerk & Master proceed to sell at public auction on the premises the part of the tract of lands in the pleadings to wit:181 acres being the balance of said tract exclusive of the parts claimed by Draper & Graham & 75 Pharis as aforesaid ... 40 days notice given (Page 174) in Gainesboro at **Highland** ... at **Granville** ....

Page 174: **Bird Cannon** & **Lucinda** his wife vs **Garret Sadler. Henry Saddler David Apple Abisha Cannon** & **Sally** his wife ... complainants failed to show that complainant Lucinda is a child of said **Owen Franklin** decd and Distributee of his estate ... bill dismissed ....

Page 174: **William G. Darwin** vs **John G. Burke** ... in presence of counsel on both sides ... defendant and complainant as his surety executed their note jointly to **Richard P. Brooks** and **William C. Burke** Administrators of **John Burke** deceased for $450 the price of a negro **Hal** purchased by Burke at public sale which note is now due ... before said note fell due Defendant being indebted and possessed of but little property except said negro Hal was about (Page 175) to remove himself and said negro out of this state as he himself alleges and was reported. Where-upon it is decreed that the Clerk & Master sell said negro Hal ... he has this day sold the negro boy attached in this cause to **Shelby B. Marsh** for $462.50 in cash ....

Page 175: **N. G. Jackson** vs **Benjamin E. Williams** ... in the presence of the parties by their solicitors when by agreement of the parties and with the assent of the court. It is ordered ... that the Clerk & Master make and state an account as to the partnership dealings of complainants and defendant in the purchase and sale of a flat boat and load and (Page 176) the purchase of dry goods and groceries and the selling of same in Gainesboro ... since 1841 to the filing of this bill how much each has paid into the partnership concern, how much each has drawn out and what has been the profits ... sell to the highest bidder for cash all the remaining stock of goods on hand ... and report to the next term ....

Page 176: **Christopher Clemons** vs **Harmon Howard** ... the Clerk & Master in pursuance of the decretal order of last term he sold the land in the mortgage deed in the pleadings to **James Crawford** and **Christopher Clemens** jointly at the price of $1,552.00 on a credit of six and twelve months ... that a lien be retained upon said land for the purchase money ....

Page 176: **Joel Lynn** vs **Josiah Copeland** & **Leroy B. Settle** ... (Page 177) in pursuance of a decretal order of last term the Clerk & Master sold the land in the pleadings which was mortgaged by Copeland to his co-defendant Settle upon a credit of 12 months to Leroy B. Settle at the price of $655.00 ... one Tract on **Jennings Creek** beginning at a stake in **John McCauleys** South boundary line of the old survey thence N. to a large sycamore standing in the creek thence N. 45º east to a stake in the N. boundary line of said old survey thence E. to ... McCauleys N.E. corner thence S. 160 poles to... McCauleys S.E. corner thence West to ... the N.E. corner of a ten acre survey made for **Saml Dixon** thence S 14 po. to a sugar tree thence W. to ... the N.E. corner of a twelve acre survey made for Saml Dixon thence S. 56 poles to a sugartree, thence West 36 poles to ... **James Young's** east boundary line thence N. 56 poles to a stake in side of said Morel field which is Jas. Young's north east corner thence west to ... the S.W. corner of said Saml Dixon's ten acre survey thence N. 14 po. to a stake inside of said **William Morel** fence thence W. to the beginning containing by estimation 150 acres ... it being the whole of two surveys one for 10 acres the other for 12 acres made for Saml. Dixon and a part of a survey made for **John McCaulley** including the house and plantation where Morel formerly lived except a tract of 20 acres ... conveyed by Morrell to **Francis Kirkpatrick** ... Leroy B. Settle to have possession of said lands ....

Page 177: **William Buchanan** & wife vs **James, Matthew, Simon Hogin** & others, heirs at large of **Edward Hogin** Decd. & **Matthew C. Hogin** Admr Debonus Now (Page 178) ... in presence of the solicitors upon both sides it appeared in the year 1838 Edward Hogin departed this life in Jackson County having first made and published his last Will and testament that **Rebecca Hogin** the widow and **Anthony Hogin** were appointed his executors and were duly qualified ... that they have both departed this life and Matthew C. Hogin was duly appointed and qualified as administrator of his estate with the will annexed and was appointed administrator of the estate of **Rebecca** . . . that James Hogin has departed this life and that the complainants and Defts are the heirs of law of Rebecca and James and also of **Sally Hogin** who also departed this life and it appearing from the will that the heirs were to share said estate as in the will and that complainant and wife were to be made equal with the balance of the legatees intended to be provided for in said Will after deducting what she may have received but it not appearing what sum had been advanced to him [*sic*] by the said Edward Hogin in his lifetime and what she has since received ... ordered that the Clerk & Master make an account of the Estate of the said Edward Hogin Decd ... that Complts & Defts are entitled to equal distributions of the estates of Rebecca, James and **Sally Hogin** ... that the land mentioned in the pleadings be sold by the Clerk & Master to the highest bidder at the court house door in Gainesboro (Page 179) ....

Page 179: **Cannon** & wife vs Cannon et al. The Depositions of the following persons **Reubin Harrison, John Catlet A. M. Catlet, George Rucker Abba Dod Samuel Johnson. Lucy Rucker** and **James Williamson** witnesses for Defendant were taken after November term 1843 and consequently are inadmissible to prove any fact except the identity of complainant **Lucinda**.

Page 179: **Bird Cannon** & wife, **Lucinda** vs **Abisha Cannon** & wife **Sally Garret Sadler**, **Henry Sadler** & **David Apple**. Complainants pray an appeal ... in this cause to the Supreme Court (Tennessee) to be held at Nashville on the first Monday of December next which to them is granted and ... Bird Cannon subscribed and took the oath that owing to his poverty he is not able to bear the expenses of this lawsuit and that he is entitled to recovery as he believes within the jurisdiction of said Supreme Court ... said appeal is accordingly granted them.

Page 179: **Wilson C. Canter** et al vs **William P. Hollimon** et al ... upon the report of the Master unexcepted to ... it appears that pursuant to a decretal (Page 180) order of last term the Master sold the land in the pleadings to **Micajah Duke** at the price of $240 $25 of which in cash and $215 in two equal payments to be due in one and two years ... retaining a lien upon the land for the purchase money ....

Page 180: **Sophia** [sic] and others by their next friend **Joseph Eaton** vs **Henry & Robert Richmond** ... deposition of Robert Richmond was objected to and overruled when it appeared from the evidence that the paper writing exhibited in the answer purporting to be the last will and testament of **John Richmond** Decd is not his will–John Richmond at the time the same was executed being of unsound mind and memory–it appearing the complainants have been in the possession of Eaton [sic] ever since the filing of the Bill at November Term of this court 1842 ... ordered he deliver them up to the defendants immediately. And the Clerk take and state an account of their hire charging Eaton with reasonable hire from the time they came to his possession up to this time and report the same ....

Page 181: **Samuel E. Hare** vs **John W Richmond** and **Henry Richmond**. The parties agree that the Master sell the negro girl **Ann** and the land in the mortgage deed in the pleadings at auction for cash on the First Monday in April next at the Court House in Gainesborough ... and ascertain what is justly due from Defendant **John W Richmond** to Henry Richmond and the amount due from ~~Joseph~~ John ichmond to **Joseph Ellison** and report to next Term.

Page 181: **Daniel Lee** Admr &c vs the Creditors of **Ab' Lee** decd. Decree ... report of the Master of the sale of the lands of **Abraham Lee** subject to his widows dower ... that in the life time of said Deceased he had sold the tract of land purchased by **Samuel E. Stone** to **James Clark** and executed to him a bond for title to the same and in consideration of said sale Clark had executed his notes to (Page 182) said deceased for the same–by consent of the parties it is decreed said land and notes be rendered null and void.

Page 182: **James Keith** vs **G. M. McWhirter** Admr &c ... ordered that the demurrer to complainant's bill be allowed ... that the complainant have leave to amend his bill ... before the first rule day after this term.

Page 182: **Hare** & **Cooke** vs **Benjamin Monroe** et al ... order made in this cause at the last term to take and state an account ...be and the same hereby revived ....

Page 182: **James McBroom** vs **David Herbert** . . . this cause be remanded to the rules for further steps to be taken thence.

Page 182: **John Love** vs **Samuel T. & Theodore Vaden** ... upon Bill & Demurrer ... ordered the Defendants demurrer be disallowed and Defendants answer complainantts Bill ... Defendants have leave (Page 183) to insist upon the reasons in the demurrer in their answer.

Page 183: **Alexander Hardcastle** vs **James & Allen Manier** ... Bill dismissed as to Allen Manier and an account be taken between complainant & James Manier ... that this case be reheard ... Complt. has leave to take the depositions of **James T. Hughs** & **Francis Sanders**.

Page 183: **William Buchanan** & wife vs **Matthew C. Hogin** et al. And Matthew C. Hogin et al vs William Buchanan et al ... ordered by the court that these causes be consolidated. Court adjourned till Court in course. /S/ **Bromfield Ridley**.

Page 184: (Blank Page)

Page 185: **May Term 1845**. The first Monday it being 5 May 1845 for the Chancery District composed of the County of Jackson ... in the Fourth Chancery Division of said state, in presence of **Bromfield L Ridley** presiding.

Page 185: **William E. Nelson** Esqr **Benjamin B. Washburn** Esqr. and **Lyttleton E.(?) Hall** Esqr ... placed upon the roll as practicing Solicitors of this Court.

Page 185: **Lewis R. Vance** vs **James T. Hughes** ... continued ... complainant is permitted to take the depositions of **Lewis Fletcher Richard Rison Thomas Smith** and **Daniel W. Hawes** ... Defendant permitted to take rebutting testimony.

Page 185: **John Scanland** vs **Isaac Hogin** et al ... this cause has been irregularly set for hearing ... ordered the same be remanded to the rules for the steps to be taken.

Page 186: **Hicklin Heirs** vs Hicklin Admr et al ... Masters report is incomplete ... by consent of Solicitors on both sides ... this cause be continued ....

Page 186: **Samuel E. Hare** vs **Henry & John W Richmond** ... Bill dismissed ....

Page 186: **Danl Lee** Admr &c vs the Creditors of **Ab. Lee** decd ... Clerk & Master to collect the balance of the money due the Estate of **Abraham Lee** decd and report to the next Term.

Page 186: **Isham Beagley** vs **Amos J. Chapman** et al ... Complainants Bill be dismissed and that he pay the cost of the same for which execution may issue.

Page 186: **Sam. E Hare** & **Watson M Cooke** vs **Benjamin Monroe** et al ... cause be continued & that the Clerk & Master report as before directed to the next Term.

Page 187: **Hogins Heirs** vs Hogins Admr et al. Bill & Cross Bill ... order made at the last Term directing the Master to take an account be revived ....

Page 187: **Letty Roberts** Executrix &c vs **James G Holloman** ... in the presence of Solicitors on both sides ... complainants Bill dismissed ... Court adjourned ....

Page 188: Tuesday **May 6, 1845**–8 o'clock. Chancellor **B. L. Ridley** presiding.

Page 188: **Lewis N. Vance** vs **James T. Hughes** ... Defendant permitted to take the Deposition of **Herald D. Marchbanks** to be read on the hearing.

Page 188: **Henry Carter** vs **James Carter** et al ... James Carter have leave to file his Cross Bill.

Page 188: **Nathan Montgomery** vs **Kinnaird & Bransford** et al. The death of the Defendant

Isabella Gailbreath was this day suggested and proved in open Court.

Page 188: **James McBroom** vs **David Herbert** ... continued ... complainant permit-ted to take the depositions of **Champ Stanton James McBroom** and Defendant permitted to take proof touching the boundary of the land in controversy.

Page 188: **Bailey Butler** et al vs Heirs of **Lucy Ursery** decd ... complainant prayed for a continuance ... by consent of the Solicitors ... it is ordered (Page 189) ....

Page 189: **A & B. S. Jones** vs **Alexander McNichol** et al ... McNichol is confined in the penitentiary of this State. It is ordered that alias subpoena issue to the Sheriff of **Davidson County** to be executed on said McNichol.

Page 189: **Perry Mahaney** vs **Edwin F. McKinney** et al ... the Master be continued receiver &c and that he report to the next Term ....

Page 189: **John M Love** vs **Saml T** & **Leoderick Vaden** . . . ordered that an alias subpoena & copy issue to the Sheriff of **Smith County** to be executed on the Defendant Leoderick Vaden.

Page 189: **Samuel E. Hare** et al vs **John Scanland** et al ... ordered that Samuel E. Hare be appointed receiver to take into his possession all the debts discovered in the answers of the Defts & collect the same ... report to the next term.

Page 189: **John W. Heady** vs **Edwin F. McKinney** et al. Complainant came (Page 190) by his solicitor and dismissed his suit ....

Page 190: **James H. Richmond** vs **John Eakle** et al ... complainant permitted to so amend his Bill by making **Christian Eakle** a Defendant to the same by paying the cost of the amendment.

Page 190: **William Hudson** vs **Thomas M. Wilson** et al. And Thomas M. Wilson vs William Hudson et al ... these two causes be consolidated and heard together ....

Page 190: **Kinnaird & Bransford** vs **David Johnson** et al. Came the parties by their Solicitors and the complainants dismiss their Bill ....

Page 190: **Ann Cox** et al vs **Mounce Gore** et al. Leave is given till the 1st Rule day for the defendant Gore to file his answer ....

Page 191: **Martin Jones** vs **Michael Price** ... agreement made and signed by the parties to this suit was exhibited ...on this 5th day of May 1845: An agreement made and entered into on this 31st day of December 1844 between Michael Price ... and Martin Jones ... both of (Jackson County) viz: ... Michael Price ... doth agree to make and give unto Martin Jones a quit claim to all the land where Jones now lives which Jones once sold to Price. The same meant land now in law between them ... the tract known by the name of the **Olly**(?) tract East of where the Jones now lives ... /S/ Michael Price by X-Mark. Martin Jones by X-Mark. In the presence of **James Carter** and **Stanton A. Carter**. And it appearing that the matters in controversy between the parties have been adjusted and settled ....

Page 191: **Samuel E. Stone** & **Leroy B. Settle** vs **Henry F Burke** et al ... report of the Master ... (Page 192) Henry F. Burke is indebted to the complainants in the sum of $191.99 1/2 and ... Henry F. as one of the distributees of **John Burke** deceased in the hands of Defts **Richard P.**

Brooks & **William C Burke** as Administrators of said **John Burk(e)** $99.99 1/2 which shows a deficit of personal effects of Henry F. to satisfy complainants debt against him of $92 ....

Page 192: **Andrew McClellan** & **Beverly Graves** vs **Alvey Graves** & others ... upon report of the Master ... there is in the hands of Defts. **Richard P. Brooks** & **William C Burke** as Admrs of John Burke decd due Alvey & wife as distributees of John Burke decd ... Alvey is indebted to the estate of John Burke ... decreed that Administrators appropriate ... the distributive share of Alvey & wife of the estate ... in their hands to the payment of the balance due on said note .... (Page 193).

Page 193: **James T. Hughs** vs **Henry Cheek** & wife **Mary & Mark Hollimon, Robert Sweat** & **Jemima Glenn** ... Complt. for the use of **Richard McConnell** in Oct 1841 recovered judgt against Henry Cheek for $85.80 ... that execution issued on the same was returned by the proper officer "nothing found." That **Thompson Glenn** departed this life having first made and published his last will & testament in which he devised all his estate both real and personal to his wife **Patsy** during her life equally divided among his six children the deft Mary being one. Patsy has also departed this life–said testator also devised to his daughter Jemima Glenn a negro girl **Sucky** and her first child. Sucky at testators death had no child after his death she had a child which died shortly after its birth She then had another child named **Amanda** and then Sucky died. It appears the Exrs have paid to Henry & his wife Mary their portion of said estate unless Mary has an interest in the negro Amanda which is contested by **Jemima** ... that Henry is an improvident man and will probably waste his wifes estate should it come to his hands and she asks the interposition of the court. The court is of opinion the negro girl Amanda is included in the property directed in said will to be divided among his ~~daughters~~ children and that deft Mary is entitled to a distributive share of said negro but the same in the hands of said executors is not subject to the debt of Complt. (Page 194) ... decreed Executors sell the negro Amanda at public sale ... & distribute the proceeds as said will directs and they pay the costs of this suit out of the share of Mary and pay the residue of her distributive share to **James Hollimon** who is hereby appointed trustee to hold the same for her separate use and maintenance.

Page 194: **Joseph Eaton Sophia** [*sic*] & others vs **Henry & Robert Richmond** ... it appeared from said report that said Eaton had received the benefit of the hire of the negroes in the pleadings mentioned three of them for two years and one for one year and nine months ....

Page 194: **Silas C. Cornwell** & Son vs **A. McClellan** & others ... from the report of the Master (Page 195) in the decree on 4 January 1845. . . sold said land at auction to ... Silas C. Cornwell ... at the price of $200–that he took bond & security for the purchase money & retained a lien upon the land ....

Page 195: **Alexander Hardcastle** vs **James & Allen Manier** ... there was no evidence to charge Allen Manier or render him liable ... decreed that the bill & petition as to Allen Manier be dismissed ... but it appearing the sum of $80 of the funds of the firm of James Manier & Complainant was included in a note executed by **Miller** to Allen Manier and the same had not been collected ... decreed that Allen Manier be enjoined from disposing of said fund or any other fund in his hands of said partners except $36 ... it appearing James Manier & Complainant were partners in purchasing & selling horses & that accounts of all their partnership transactions & report the same to the next term ... (Page 196) ....

Page 196: **Nathan Pharis** vs **Sam E. Hare**. Decree ... there being no proof to sustain the allegations in complainants bill ... it be dismissed and Defendant recover against Complt &

Samuel E. Stone & **Sampson W. Cassetty** his security in the injuction bond $2000.00 ....

Page 196: **Nathan Montgomery** vs **Thomas L. Bransford, Russel M Kinnaird Thomas J. Gailbreath Isabella Gailbreath** and **William A Gailbreath**. Decree ... on 6 July 1842 Isabella Gailbreath executed to the complainant a deed of Trust conveying to him two undivided tenths of tract of land of 200 acres in Jackson County for the purpose among other things of _ifying the said Montgomery in the payment of a judgement ordered at the March (Page 197) Term 1843 of the Circuit Court of Jackson county in favor of the Branch of the Bank of Tennessee at **Sparta** vs T.J & Isabella Gailbreath and complainants for $200 besides interest and costs and it further appeared Isabella held and had right to one of the undivided tenths of the tract of 200 acres of land by virtue of deed of conveyance executed to her by the deft Wm A Gailbreath on 28 May 1839 and she held and had right to the other undivided one tenth so conveyed to complainant by virtue of her character as widow and relict of her decd husband **William Gailbreath** ... on 9 March 1843 Isabella conveyed her interest as doweress in the lands of her decd husband and that Wm A. likewise on 9 March 1843 by his attorney in fact Thomas J. Gailbreath conveyed to **Kinnaird & Bransford** his undivided one ninth of said tract of 200 acres being the same interest previously conveyed to Isabella. But because it appears to the deed executed by deft Wm A. to deft Isabella and that executed by her to complainant are both older than the deeds executed to defendants Kinnaird & Bransford and being first in time are best in right ... decreed ... that the Deeds by the William A. & Isabella executed to Kinnaird & Bransford are not for nothing so far as they affect the interest of complainant ... Clerk & Master ordered to sell the undivided one tenth conveyed by Wm A. and said Isabella ... (Page 198) and report to the next term of this court.

Page 198: **John Carver** vs **Joseph Carver** ... said bill be dismissed and it appearing there yet remains of the judgements which the Deft. recovered against the complt before **I. Young** Esqr of **Macon County** and which were enjoined by the order of the Court the sum of $88.15 unpaid by the complainant and ... that **William Kirby** and **Thomas Haile** are the securities for complainant in the injunction bond ....

Page 198: **Buchanan** & wife vs **Matthew C. Hogin** et al. Decree. By agreement of the parties by their solicitors and the consent of **James T. Quarles** and Matthew C. Hogin the purchasers it is ordered that the sale of the land made by the Clerk & Master to Matthew C. Hogin and of the town lot to James T. Quarles since the last term of this court be set aside and (Page 199) it is agreed ... that the Clerk & Master ... sell said land on the premises and town lot at publick sale ... And upon petition of the parties this day filed in court it is ordered that the confirmation of the sale of the land made to **Allen Manier** reported to this term by the Clerk & Master be suspended ... that said Allen be served with a copy of said petition.

Page 199: **Christopher Clemens** vs **Harmon Howard** & wife, **Thomas Howard** & wife and **Sampson Allen** and wife ... upon the report of the Clerk & Master made at last term and amendments made to the present term ... the estate of **John Clemens** deceased is indebted to complainant in the sum of $912.07 and that the administrator of said estate has in his hands $353.53 which being deducted from said $912.07 leaves a ballance due complainant from said estate of $558.54 ....

Page 200: **Nathaniel G. Jackson** vs **Benjamin E Williams**. It appearing ... that the parties have settled between themselves the matters ... suit dismissed ....

Page 200: **Wm C. Burke** et al vs **Henry & Robert Richmond** ... complainants are entitled to distribution of the estate of **John Richmond** deceased more than two years having expired before the filing of this Bill since the qualification of the Defendants as administrators of said decd ... Clerk & Master to take an accounting of the administration of said defendants showing the balance due to each distributee ... that said judgment will exceed the distributive share of said William C. the sum of $200 and that the judgement aforesaid has been enjoined and that **Merlin Young**, **John Scanland** & **Nathan Pharis** (Page 201) are the securities of complain-ant Wm C in the injunction bond ... Court adjourned ... /S/ **Bromfield Ridley**.

Page 201: 3 November 1845. Chancery Court for the Chancery District composed of the County of Jackson in the 4th Chancery Division at ten o'clock the Chancellor not being present the Clerk & Master of said court and the Sheriff of said county to open and adjourn the same till tomorrow morning 9 o'clock.

Page 201: Tuesday Morning 9 o'clock The Chancellor not being yet present the Master ordered the Sheriff to open and adjourn said court till tomorrow morning 9 o'clock. Wednesday morning 9 o'clock. The Chancellor not yet having arrived the Master caused said court to be opened and the same was kept open until 4 o'clock P M of Wednesday where the Chancellor not having arrived said court was by the Master adjourned to the court in course. /S/ **G M McWhirter** C & M.

Page 203: **January Term 1846**. It being Thursday after the 4th Monday of January 1846 ... Chancery Court ... **Bromfield L. Ridley** Chancellor presiding.

Page 203: **William H. Wilson** et al vs **Wilson T. McColgin** ... the Master take proof and report what amount of money arising from the sale of the land mentioned in the pleadings is due from **John N. Gates** the purchaser thereof to the Heirs of **Saml Wilson** Decd respectively.

Page 203: **Bailey Butler** et al vs **Mary Davis** et al ... cause remanded to the rules and leave is given both parties to take proof generally to be read on the hearing.

Page 203: **Christopher Clemons** vs **Harmon Howard** et al ... (Page 204) ... the Clerk and Master after retaining a sufficient sum to pay the costs heretofore adjudged and five per cent on the amount collect pay to complainant and defendants the residue of the monies ensuing from the sale of the lands in the pleadings ...

Page 204: **Hicklins Heirs** vs Hicklins Admr. ... continued on account of the absence of counsel on both sides.

Page 204: **Joel Lynn** vs **Josiah Copeland** et al ... ordered by the court that the Master ... pay the money in his hands first to the claim of **Leroy B. Settle** Mortgagee of the lands sold and then to the complainant any balance ....

Page 204: **Richmonds Heirs** vs Richmonds Admrs ... cause continued on account of the absence of counsel on both sides.

Page 205: **Asa Lynn** vs **Joseph J. Walker** ... continued ... leave given Walker to take the depositions of **Robert Gr_shill, William Amonett David Majors Robert O. Brown** & **Reas___**.

Page 205: **James McBroom** vs **David Herbert** ... continued on account of the absence of counsel on both sides.

Page 205: **Alex. Hardcastle** vs **James Manier** ... continued ....

Page 205: **Amon Hale** vs **Absalom Johnson** et al ... dismissed ....

Page 205: **Amon Hale** vs **Absalom Johnson** et al ... Came the plaintiff and dismisses his suit ... he pay the cost of the same in the first instance but have his judgment over against the defendants for the same ....

Page 206: **John R. James** vs **Z. B. Roberts** ... dismissed.

Page 206: **Kinnaird** & **Bransford** vs **Z. B. Roberts** ... dismissed.

Page 206: **Sam E. Hare** et al vs **John Scanland** et al ... cause remanded to the rules ... on motion complainants Bill is taken for confessed as to Deft. John Scanland.

Page 206: **Ann Cox** et al vs **Gore & Cason** ... continued ... leave given complainants to take the depositions of **John VanHooser Hiram Minor** &**Thompson Cason** ....

Page 206: **Lewis R. Vance** vs **James T. Hughes** ... continued and leave given complainant to take the Depositions of (Page 207) **Lewis Fletcher Richard Benson Thomas Smith** and **Danl W Hawes** ....

Page 207: **Nathan Pharis** vs **Sam. E Hare** ... Defendants answer fully met and devised all the equity fore ordered that the injunction granted in this cause on the Bill ... is hereby dissolved ... and Defendant upon entering into bond and security ... shall be entitled to his execution as heretofore ordered ...

Page 207: **James Draper** vs **Richard P. Brooks** et al ... ordered that the injunction granted in this cause be (Page 208) ... dissolved and that upon entering into bond and security ... Defendants shall be entitled to recover of complainant James Draper and **Milton Draper** and **William H. Kirby** his securities ....

Page 208: **John Scanland** vs **Isaac Hogin** et al ... continued ... on account of the absence of counsel.

Page 208: **James Keith** vs **G M McWhirter** Admr &c ... This cause by consent is set for hearing and continued till next Term of this court.

Page 208: **William Gipson** Admr &c vs **Randal M Gipson** et al ... ordered that the Master report ___ as to the indebtedness of complainants intestate and also what quantity of the lands described in the petition should be sold to pay the same....

Page 209: **Sam E. Hare** et al vs **John Scanland** et al ... leave is given defendant **William Scanland** to file his cross bill against the complainants and the Defendant John Scanland.

Page 209: **Nathan Montgomery** vs **Kinnaird & Bransford** et al ... upon the report of the Clerk & Master of the sale of the land in the pleadings ... and the Clerk execute to **Thomas Murry** the purchaser of the land a deed for the portion so purchased ... and retaining a lien upon the same for the purchase money ....

Page 209: **Hare & Cooke** vs **Ben. Monroe** et al ... upon the report of **William Davidson** a receiver appointed by a former decree of this court to receive and collect the debts attached by complainants Bill ... (Page 210) ordered by the court that **Saml E Hare** be appointed receiver in his stead ... cause continued ....

Page 210: **William Gipson** Admr &c vs **Randal M Gipson** et al ... it appearing to the satisfaction of the Court from the report of the Master that the allegations in complainants petition are true. It is there upon ordered and (Page 211) decreed by the Court that the Clerk and Master after giving 30 days notice ... proceed to sell all the lands in complainants petition ... and retaining a lien upon the land for the purchase money. Said lands to be sold subject to the widow's dower ....

Page 211: **William H Wilson** et al vs **Wilson T. McColgin** ... upon the report of the Master ... the respective shares of **Saml. T. Wilson. Narcissa J Wilson, Elizabeth B Wilson** and **John A Wilson** in the funds arising from the sale of the lands in the pleadings mentioned is $271.81 ... that the shares of **Golder** & wife, **Chism** and wife and **Martin** and wife are each $3.22 ... and **James T. Golder** having exhibited to the court here a record of the County Court of **Monroe County, Kentucky** properly authorized appointing **Samuel T. Wilson** Guardian of the said Narcissa J Wilson, Elizabeth B. Wilson and John A Wilson and also a Power of (Page 212) Attorney executed and properly authenticated constituting said Golder ___ and Attorney in fact for said Samuel T. Wilson as well for himself as for him as guardian as aforesaid to demand and receive said fund and accept for the same ... that the Master ... pay to said James T. Golder against as aforesaid the amount belonging to said Samuel T. Wilson and his wards the said Narcissa J. Elizabeth B. and John A Wilson and that the Master also pay to said Golder the amount belonging to himself & wife in said funds also pay to Chism & wife to Martin & wife the amt belonging to them and to **John N. Gates** the residual of the funds collected.

Page 212: **Perry Mahanay** vs **E. F. McKinney** et al. The Master is continued recover [sic] in this cause and directed to report to next Term. Adjourned until next Court in course. /S/ **Bromfield Ridley**.

Page 213: **July Term 1846**. Chancery Court began and held at the Court House in Gainesborough for the ... 4th Chancery Division ... Wednesday after the 4th Monday being 29 July 1846 ... **Bromfield L. Ridley**.

Page 213: **John Scanland** vs **Matthew C. Hogin** et al ... that further time ... be allowed Deft. Matthew C. Hogin Admr &c to file his answer in this cause.

Page 213: **Daniel Lee** Administrator of **Abraham Lee** Decd vs The Creditors of said Abraham Lee Decd ... this cause came to be heard on 29 July 1846 ... the Clerk and Master has in his hands a fund belonging of right to the Defendants ...having here collected either as assets of said Decd or for lands sold by sale Clerk ... and decreed by the court that the Clerk and Master proceed to take an account in this cause and to distribute all the assets pro rata among said defendants ... (Page 214) ....

Page 214: **Perry Mahanay** vs **Edwin F McKinney** et al ... continued ....

Page 214: **Hogins Heirs** vs Hogins Admr et al ... the order requiring the Clerk & Master to take an account be and the same is hereby reversed and the Master is directed to report to next term.

Page 214: **Hogins Heirs** vs **Allen Manier** ... (Page 215) upon the agreement of the defendant Allen Manier and the report of the Clerk and Master touching the mini-mum value of the land in controversy ... the Master heretofore sold the land in the pleadings ... to Allen Manier for

$187.50 and ... that on 20 July 1846 said Defendant and Complainant **Rawlins Hogin, Matthew C. Hogin** and others and said Defend-ant agreed that the sale should be set aside and said land be sold again and plain-tiffs agreed that Defendant should not be charged for any rents of said land while in his possession ... that the Clerk and Master after giving 30 days notice ... in **Granville** and at three other public places in Jackson County proceed to sell the land ... that complainants pay the cost of the former sale ... that the same be deducted from the fund of the Estate of **Sarah Hogin** Decd to be distributed.

Page 215: **James H Richmond** vs **Henry Eakle** et al ... complainant by his Solicitor ... dismissed his suit ....

Page 215: **Richmonds Heirs** vs Richmonds Admr ... continued (Page 216) till the next term ... the Defendants Solicitor is undisposed and unable to attend ....

Page 216: **James McBroom** vs **David Herbert** ... the Defendants Solicitor is indisposed and unable to attend ... cause continued ....

Page 216: **Lewis R. Nance** vs **James L Hughes** ... continued ... that the Defendant recover of the Complainant all the costs that have accrued ... up to this date–And leave is granted complainant to take the depositions of **William R. Nance, Lewis Fletcher, Mary A. McNichol** and **Richard Benson** and to retake the deposition of **Daniel Hawes** ... Defendant is permitted to take rebutting testimony ....

Page 216: **A & B S Jones** vs **A B McNichol** ... cause be remanded to the rules for further steps.

Page 217: **James Draper** vs **Nancy Anderson** et al ... came the Plaintiff by his Solicitor and dismissed his suit ....

Page 217: **D. G. Shepherd & Co.** vs **Lawson Clarke** et al ... decreed ... that the Bill and Attachments be dismissed as to the defendants **Mark Harper** and **Thomas Hudelston** ... that said Defendants be dismissed hence without cost. And it appearing the Defendant Lawson Clark [*sic*] is indebted to the complainants ....

Page 217: **Charles F. Burton** vs **Lawson Clarke** et al ... (Page 218) complainants Bill be and the same hereby dismissed as is also his attachment as to the Defendants **Mark Harper** and **Thomas Huddleston** and said Defendants are dismissed hence without cost. And it appearing that the defendant Lawson Clark is indebted to the plaintiff and that his property is attached ....

Page 218: **Wilson C. Canter** et al vs **Levi Canter** et al ... Clerk and Master proceed to distribute the amount of money in his hands arising from the sale of the land ordered to be sold at a former term of this court ....

Page 218: **Ann Cox, Robert Cox, Rebecca Cox, Elizabeth Cox, Sally Cox** and **Matilda Cox** by their next friend **Nathaniel M Cox** vs **Edward M Cason** and **Mounce Gore**. (Page 219) (All words are scratched through. The term "Rescind" is written across the body of the text.)

Page 219: **William Gipson** vs **Randall McGipson** et al ... upon the report of the Clerk and Master ... the Master proceeded to sell said lands ... at public sale at the Court House door in Gainesboro on 6 April 1846 ... the same was purchased by **Tobias McGipson** ... at the price of $73 ... the Master besides taking bond and security retained a lien upon said lands for the purchase price ... that the title to said lands be and the same hereby divested out of all the

Defendants except the widow of **George McGipson** decd who has dower therein and the said Tobias McGipson the purchaser ....

Page 219: **James Keith** vs **Geo. M McWhirter** Admr &c of **James Marshall** Decd ... (Page 220) the Bill Single upon which the judgement enjoined in this cause was attained was delivered by the complainant as an Escrow and that the condition upon which the same was delivered was never complied with by James Marshall in his lifetime or **George M McWhirter** Administrator as aforesaid since his death. It is ... decreed by the court that said George M McWhirter Admr as aforesaid together with all other persons, whether as principal agents or attorneys he and the same are hereby perpetually enjoined from proceeding any further in the collection of said judgement or any part thereof (the same having been recovered in the Circuit Court of Jackson County ... and that said complainant recover judgment over against said George McWhirter for said erat(?) to be levied of the assets of James Marshall Decd in his hands to be administered.

Page 220: **Henry Carter** vs **James Carter** et al ... continued on account of the indisposition of complainants solicitor-and for reasons appearing by affidavit of **Dale Carter** permission is given complainant to take the depositions of **John B Pointer**, **Peter G. Cox** in chief in this cause and he is also permitted to (Page 221) take what testimony he thinks proper touching the general character of **Rebecca Stypes** by paying the cost of all that he takes and provided said depositions are taken within three months from this date ....

Page 221: **Hare & Cooke** vs **Polly Henry** et al ... the solicitor of complainants is indisposed and unable to give his attention to his clients interest ... continued till next term. Court adjourned ... /S/ **Bromfield Ridley**.

Page 221: Thursday morning **July 30 AD 1846**. **B. L. Ridley** Chancellor &c presiding.

Page 221: **William Hudson** vs **Thomas G. Wilson** and others. And Thomas G. Wilson vs William Hudson et al. Bill and Cross Bill ... that **Nathaniel Coons** in 1841 fraudulently procured the complainant in the Cross Bill, Thomas G. Wilson to sign a note of that date for $100 as his security to William Hudson alleging that **Polly Christian** would sign the same note as his security (Page 222) ... that Thomas G. Wilson did sign said note ... upon condition that Polly would sign it also and not otherwise and ... that Polly had not signed the same and ... the complainant in the original bill had no equity ... that Hudson had recovered a judgement at law against Wilson in his said bill in seeking to subject a tract of land to satisfy the same ... it is ordered ... that the complainants original Bill be dismissed and Hudson be perpetually enjoined from all further proceedings at law upon said judgement against Thomas G. Wilson that the Cross Bill be dismissed as to Polly Christian and ... William Hudson pay all the costs in these suits except the cost of making Polly Christian and her husband **Cornwell** parties which is to be paid by Thos G. Wilson ....

Page 222: **A. M. Cox** next friend &c vs **E M Cason** & **Gore** ... the deed executed **James Cason** to Defendant Cason was executed since the making of his will by said James Cason was not procured by fraud or undue influence & that James Cason was of sound mind at the time of the execution of said deed & the court set out in the pleadings in this cause ....

Page 229: **Hare & Cooke** vs **Benjamin Manier** & others ... continued ... **Samuel E. Hare** is continued receiver in the same ....

Page 229: **Samuel E. Hare** vs **William Fraim** et al ... cause be remanded to the rules and during the term of five months from this date.

Page 229: **Stephen D. Burton** vs **Bird C. Kinslow** & **John Dowell** ... By consent ... time is given the Defendants until September rules to their answers ....

Page 229: **John A Hall** vs **William Toney** ... leave is given the complainant to take the Depositions of **Samuel DeWhitt, Henry Crowder, Elisha Sanders Jr** and **Reuben Price** ... (Page 230) Defendant is permitted to retake the deposition of **Joseph Spivey** at his own cost.

Page 230: **Nelson Sadler** vs **Merlin Young** ... it appeared ... that **John Scanland** who is a non resident of the State of Tennessee has interest in this suit which should be protected and that John Scanland is not a party to the same ... this cause remanded to the rules and that complainant have leave to amend his Bill so as to bring John Scanland before the Court provided the same is done on or before the next September rules ....

Page 230: **David G. Shepherd & Co** vs **Lawson Clark** ... Defendant is justly indebted to the Complainant upon the several notes, bills single and accounts (for) ... $313.99 ... complainant recover against the Defendant ... (Page 231) ....

Page 231: **D. G. Shepherd & Co** vs **Christopher Shaw** & others. On motion of complainants solicitor ... **Rawlins Hogin** is appointed Guardian per dente lite of ~~Arta Shaw Thomas J. Shaw~~ & **Rebecca C Shaw Matilda Shaw Jane Shaw Burcky Shaw**, minor heirs of **George W. C. Shaw** decd ....

Page 231: **James M. Shepherd** Admr &c vs **Christopher Shaw** et al. On motion of complainants solicitor ... **Rawlings Hogin** be appointed Guardian perdente lite of **Matilda Shaw, Jane Shaw, Burckey Shaw** and **Rebecca C Shaw** minor heirs of **George W. C Shaw** decd ....

Page 231: **Samuel E. Hare** vs **Levi McGipson** et al ... When the Chancellor being satisfied that the demurrer is not well taken adjudges that the same be corrected and the defendants have leave to answer in one months ... **Samuel Turney** who appeared as solicitor for the Defendants declined to answer, whereupon the Chancellor is pleased to order that said Bill be taken for confessed ... and that Defendant McGipson be perpetually enjoined as well as all persons for him from proceeding any further in the collection of the judgement obtained before **Reuben H Doll_ll** Justice of the peace ... (Page 232) ....

Page 232: **Nathan J. Goss** et al vs **James Guffy** ... Defendant granted leave to withdraw his demurrer filed in this cause ....

Page 232: **Joseph J. Walker** vs **Asa Lynn**. Came the plaintiff in proper person and dismissed the appeal by him prayed ....

Page 232: **James Keith** vs **Geo M McWhirter** ... defendant prays an appeal from the decree of the Chancellor pronounced him at the present time to the next Term of the Supreme Court of the State of Tennessee to be held at the Court House in Nashville on the First Monday of December next which to him is granted without security he being sued in capacity of Administrator of **James Marshall** ....

Page 232: **Hicklins Heirs** et al vs Hicklins Admr.s et al ... (Page 233) cause came on to be further heard upon the suggestion of the death of **Samuel Olive** one of the heirs and on the application of **Aaron Biggerstaff** ... Clerk and Master take evidence and report whether the said Samuel Olive has departed this life and also that he report to the next term ....

Page 233: **Henry Carter** vs **James Carter** et al. And James Carter vs Henry Carter ... leave is given James Carter to retake the depositions of **Lee Sadler** and **Ridley Roberts** to be read on the hearing if taken at his own cost in three months and Henry Carter is permitted to take rebutting testimony.

Page 233: **Alexander Hardcastle** vs **James Manier** ... it appeared to the court from the report of the Clerk and Master that Deft James Ma<u>near</u> is indebted to complainant for $36.31 ... complainant to recover from defendant ....

Page 234: **Argyle R. Jarvis** vs **John N. Gates** & **Whitfield Button** ... upon Bill, answer, Judgement <u>pro confesso</u> and replication where it appeared to the Court that complainant had heretofore sold the land in the pleadings mentioned to Defendant Gates and that there yet remains due the complainant $337.22 1/2 of the purchase money ... and it further appearing to the Court that Complainant is bound by judgement in favor of **William P. Welch** for the use of Whitfield Button as the security of the Defendant Gates in the sum of $121.51 ... ordered that the Clerk and Master proceed to sell the lands mentioned in the pleadings at the court house door in Gainesboro for cash in hand ....

Page 234: **Nathan Farris** vs **Saml E Hare** ... complainant prays an appeal at the present term to the next Supreme Court which is granted ... (Page 235) ... Court adjourned till the regular term. /S/ **Bromfield Ridley**.

Page 236: **January Term 1847**. Chancery Court began and held at the Court House in Gainesborough on Wednesday after the Fourth Monday it being 27 January 1847, forth [*sic*] Chancery District composed of the County of Jackson in the Fourth Chancery Division ... in the presence of **Bromfield L. Ridley**, Chancellor.

Page 236: **John Barnes** et al vs **George Welch** et al ... ordered ... that **Levi Murphey** be appointed Guardian perdente lite for **Jesse Welch** & **Alvira Welch** ... and that Defendant **George Welch** have till the 2nd rule day to file his answer ....

Page 236: **Green Garrett** vs **Bird C. Kinslow** ... leave given defendant until the second rule day to file his answer ....

Page 236: **Stephen D. Burton** vs **Bird C Kinslow** et al ... came the plaintiff by his solicitor and dismissed his suit and came also the defendants and assumed the cost herein ... (Page 237) ....

Page 237: **Nathaniel G. Jackson** vs **Nathaniel M Cox** & al ... cause continued until next term ... leave given complainant to take the depositions of **Joel Lynn William Davidson**, **George M McWhirter** and **Holland Denton** ....

Page 237: **Daniel Lee** Admr &c vs The Creditors of **Abram Lee** decd. The death of the complainant being suggested ... ordered this cause be revived in the name of **David H. Draper** Admr of said Daniel Lee decd ....

Page 237: **Hare & Cooke** vs **Benjamin Monroe** & al ... the order heretofore made in this cause is hereby revived ....

Page 237: **Perry Maha<u>ny</u>** vs **Edwin F McKinney** & al. It was this day (Page 238) suggested to the Court and admitted by complainants solicitor that ... complain-ant Perry Mahany has departed this life in Jackson County intestate since the last term of this court.

Page 238: **John A Hall** vs **William Toney** ... (it) appeared there was no partnership at any time existing between the complainant and defendant in boating and farming as alleged ... bill dismissed and complainant pay the cost ....

Page 238: **James & Littleberry Young** vs **Lawson Clark**, & others ... that conveyance of the lands from the Defendant Lawson Clark to the Defts **Thomas Huddleston** & **Mark Harper** ... was bonafide and without fraud ... complainants bill dismissed as to Huddleston & Harper, it further appearing ... Lawson Clark is in indebted to the complts (Page 239) but the sum not appearing ... Clerk and Master to take and state an account of indebtedness ....

Page 239: **Matthew Rogers** vs **Lawson Clark** & others ... to the satisfaction of the Court the conveyance of the land from Deft Clark to Defendants **Huddleston & Harper** in the pleadings was bona fide and without fraud ... complainants bill dismissed as to the Defts **Tho Huddleston & M. Harper** and also the attachment and it further appearing ... that the Defendant Lawson Clark is indebted to the complainant and his property has been attached ... Clerk and Master to take and state an account of the indebtedness ....

Page 239: **Charles F. Burton** vs **Lawson Clark** ... upon the report of the Clerk and Master of the indebtedness of the Defendant to the complainant ... (Page 240) is the sum $165.50 ... Complainant to recover from Defendant ....

Page 240: **Matthew Rogers** vs **Lawson Clark** ... upon the report of the Clerk and Master of the indebtedness of the Defendant to the Complaints ... in the sum $544.95 ... Matthew Rogers recover of the Defendant Lawson Clark $544.95 ... Court adjourned till tomorrow.

Page 241: Thursday morning 8 1/2 o'clock **January 28 1847**. **Bromfield L Ridley** Chancellor presiding.

Page 241: **Rebecca S. Henderson** vs **Kinman W. Henderson**. Decree for Divorce ... about three years before the filing of this Bill the Defendant and complainant intermarried and that in a very short time thereafter the Defendant maliciously and without good cause abandoned complainant and that they have continued to live separate and apart for more than two whole years next before the filing of the Bill ... decreed ... that the bonds of matrimony ... are hereby dissolved ....

Page 241: **Nathan J. Goss** and **James A. Davis** vs **James Guffy**. Decree ... in 1841 Goss sold to Defendant a tract of land in Jackson County in District No. 13 of 118 acres for the price of $250.00 for which defendant executed his two several notes for the same ... afterwards Goss transferred one of said notes to his cocomplainant and that no part of said notes (Page 242) have been paid by Defendant ... they still remain due and unpaid ... ordered ... that the Clerk and Master ... sell said land to the highest bidder at the court house door in Gainesboro for cash in hand ....

Page 242: **James A. Spurlock** Esqr ... placed upon the roll of practicing solicitors of this court.

Page 242: **Andrew Wossom** Admr &c vs **Margaret Erwin** ... continued ... complainant permitted to take the Depositions of **Henry Garrison, Elizabeth Garrison, John Garrison, George W Clinton Hannah Clinton, Jesse R. Clinton John L Clinton Nancy Paul Peter Anderson, Sally Anderson Elizabeth Erwin James Erwin, John Scarlett, Thomas Scarlett, Elizabeth Scarlett, Joshua White, Moses Scarlett, Eliza Car, Andrew Wossom Jr. Harriet N. Wossom, Rebecca Wossom, William Stone, Nathan Judd, Dice Erwin William H Barnes,**

Angeline Scarlett & **Squire L. Harrison** if taken in three months ....

Page 243: **William W. Goodall** vs **Francis Duffy** ... appeared ... that all the Equity alleged in the complainants Bill is fully answered and denied by the Defendant and that there is no proof to sustain the allegations ... Bill dismissed ....

Page 243: **James McBroom** vs **David Herbert** ... by consent of the parties this cause be opened for proof ... for the space of four months from this date.

Page 243: **Zadock B. Roberts** et al vs **Ridley Roberts** et al ... this cause be remanded to the rules for further steps to be had therein.

Page 243: **James Draper** et al vs **Nancy Anderson** et al ... ordered ... that $12.50 fees of the Jailor of Jackson County for keeping certain negroes in the jail (be paid) ... on which the execution enjoined in this cause was heard by the Sheriff of Jackson County ....

Page 244: **John M. Love** vs **Samuel L Vaden** and **Leoderick Vaden** ... there is no proof to sustain the allegations of the Bill ... therefore ordered ... that complain-ants Bill be dismissed without prejudice to complainants right of recovery in any subsequent suit that may be instituted by said complainant for that purpose ....

Page 244: **James T. Hughs** vs **Christopher Shaw** Admr & al ... the affidavit of **James M. Shepherd** showing that he as administrator of **John Shepherd** and that himself & **David G. Shepherd** are interested in the matter of controversy in the suit ....

Page 244: **Sterling Harris** vs **Joseph J. Walker** ... (Page 245) the court was of opinion that all the equity set up in the bill is fully not ____ bye the answer & that the allegations of the bill are not sustained by proof ... bill be dismissed ....

Page 245: **Alfred & Bird S. Jones** vs **A. B. McNichol** & **Thomas A Lancaster** ... on 15 November 1841 Defendant McNichols recovered a judgement by confession against the complainants Alfred & Bird S. Jones in the Jackson Circuit Court for $225 & costs of suit ... it was agreed between Jones & McNichol that said complain-ants should have the privilege of paying on said judgement a horse at valuation ... and it further appearing that said judgment ... was transferred for value received by said McNichols to **John Congo** and by said Congo to **Costillo & Brothers** & by Costillo & Brothers to the Defendant Thomas (Page 246) A. Lancaster and the court being of opinion that said Complainants are entitled to have said sum ....

Page 246: **Hare** & **Jackson** vs **Wm Scanland** & others. Inj. Bill. And **William Scanland** vs Hare, Jackson & others. Cross Bill. ... upon bill, cross bill, answers to each & replications thereto of all the parties except **John Scanland** against who said Bills have been taken for confessed & set for hearing exparte as to him & proof in the cause and it appearing ... that John Scanland is indebted to Jackson & Hare as alleged in their bills and that (Page 247) he is a nonresident of this state as charged but it appearing ... the effects to wit the books notes & accts of John Scanland & Co attached in their Bill belongs to the firm of John Scanland & Co which firm is comprised of John Scanland & William Scanland . . . and William is entitled to a prior lien upon said effects for the payment of the partnership debts ... that **Samuel E. Hare** has heretofore been appointed receiver in this case ....

Page 247: **Samuel E. Hare** vs **William** & **John Fraim** ... complainant by his Solicitor dismissed his suit ....

Page 247: **Wm C Burke, Hannah D Burke, John W. Richmond, James M. Richmond George C Darwin Jr. Margaret Darwin, Dudley B Hale Julia Hale, Thaxton Carter** & **Jane Carter** vs **Henry Richmond** & **Robert Richmond** Administrators of **Jno Richmond** decd ... (Page 248) in the presence of solicitors on both sides ... decreed ... that the Defendants' exceptions be disallowed and it appearing from the masters report that the complainants and **Henry Richmond** are the heirs of **John Richmond** decd. that the Defendants were the Admrs of said Decd and as such have in their hands a fund which of right should be distributed to complts **Thackston Carter** & wife $56.71. To James M. Richmond $10.97 to **Dudley B Hail** & wife $70.78 and that the Defendants have overpaid to the complainants as follows to **William C. Burke** & wife $45.33. To John W. Richmond $67.14 to **G. C. Darwin** & wife $61.40 ... complainants to recover from the defendants ... (Page 249) Court adjourned ... /S/ **Bromfield Ridley**

Page 249: Friday morning 8 o'clock Jan. 29. 1847. **B. L. Ridley** presiding.

Page 249: **Lewis R. Nance** vs **Alexander Dillard** and **Henry B McDonald** Ex of **John Congo** ... in the presence of solicitors on both sides ... the court being satisfied from the proof in the cause that the complainant was sober and in his proper mind at the time the contract was made and the $500 note and deed of trust in the pleadings were executed ... court orders the Clerk & Master to take and state an account of the consideration that said **John Conger** paid to and for complain-ant as a consideration for said $500 note and deed of trust ... the amount of the rents and profits received by the trustee Dillard .... that the complainant file with the Clerk and master the written obligation of John Conger for the payment of the money to **James F. Hughes** and in stating said account will look to the proof already taken ....

Page 250: **Nathan Montgomery** vs **Thomas L. Bransford** & others ... Clerk & Master confirmed that he sold the land and **Thomas Murry** became the purchaser at $175 and executed his note with Thomas L Bransford and **Russel M Kinnaird** his surety which fell due 7 January 1844 with interest ... decreed that complainant recover from the said Murry, Bransford & Kinnaird the said sum ....

Page 250: **James Tinsley** vs **Thomas H Butler** et al ... leave is given Thomas H Butler until April Rules to file his cross Bill ....

Page 250: **James T. Hughes** vs **Christopher Shaw** et al ... that **William B Holmes** be appointed receiver in this cause to take into his possession and rent out the lands sought to be sold in this cause ... and report to next term.

Page 250: **Lewis R. Vance** vs **James T. Hughes** ... (Page 251) deft became the purchaser of the lands in the pleadings mentioned at execution sale for the sum of $___ (blank) that said Deft ... recovered judgement for possession &c–that a writ of possession issued & complainant not wishing to be dispossessed acknowledge himself Defendants tenant and executed his note to Defendant for $70 for the rents and profits of said land ... there is no equity in complainants bill ... complainant's bill dismissed ....

Page 251: **James Young** and **Littleberry Young** vs **Lawson Clark** et al ... the indebtedness of Defendant Lawson Clark to the complainants for which his property was attached in this cause together with interest thereon up to this date is $76.30 ... ordered ... (Page 252) complainants recover against said Defendant ....

Page 252: **Lewis R. Vance** vs **Harold D Marchbanks** & **Thomas Marchbanks** ... Chancellor thinks fit to submit the same to a jury ... at its next Term ... on the following issues. 1. Deed to Deft Marchbanks in Decr 1840 was he in the full possession of his right reason & intelligence? 2. If not & the Deed was executed when drunk did he Vance afterward when sober satisfy & confirm the contract? (Page 253) ... continued till July term ....

Page 253: **John Scanland** vs **Isaac Hogin** et al ... by consent cause continued ....

Page 253: **Hicklins Heirs** vs Hicklins Admrs ... the report in all things confirmed, from which it appeared there is a balance in the lands of the Defendant **James Nevins** in favor of **Elizabeth Walker** of $49.89–in favor of **Parish** and wife of $29.38–in favor of **Nunnelly** & wife of $3.52 and to the Heirs of **Thomas Hicklin** decd $75.54–to **Joseph Olive** of $211.54 and to **Samuel Olive** of $211.54 and to **Landon Armstrong** of $10.09 after deducting the share of James Nevins & wife ... that **Aaron** (Page 254) **Biggerstaff** is in debt to the estate for land purchased by him at the sale by the Clerk of the Circuit Court in the sum of $229 with interest up to the first November 1845 ... further decreed that the matter of the death of Samuel Olive be continued until the next term to take further proof ... that unless the Deft Nevins and the said Biggerstaff pay said sums so decreed by the May rules then the Clerk & Master to issue executions for the same ....

Page 254: **Samuel E. Hare** & **Watson M. Cooke** vs **Polly Henry** & **James Henry**, **William Jordan Henry** & **Michael Henry** and others ... (Page 255) that Defendant Polly Henry being indebted to complainants to secure the payment of the same executed to them a mortgage deed to her dower as widow & relict of Michael Henry decd of the lands lying in Jackson County of which her said husband died seized and possessed ... Polly also authorized and empowered complainants to procure her dower to be laid off and assigned. And it also appearing to the Court that the other Defendants are the heirs at law of said Michael decd .... Clerk & Master ordered to take an account between the complainants and Deft Polly and report to next term. And it is further ordered that the Sheriff of this county summon on five freeholders unconnected with the parties by affinity or consanguinity and that they allot and assign to said Polly one third part of the lands mentioned in the pleadings including the mansion house as her dower ....

Page 255: **William Buchanan** & wife **Jane** vs **M. C. Hogin** Admr &c & others. O.B. And M. C. Hogin Admr &c & others vs **Wm Buchanan** & wife and others. Cross Bill ... in pursuance to an interlocutory order pronounced in this cause and upon exceptions by complts solicitor to the report of the master as to the amount advanced to Wm Buchanan & wife out of the Estate of **Edward** (Page 256) **Hogin** deceased and it appearing to the Court the report is erroneous in that particular and complainants exceptions are therefore sustained ... it appears the lands laid off to **Rebecca Hogin** under the Will of said Edward descends to her heirs at law equally ... ordered adjudged & decreed ... that the said Administrator, **Matthew C. Hogin**, pay over to each of said distributees the amounts found in their favour [*sic*] from the estate of said Edward Hogin and from the estate of **Sarah Hogin** & the estate of Rebecca Hogin, first retaining out of said fund the costs of their causes, except the proceeds of the real estate of Rebecca Hogin & Sarah Hogin which is not yet collected ... that the amount given in the Will of said **E. Hogin** to Complt Jane Buchanan is given to her during life then to go to her son **John** and ... that William Buchanan is an improvident man. It is ordered ... that the amount coming to said Jane from said E. Hogin's estate be settled on her during her life & then to vest in said John, and that whatever amount may be coming from the estates of Rebecca & Sarah Hogin be settled on said Jane from the debts and contracts of her said husband Wm Buchanan ... (Page 257) that the (solicitor fees) be paid out of the fund coming to said Buchanan & wife to their Solicitors **Wm B Campbell**, **Samuel M Fite** & **Samuel Turney** ... ordered that Matthew C. Hogin Admr &c

recover of **Elvis Taylor** & **Rawlings Hogin** his security the balance reported against said Taylor and wife ... that said Admr recover of **Daniel Hogin** and Rawlings Hogin his security the sum reported in said report against said Daniel Hogin ....

Page 257: **Henry Carter** vs **James Carter** & al. Inj. Bill. And James Carter vs Henry Carter. Cross Bill ... complt Henry in the year 1834 left the negro woman **Charlotte** & her two children **Winney** & **Hannah** in the possession of James Carter ... that said woman has since had the other three (Page 258) **Hampton**, **Leroy** & **Benjamin** and the court being of opinion that the deeds of Gift made by said Jems [sic] to the other parties for said negroes are void being executed and devised with a knowlege [sic] of the rights of said Henry and ... that if it should be found that the services of said negroes have been worth more than the expense of taking care of them that James should be charged therewith ... cause continued ....

Page 259: **Thomas L Bransford Esq** ... placed upon the roll as practicing solicitor of this Court.

Page 259: **Argyle R. Jarvis** vs **John N. Gates** ... after taking the steps directed by an interlocutory decree pronounced in this cause at the last term sold the lands in the pleadings mentioned at public auction to **Erwin F. Langford** for $489 ... and Langford being the beneficiary in said sale no money was exacted ... decreed that the title to said lands in the pleadings to wit, One lying in Jackson County on the north side of **Cumberland River** containing 76 1/4 acres beginning ... in the East boundary line of **Gwinn's**[10] 640 acre tract 20 poles south of his N.E. corner running S. with Gwinn's line 122 poles to a beech & two sweet gums, thence east 120 poles to a beech on the bank of the river, thence N. 122 poles to a stake, thence W. 100 poles to the beginning. One other tract containing 5 acres beginning at a beech in the N. boundary line of said 76 1/4 acre tract running N. 20 poles to a beech thence W. 40 poles to a sugar tree and beech, thence S. 20 poles to a stake, thence East with the N. boundary line of said 76 1/4 acre tract to the beginning (Page 260) be divested as to said John N. Gates and said Argyle R. Jarvis and vested in said Erwin F. Langford and his heirs forever and that the money arising from the sale of said land be appropriated first to the payment of $33.22 1/2 the amount due from said Deft Gates to Complt ... and the residue to the payment of the **Whitfield Button** debt in the pleadings mentioned and the surplus if any after said payments to be paid over to said John N. Gates ... Court adjourned ... /S/ **Bromfield Ridley**.

Page 261: Chancery Court ... held at the Court House in Gainesboro for the Chan-cery District composed of Jackson County, 4th Chancery Division, on Wednesday after the 4th Monday, **28 July 1847**. **Bromfield L. Ridley** Chancellor presiding.

Page 261: **George M. McWhirter** vs **Jackson T. Wood** & others. Decree ... answer of Deft **John M Richmond** in presence of complainant and said Defendant Richmond where by consent of parties it is ordered ... that the complainant he being Clerk & Master proceed to take an account of the expenses that the said Defendant together with the other securities of **William Wood** for the appearance of the said William W.ood at the Circuit Court of Jackson County to answer the State of Tennessee on a charge of counterfeiting incurred by being such security and then he report the same to next term and what indemnification if any has been made to said securities otherwise than by the conveyance of the lands attached in this cause ... said complainant have leave to file an amended Bill in this cause so as to bring **Abner Lee** the conveyor of the land attached to Jackson T. Wood before the court as a party Defendant to this suit ....

Page 262: **John Barnes** & others vs **George Welch** & others. O.B. ... by their solicitors and on

---

[10] The writing is quite legible, but the exact spelling can not be determined. Another possibility is "Given's" or " Givinen's."

motion leave is given his co-defendants to take the Deposition of George Welch ....

Page 262: **Hare & Cook** vs **Benj. Monroe** & others ... order for the Clerk & Master to take an account is revived.

Page 262: **William Buchanan** & wife vs **Matthew C. Hogin** & others. Came the parties by their Solicitors and the death of the complainant William Buchanan was this day suggested ... and admitted by Defendant and **John A. Buchanan** produced ... a power of attorney ... authorizing him ... to receive and receipt any moneys which of right belong to Complainant **Jane Buchanan** arising from the estates of **Edward Hogin** decd, **Rebecca Hogin** decd & **Sarah Hogin** deceased ....

Page 262: **James T. Hughs** vs **Christopher Shaw** & al. Came the parties by their Solicitors and on motion & by consent this cause is remanded to the rules. It is further ordered that the same be consolidated with the cause of (Page 263) **James M. Shepherd** Admr &c vs said Christopher Shaw & others and **David G. Shepherd** & Co. vs Christopher Shaw & others.

Page 263: **Samuel E. Hare** & al vs **William Scanland** & others and **Wm Scanland** vs **Sam E. Hare** & others ... the decree herein announced at a former term directing the Clerk & Master to take an account in this cause ... is hereby revived ... report to next term.

Page 263: **Zadock B. Roberts** & others vs **Ridley Roberts** & others. Complainants dismiss their suit.

Page 263: **Nathaniel G. Jackson** vs **Nathaniel M. Cox** & al. Complainant dismisses his suit.

Page 263: **Holland Denton** & al vs **A. J. Hoodenphyle** &al. Complainants dismiss their suit.

Page 264: **Watson M. Cook** vs **John Dowell** & al. Complainant dismisses his suit.

Page 264: **Nathan J. Goss** & al vs **James Guffy** ... the decree herein pronounced at last term is hereby revived and the clerk directed to proceed as ordered ....

Page 264: **John Scanland** vs **Isaac Hogin** and **Matthew C. Hogin**. Decree Final ... on 22 March 1837 complainant became bound as security of Defendant Isaac in two judgements rendered in the Circuit Court of Jackson County ... making in all the amount $88.81. It further appeared ... that Defendant Matthew C. as administrator of **Edward Hogin** decd of **Rebecca Hogin** decd and of **Sarah Hogin** decd has in his hands a fund of 30 cents belonging to said Defendant Isaac ... It further appeared to the court that as required by decree pronounced at a former term of this court in the case of **Buchanan** & wife against said Matthew C. Hogin (Page 265) & others the lands & town lot of the estate of Sarah Hogin decd were sold for $396.50 and that said sum will in a short time fall due ... that Isaac is entitled to a distributive share of 1/13 part of said fund when collected ... that Complainant recover of Isaac Hogin $88.81 ... that the Clerk & Master proceed to collect and distribute the fund arising from the sale of said land ... Court adjourned ....

Page 265: **29 July 1847**. Court met pursuant to adjournment. **Bromfield Ridley** Chancellor, presiding.

Page 265: **John Sommers** & wife **Margaret** vs **Solomon Dill, Stephen Dill, Elijah Dill Elizabeth Dill Sutton Polly Rutledge Archibald Dill Rowland C. Dill, Stephen Dill jr.**

Solomon Dill jr Dorcas Williams Emanuel Williams. Aner Medlen, Samuel Medlen and **Milly Loftis** ... (Page 266) it appeared **Archibald Dill Senr.** Died ... possessed of the lands in the pleadings and complainants and Defendants are heirs and distributees of s̲d̲ decd and said lands are not susceptible of division for distribution ... ordered lands be sold for the purpose of distribution and a lien taken upon the land for the purchase money ... report to next term.

Page 266: **Hicklins Heirs** vs Hicklins Admrs et al ... Clerk ordered to collect as before directed and pay over to all of defendants as heretofore decreed except the share of **Samuel Olive** which shall be retained by the master ... both parties are permitted to take proof as to the death of said Samuel Olive and if dead whether he left any heirs or representatives other than complainants and defendants ....

Page 267: **Daniel Lee**, Admr &c vs The Creditors of **A Lee** Decd. ... Clerk and Master proceed to pay out to each of the creditors of **Abraham Lee** Decd the amounts to which they are respectively entitled by said report ... that he proceed to collect the residue of the debts of said estate and report to the next Term &c.

Page 267: **Henry Carter** vs **James Carter** et al. And James Carter vs Henry Carter. Bill and Cross Bill ... it appeared ... that James Carter contracted with Henry Carter to take and keep the negroes in the pleadings mentioned for their victuals and clothes and that therefore the said James Carter is not entitled to an account of services rendered to said negroes as a physician or otherwise ... Cross Bill is dismissed ... that all of the negroes in the pleadings mentioned be delivered up to said Henry Carter or his authorized agent ... (Page 268) It is further ordered that James Carter produce the Negro girl **Winney** here at the next term of this court.

Page 268: **James McBroom** vs **David Herbert.** Decree final ... that in a former suit litigated in this court the Defendant had obtained a decree to redeem a tract of land adjoining the 100 acre tract of complainant and that in taking out the writ of possession the Defendant claimed to include the house of ~~defendant~~ complainant and to cross the lines of said hundred acre tract- and it appeared to the court that the boundary of said lands were not litigated or made a question in the former suit and that the parties had agreed the boundary of said hundred acre tract should be the line dividing their land therefore it is ordered that complainant be quieted in the possession of his said hundred acre tract ... and the defendant be enjoined from taking possession or interfering with the same ....

Page 269: **Nelson Sadler** vs **Merlin Young** et al ... it appeared that Defendant **Scanland** was indebted to the complainant in the sum of about $1000 paid for him as security that Scanland had left insolvent to parts unknown that whilst he was Sheriff of (Jackson County) he was entitled to various sums in costs which came to the hands of said Young who was then the Clerk of the Circuit Court for Jackson County that then fees were owing to Scanland but because it does not appear how much money of said Scanland has come to the hands of the s̲d̲ Young. It is ordered ... the Clerk & Master take an account charging said Young with the amount of fees of said Scanland which he has received or collected crediting him with whatever Scanland may have collected of fees due Young and not accounted for ....

Page 269: **Lewis R. Vance** vs **H. B. McDonald** Exr &c of **John Conger** Decd and **Alexander Dillard** Defendants ... in the presence of solicitors on both sides upon report of the Clerk and Master made in pursuance of an interlocutory decree pronounced in this cause at the last term of this court and the exceptions on both sides when it appeared the exceptions of complainant to the allowance of $115.50 to the trustee for his services are well taken ... (Page 270) it appears the complain-ant was indebted to John Conger Decd on 10 Sept 1841 ... also to **James**

T. Hughes ... it is considered by the court that Deft H B McDonald as Executor recover against Lewis R. Vance ... and said Executor recover against Alexander Dillard ... and Dillard is to pay **Henry B McDonald** $50 for his services as solicitor ... and the Clerk & Master after giving 20 days notice of time and place of sale in writing at Gainesboro, **Granville** and some public place (Page 271) in the neighborhood of the land proceed to sell the land ... at public sale for cash in hand ....

Page 271: **Andrew Wossom** Admr with the will annexed of **Andrew Erwin** Decd vs **Margaret Erwin** ... it appeared to the court Andrew Erwin departed this life leaving a last will in which he devised that all of his property should left to the use of his father and mother, **Benjamin Erwin** and wife. It appeared Benjamin Erwin and wife ... have departed this life. It further appeared that previous to his death Benjamin had purchased a tract of land on which the defendant now lives ... that the whole of the fund of Andrew in the hands of Benjamin had come to the hands of Defendant at the death of Benjamin ... that Margaret had lived with Benjamin and wife previous to their death her and her children and that since their death she has occupied the land and took the rents and profits ... it is ordered that the Clerk & Master take an account and report to next Term whether the tract of land was purchased with the funds of the Estate of said Andrew (Page 272) Decd mentioned in his will in all or in part, how much of the personal Estate of Andrew decd remained unconsumed at the death of the father & mother, how much came to the lands of Margaret–what if any thing the defendant Margaret is entitled to for her service by contract or otherwise in attending upon the father and mother of said Andrew decd and what would be a reasonable compensation to her, let him report what would be a reasonable rent for the land since the death of the last one of the old people, and whether the defendant has occupied the same. That in making the allowance to Deft. the fact of her children being with her and all of the circumstances be taken into the estimate ....

Page 272: **Lewis R. Vance** vs **Herald D Marchbanks**. Came the parties by their solicitors and then came a jury of good and lawful men to wit–**Adam C Hamilton**, **Benjamin Scanland**, **Andrew Wassom**, **William Gipson**, **Thomas D. Cassetty**, **James Carter**, **Overton Pate**, **George Apple**, **Benjamin Erwin**, **Watson M Cooke**, **Andrew Poston** and **Charles N Price** who being elected ... upon their oath do say they can not agree where by consent Watson M Cooke one of the jurors aforesaid is withdrawn and the balance of the jury aforesaid from rendering their verdict are discharged and this cause is continued until next Term (Page 273) ....

Page 273: **George Apple** vs **Willis Halford** et al. Leave given complainant to take what proof he may think necessary ... within three months ... Defendants permitted to take rebutting testimony.

Page 273: **Nathan Montgomery** vs **Thomas L Bransford** et al ... before paying out any part of the funds arising from the sale of the land herein directed to be sold ... the Clerk & Master shall require a refunding bond with good security ....

Page 273: **Samuel E. Hare** vs **Nancy Griffith** et al ... the matters contained in complainants Bill are not sufficient in law to sustain the same and find relief as prayed ... (Page 274) complainants Bill dismissed ... complainant prays an appeal to the next term of the Supreme Court of the State of Tennessee to be held at

Nashville on the First Monday of December next which to him is granted upon his executing bond and security ....

Page 274: **Henry** & **Garrett Sadler** vs **Abisha Cannon** et al. It appearing to the court that **Jane**

Cannon, Martin V. Cannon Henry H Cannon and **Abisha Cannon Jr** Defendants are minors and have no regular guardian on motion it is ordered that **James M. Shepherd** be appointed guardian <u>perdente lite</u> ....

Page 274: **Hare & Cooke** vs **Polly Henry** et al ... ordered ... that the order directing a writ of dower and the taking and stating of an account be revised and that the master report to next term. And it is further ordered that **Mounce Gore** be appointed guardian of the Minor Heirs of **Michael Henry** Decd in the place of Deft Polly Henry. Court adjourned till court in course. /S/ **Bromfield L. Ridley.**

Page 275: Chancery Court convened on the first Wednesday after the Fourth Monday it being **26 January 1848**. **Bromfield L Ridley** Chancellor of the 4th Division presiding at the Court House in Gainesboro.

Page 275: **Hicklins** Heirs vs Hicklins Admr. ... order heretofore made is revived and the parties are permitted to take proof if taken before the next term.

Page 275: **Perry Mahanay** vs **Edwin F McKinney** et al. Came the complainant by his Solicitor on motion this cause continued ....

Page 275: **William Scanland** vs **Clayton Rogers** et al. Came the complainant by his solicitor and on motion ~~Nelson Sadler~~ **Benjamin Scanland** is appointed receiver in this cause ....

Page 276: **Lewis R. Vance** vs **Herald D Marchbanks.** Came the parties by their Solicitors and came a jury of good and lawful men, to wit, **William A. Hall Thomas Gentry Alexander H. Montgomery Nicholas Hail, Thomas Smith John Lock, John Leach Absalom Taylor, Alexander Cassetty Jefferson Roberts William Brooks Hiram Crabtree** ... because there is not time to go through the trial this evening the persons aforesaid are permitted to disperse to meet here again tomorrow morning. Court adjourned.

Page 276: Thursday Morning Jan. 27, 1848. **Bromfield L Ridley** Chancellor & presiding.

Page 276: **Goss** and **Davis** vs **James Guffy.** Came the complainant by his solicitor and the Clerk not reporting any sale of the land ... ordered to proceed to sell said lands ....

Page 277: **Nelson Sadler** vs **Marlin Young** et al. Cause continued.

Page 277: **Jared H. Graham** et al vs **Zadock N B Roberts** et al. Suit dismissed.

Page 277: **William Mansell** vs **Saml Mansell** et al. It appearing ... that Defendants had taken the depositions of **Henry Bohanan, Michael Moore, John B Pointer, John West, James Brock, John L. H. Huddleston** and **William Norris** ... which depositions were excepted to by the complainant for want of notice ... Defendant is permitted to retake the depositions of said witnesses upon giving notice.

Page 278: **Hogin's Heirs** vs Hogin's Administrators ... it appeared by report of the Master that he had in his hands arising from the sale of the Real Estate of **Rebecca Hogin** decd and **Sarah Hogin** Decd the sum of $1499.81 which at right belonged to complainants and defendants. It further appeared there are thirteen heirs and representatives of said Rebecca and Sarah Hogin Decd to-wit: **Rawlings Hogin, Martha Shaw, Jane Buchanan, Matthew C. Hogin, Richard Hogin Elvis Taylor** and wife, **Daniel Hogin, Isaac Hogin William C Hogin, Anthony Hogins** children, **Ira Cowan's children**, **Simon Hogins** Estate and **James Hogins** Estate and that a distributive share in said fund is $115.37 to each of said heirs ... Richard Hogin had transferred his interest in said funds by deed properly authenticated and here exhibited to the court to William C Hogin & that Jane Buchanan by Power properly executed and authenticated has transferred and set over her interest in said fund to **John Hughes** and that Isaac Hogin had by Deed properly executed and authenticated transfer and set over his interest in said fund to **George M McWhirter** all of which deeds and powers are submitted here for the inspection of the court ... It further appeared to the court that John H.ughes is the Administrator of the Estate of James Hogin Decd and that Rawlings Hogin is the Administrator of Simon Hogin Decd. It further appeared to the court that Daniel Hogin had executed a power of attorney properly authenticated authorizing ... Rawlings Hogin to demand and receive from Matthew C. Hogin Administrator of said Sarah and Rebecca Hogin his share of said funds. And it further appearing that said Matthew C. Hogin by decree 29 January 1847 recovered judgement against **Elvis Taylor** and Rawlings Hogin his security for $153.40 ... (Page 280) ... George M McWhirter Clerk & Master be allowed to retain as his own property all that part of the share of Isaac Hogin in said funds except such portion as is included and adjudged to **John Scanland** in the decree pronounced at the last term of this court in the case of John Scanland against Isaac Hogin ... and that he proceed to pay William C Hogin the share of the said Richard Hogin, that he pay John Hughes the share of Jane Buchanan and also the share of the estate of James Hogin Decd–that he pay to Rawlings Hogin Admr the share of is [sic] belonging to the Estate of Simon Hogin Decd and that he pay to Matthew C. Hogin Admr the share of Daniel Hogin ....

Page 281: **Martha Wright** vs **Matthew C. McKinly** & al. Upon the plea of Statute of limitation of two years and the demurrer of the complainant and the demurrer was sustained by the Court & the plea ordered to be stricken out and Deft McKinly ordered to answer the bill with leave to rely [sic] in answer upon the statute of limitations ... and an alias subpoena and copy of Bill is ordered as to Deft. **Graham** directed to the Sheriff of **Marion County**.

Page 281: **Samuel Turney** vs **Samuel E. Stone**, **Thomas L. Bransford George M. McWhirter**, **Thomas Johnson** & others. The tracts of land mortgaged by Thomas Johnson and conveyed to **Jefferson Johnson** be sold as the property of Thomas and Jefferson Johnson and out of the money arising from the sale **Botts & McWhirter** is first to be paid their mortgaged debt ... leaving the **Petty** tract which is first upon the sale therof [sic] next to George McWhirter ... then the debt of the complainant Samuel Turney is to be paid next giving the Petty land to the McWhirter debt and ... should the Petty tract which is to be sold subject to the dower of the Widow not be sufficient to pay said debt due to McWhirter ... then should any remain of the other tracts after paying the debts mentioned then the residue thereof shall be appropriated to the balance ... that **William Davidson** be appointed commissioner and he proceed to sell the land ... should the Petty tract realize more than sufficient to pay the debt ... the remainder if any to be paid to Deft Thomas Johnson.

Page 283: **John Hughs** Admr &c. Exparte. It appears that the outstanding debts against the estate of **Letty Roberts** decd exceed the perishable property and chooses in action of said decedent which has come to the hands of petitioner as administrator and that there are two negro slaves of said estate, **Polly** aged 7 or 8 years and **Jane** aged one year and that there are eight distributees of said estate. Ordered by the court to sell said negro slaves at public sale upon a credit of six months for the purpose of paying debts of said estate and for distribution of the residue if any ... giving notice of sale at Gainsborough, **Granville** and some other public place in said county ....

Page 283: **Matilda Shaw, Jane Shaw, Burchet Shaw Rebecca Shaw** by their next friend

Rawlings Hogin and **Martha Shaw**. Exparte-Petition. Ordered that the Clerk report whether it would be to the interest of petitioners that the lands in the petition be sold for the purpose of distribution ....

Page 283: **Matilda Shaw, Jane Shaw, Burchet Shaw Rebecca Shaw** by their next friend **Rawlings Hogin** and **Martha Shaw**. Exparte Petition. (Page 284) ... it appeared to the court that petitioners as heirs and widow of **George W. C. Shaw** are seized and possessed of the land in the petition and the same is not susceptible of partition among said petitioner and said widow consents to take her dower in money ... ordered ... that the Clerk sell the land at public sale upon a credit of twelve months ... and retain a lien upon the land for the purchase money and report to the next term of this court ... Court adjourned ... /S/ **Bromfield Ridley.**

Page 284: Friday Morning **January 28. 1848**. Court met with **Bromfield L Ridley** presiding.

Page 284: **George M McWhirter** vs **John M Rich** and [sic] and **Jackson T Wood.** Decree ... (Page 285) upon report of the Clerk ... **John M Richmond** and his co-securities had sustained loss by being security of **William Wood** in procuring his attendance before the Circuit Court to answer the state of Tennessee on a charge of counterfeiting to the amount of $78.25 for the securing of which the Deed was executed by Defendant Jackson T. Wood to his co-defendant John M Richmond ... that Jackson T. Wood is indebted to complainant George M McWhirter by note due 1st Monday in November 1846 in the sum of $100 ... with interest ... that Jackson T. Wood is a non resident of the State of Tennessee so that ordinary process of law cannot be executed on him ... it further appearing from the answer of Richmond that the Deed executed to him by his codefendant although absolute on its face was intended by the parties to operate as a mortgage to secure Richmond and his cosecurities against loss in the matter of their security for the appearance of William Wood ... (Page 286) that complainant recover of Jackson T. Wood said sum of $100 and interest ... that said tract of land conveyed has been attached in this cause ... ordered **James T. Quarles** be appointed a special commissioner to sell said land ... the proceeds of sale be applied first to the cost of this suit, then to the amount of $79.50 to Richmond and his cosecurities then to the decree of $107 of complainants and the balance if any paid over to Jackson T Wood ....

Page 286: **Heare** [sic] & **Jackson** vs **John Scanland** & others. And **William Scanland** vs **Hare** & others. Bill and Cross Bill ... upon report of the Clerk & Master made in pursuance to the interlocutory decree pronounced in a former term it appears that William Scanland was a partner (Page 287) in the firm of John Scanland & Co. and William has paid out of his own private funds for said firm $1,550.00 & that William is first entitled to be reimbursed said sum out of the effects of said firm ... **Samuel E. Hare** has as receiver collected $405.14 and he is entitled as a credit on that sum for expenses costs &c and for his services as receiver ... that Samuel E. Hare pay to William Scanland $266.57 ... that in collecting said sum Hare obtained the note of **Joel & Benj Richardson** & endorsed the same himself and said note was discounted in Bank of Tennessee at **Sparta**. It is therefore ordered ... that Wm Scanland give bond and security to indemnify said Hare from any liability on account of said Richardson note of about $93 ... (Page 288).

Page 288: **Lewis R. Vance** vs **Alexander Dillard** and **H B McDonald.** Decree ... upon an application to open the bidding upon the land sold as the property of Lewis R. Vance by the Clerk & Master on the 22nd Inst. under the decree of last term and purchased by **James A. Spurlock** for $300 ... and whereas the creditor H. B. McDonald & purchaser James A. Spurlock & Lewis R. Vance and **Edward Anderson** the original owner of said land entered into the following agreement desiring that Edward Anderson be subrogated to all the rights of the original purchaser and all subsequent rights under said purchaser ....

Page 289: **James Tinsley** vs **Thomas H Butler** & others. And Thomas H. Butler Executor & others against James Tinsley. Bill and Cross Bill ... after exhausting the funds left in the Will of **Bailey Butler** to wit $2092.82 which had been paid by the executor to the payment of the defalcation of **Franklin W. Butler** there still remained the sum of $1061.63 to be paid by the intestate Bailey Butler or his executor (to) the complt James Tinsley and **William Hawkins** and that Thomas H. Butler the executor has paid of this sum $795.63 and James Tinsley has paid $266 ... William Hawkins the other security is wholly insolvent ... (Page 290) ordered that the Clerk also take an account ... and report the same to the next term ....

Page 290: **James T. Hughs** vs **Christopher Shaw** & others. Injunction, Bill, Amended Bill & Supplemental. **James M. Shepherd** admr of **John Shepherd** decd vs Christopher Shaw & others. O.B. **David G. Shepherd** & James M. Shepherd vs Christopher Shaw & others. O.B. . . came to be heard ... in presence of counsel ... it appeared ... that in the settlement of said Christopher Shaw as Admr of **Samuel Shaw** decd the item of judgements before **John Hughs J.P.** for $218.15 set down as a credit to said Christopher was improperly allowed and the same is stricken out ... that the personal estate and chases [sic] in action which were of said Saml Shaw Decd has been exhausted in the payment of debts due by said estate and that complainant James M. Shepherd as Administrator of John Shepherd decd and complainants David G. Shepherd and James M. Shepherd have outstanding claims against said estate which are ... (Page 291) due and unpaid and complainants are to be preferred to have their claims satisfied out of the estate of said Samuel Shaw before complainant James T. Hughes who is a creditor of Christopher Shaw ....

Page 291: **Martha Wright** vs **Ridley Roberts** et al. Came the complainant by her solicitor and with the assent of the court enters a nolle prosequi in this cause as to the defendant **John Graham**.

Page 291: **James T. Hughes** vs **Christopher Shaw** et al. Injunction & Amended & Supplemental Bill. And **James M. Shepherd** Admr &c vs Christopher Shaw et al. O. B. And David G. & James M. Shepherd vs Christopher Shaw et al. O. B. ... Christopher (Page 292) Shaw Administrator of **Samuel Shaw** Decd is indebted to James M. Shepherd Administrator of **John Shepherd** in the sum of $327.22 and $1.62 1/2 cents cost of suits and to David G Shepherd and James M. Shepherd in the sum of $131.64 and $1.75 costs ... ordered that the Clerk sell the lands in the pleadings on a credit of 12 months ... and retain a lien upon the land for the purchase money and report to the next term ... that Christopher Shaw is individually indebted to complainant James T. Hughs ....

Page 292: **Lewis R. Vance** vs **Hearld D. Marchbanks** & others. Came the parties by their Solicitors and came again the same Jury elected impanelled & sworn in this cause (Page 293) ... they find issues in favor of the plaintiff ... And the Defendants by their Solicitor moved the Court for a new trial in this cause which motion is by the Court overruled and the Master directed to report to next term.

Page 293: **John Sommers** & others vs **Roland C. Dill** & others . . . (Page 294) it appears that the master on 16 October 1847 sold the lands in the pleadings at public auction to **James M. Loftis** for $171 for which the sd James M. Loftis executed bond together with **Achilles Hare** & **Watson M. Cooke** his securities ... And the said James M. Loftis appearing here in open court and asserting his willingness to pay for said land in cash ... that $25 would be a reasonable fee for the services of **Messrs Hall** & **Washburn** as Solicitors in this cause ....

Page 294: **Samuel E. Hare** & **Watson M. Cooke** vs **Polly Henry, Michael Henry William Jordon Henry, James Henry, Mounce Gore** & others ... (Page 295) jury summoned to allot and set apart the dower of said Polly Henry widow of Michael Henry decd out of the lands mentioned in the pleadings of which said Michael died seized and possessed ... We the undersigned Citizens & Free holders of Jackson County, Tennessee, unconnected to Polly Henry widow & relict of Michael Henry or the heirs of Michael Henry or to Samuel E. Hare & Watson M Cooke either by affinity or consanguinity and entirely disinterested in the estate of Michael Henry decd ... set off to said Polly Henry ... her dower in all lands ... consisting of one tract containing 138 acres in said county Dist No 9 on the South side of **Roaring River** have set off to said Polly Henry 53 acres beginning at a stake on the Bank of Roaring River 30 poles below the beginning corner of said tract of 138 acres running thence South 23º 1/2 poles thence South 1º East 26 poles, thence South 3º West 27 poles thence South 7 1/2 E. 12 poles, Thence South 50º West 14 1/2 poles, thence South 78º West 32 poles, thence South 73º West 29 poles to **Robert Young** decd's line thence South with Young's line 52 poles to a stake said Young's corner, Thence East 53 poles to a stake thence North 40º East 135 poles to a stake, then North 53ºWest 77 poles to the beginning including the mansion house of the said Michael Henry decd which above described lot of 53 acres does in our opinion constitute one third part in value of the lands of which the said (Page 296) Michael Henry decd died seized ... 25 January 1848 /S/ **Thomas Gaw, John Stamps, John M Burns, Joseph Stafford** by X-mark, **William Gray**. Test: **H Denton**, Sheriff ... ordered by the Court that the Clerk sell the lands so set apart and allotted to said Polly as her dower aforesaid at public sale upon a credit of 12 months ... retaining a lien upon the land for the purchase money (Page 297) ....

Page 297: **Mary H Brooks** vs **Richard P. Brooks**. Decree ... about 27 March 1828 complainant and defendant were carefully joined together as husband and wife ... that complainant has eight children five daughters, and three sons, born during wedlock, and who are all minors living with complainant. That complainant during the whole time she lived with her said husband and until the present time has been a chaste, loving and dutiful wife. That said defendant about 4 October 1846 abandoned said complainant without any just or lawful cause he having been during coverture guilty of sexual acts of adultery and that said Richard P. Brooks, at, before and since the Bill was filed lived with a certain **Lethe Jane Bowman** in adultery, and now lives with Lethe Jane ... complainant is now and had been for more than two whole years next before this Bill was filed, a citizen and resident of the county of Jackson and state of Tennessee ... Richard P. Brooks is seized and is owner of property real and personal in said county ... decreed by the court that the Bonds of Matrimony ... be dissolved (Page 298) and that said complainant be divorced ... and that all personal property including household and kitchen furniture, farming utensils, horses, cattle, hogs, sheep, chooses [sic] in action &c as well as all other personal property which Richard P. Brooks owned in Jackson County except negroes be divested as to said Richard P. Brooks and vested absolutely in the complainant. It is further decreed that the title to the negro slavs [sic] of said Richard P. Brooks mentioned in complainants Bill to-wit: **George, Anna, Martha, Cinda, Jack, Jim, Charles, Rachel, Laura, Ridley, Martin Tom** and **Marion** a child of Cinda's have since this Bill was filed and their future increase be divested as to said defendant and vested in complainant during her life and remainder after her death be vested in her children, to-wit: **Albert W. W. Brooks, Cyprissa C Brooks Angeline A Brooks, Mary Jane Brooks, John S. Brooks, Richard V. Brooks, Ellen W Brooks, Elvira A Brooks** and their heirs forever. And it is further decreed by the Court that the title to the following described tracts of land lying in said county of Jackson and State of Tennessee to-wit: one tract containing 293 3/4 acres conveyed to Richard P. Brooks by **William Scanland** by deed dated 10 August 1840 and bounded as follows Beginning at ... the mouth of **Rocky Branch**, the lower corner of the __an 256 acre tract running thence East 180 poles to ... the N.W. corner of the **Settle, Whitley** & **Smith** 160 acre tract. thence south with their line to their corner in the North boundary line of their 100 acre tract. thence West with their line 35 poles to a sugar tree their North West corner. thence south 22 poles to an oak and sugar tree thence West 285 poles to an Elm tree sugar tree and buckeye thence North crossing a small tract at 25 poles in all 50 poles to a red oak on the river bank. thence up the river with its meanders to the (Page 299) beginning. Also the tract on which Mary H Brooks now lives. Composed of two tracts the 1st being one half of the old (illegible) purchased by said Richard P. Brooks of **John Brooks** and divided between the said Richard P. and William Scanland and also a small tract of 62 acres beginning at a sycamore on the North bank of **Cumberland River** thence N. 31º E. 126 poles to ... the road leading to **Brook's ferry**. thence S. 83º E 172 poles to ... the bank of Cumberland River below Brook's ferry. thence down the river to the beginning. the whole of said lands when consolidated being bounded by Cumberland River on the East and South and by the lands of **Nelson Sadler** on the North and West. Also all the interest which the said Richard P. Brooks had by purchase or otherwise in the lands that were of **John Brooks** Decd lying in Jackson County whether of possession or reversion consisting of three shares to-wit: the share of **James W. Burke**, **William C Burke** and **Esom L Burke** and the reversion of the Dower of the widow of said **John Burke**, for a more particular description of said lands reference is had to the proceedings now of record in the Circuit Court of Jackson County praying for partition of dower &c–The **William G. Darwin** tract and the **Daniel Ramsey** tract being excepted they having been decreed absolutely to the said Mary H. Brooks. Also the **John Ramsey** tract is vested in the said Mary H. during her natural life with reversion to her children &c. and also a tract of one acre in the river bank above the mouth of the spring branch. Said tract and the John Ramsey tract being a portion of the lands that were of said John Burke Decd. (Page 300 is a blank page.) (Page 301) be divested as to Richard P. Brooks and vested in complainant during her natural life remainder after her death in all of said lands be vested in her children ... that the title to town lots No. 98 in Gainesboro. Also one other tract of land in Jackson County containing 200 more or less bounded as follows. Beginning at the mouth of **War Trace Creek** and running with the meanders there of to **Henry Jones** corner thence with his line to the top of the ridge. thence East with the old line to the mouth of **Indian Creek** thence down Cumberland River with its meanders including one acre the ferry landing on the South side of the river. thence to the beginning. Also Lot No. 4 in the town of **Celina** Also Lot No. 6 in the town of Celina. (Page 302) Also Town Lot No. 4 in the town of Gainesboro the same sold to **Achilles Hare**. Also one tract of 100 acres know [sic] as the Daniel Ramsey tract. Beginning on a small beech standing 4 poles above the mouth of a draw or hands with a mulberry. hornbeam & sugartree pointers, **Matthew Brooks** maple corner on the bank of the river & running with the line made by Daniel Ramsey and Matthew Brooks thence S. 66º East 120 poles to a large poplar and two dogwood pointers thence N. 63º East in all 51 poles to a corner made between **Jesse McClenden** and **George White**. thence with their division line North 16 poles to ... Jesse McClendon's & **William** and George **White's** corner thence North 37º West 200 poles to ... Wm Whites corner on the river. thence down the river with its various meanders to the Beginning be divested as to said Richard P. Brooks and vested in the complainant ... further ordered that the Master report whether the said Richard P. Brooks is the owner of any other lands in Jackson County and if any they are hereby divested as to Richard P. Brooks and the title vested in said complainant during her life and the remainder vested in her s<u>d</u> children as before named ... that the tract of 50 acres of land sold by Richard P. Brooks to **Nelson Sadler** is not included in this decree.

Page 302: **Hare & Cook** vs **Benjamin Monroe** & others ... (Page 303) Defendant **Nathan Montgomery** by consent of the Complainant, said Montgomery is permitted to amend his answer filed in this cause ....

Page 303: **Edward B. Draper Exr** &c vs **John Rogers**. Inj. Bill ... in the presence of counsel on both sides when it appeared ... that complainants testator and the Defendant were the accommodation endorsers of **Lawson Clark** on a bill of exchange payable to **Martin & Collier** the Defendant being first endorser ... the Complainant seeks to make the property of Defendant indemnify him without his having incurred loss ... there is no equity in Complainants Bill ... bill dismissed ....

Page 303: **J. G. Frazier** appeared in open Court ... It is ordered he be place upon the roll as a practicing Solicitor at this bar.

Page 303: **Andrew Wassom** Admr &c vs **Margaret Erwin** ... (Page 304) being satisfied the Nuncupative Will of **Andrew Irvin** decd vested absolute right in the property devised by the same to **Benjamin Erwin Sr.** and Benjamin Erwin Sr. disposed of the same to the Defendant as he had a right to do ... bill dismissed ... And the complainant by his Solicitor prayed an appeal from the next term of the Supreme Court of the State of Tennessee to be held at **Nashville** on the first Monday in December next which to him is given ....

Page 304: **John Barnes** & others vs **George Welch** & others ... dismissed ....

Page 305: **George Apple** vs **Willis Holford** ... continued ... complainant is permitted to amend his Bill so as to make **Ridley Apple** a complt to this suit ....

Page 305: **Thomas D. Simpson** vs **Milton Draper** et al ... leave given complainant to amend his bill and ... Milton Draper is permitted to file his Cross Bill ....

Page 305: **Danl. Lee's** Admr vs Creditors of **A Lee** Decd ... it appearing ... the amount of money charged in the inventory of **Daniel Lee** Admr of A Lee Decd as having arisen from the sale of the tobacco is in the hands of Deft **Samuel E. Hare** and the same now came to the hands of the said Admr ... (Page 306) ....

Page 306: **Willis Holdford** Guardian &c vs **George Apple** et al ... leave is given defendants to file their answer ....

Page 306: **Aletha Carver** et al vs **Cornelius Carver** ... contract contended for in complainants Bill for the lands therein mentioned was rescinded by the said **Hiram C Carver** and Cornelius Carver ... (Page 307) that complainants Bill be dismissed and that Defendant pay to complainant the administration of said Hiram C Carver $266. 66 1/2 ... and $26.60 interest on the sum from the time of the payment of the same till the present time as assets of the Estate of said Hiram C. and complainant agrees to surrender possession of said land to said defendant ....

Page 307: ...ordered by the Chancellor that all the cases decreed at the present term be enrolled ... Court adjourned to .... /S/ **Bromfield Ridley.**

Page 308: Blank page.

Page 309: **July 26 1848**. Court ... held at the Court House in Gainesborough for Chancery District (Jackson County) ... Fourth Chancery Division on Wednesday next after the Fourth Monday. **Bromfield L. Ridley** Chancellor presiding.

Page 309: **Hicklins Heirs** vs Hicklins Admr. & others ... continued ... Master to report next term ... that notice be served on **Saml. Turney** Esq., complainants Solicitor ....

Page 309: **Daniel Lee** Admr &c vs The Creditors of **Abraham Lee** Decd. Master is directed to report to the next term ....

Page 310: **Hare & Cooke** vs **Benj. Monroe** et al ... continued ....

Page 310: **Perry Mahanay** vs **Edwin F McKinney** et al ... continued ....

Page 310: **George Apple** vs **Willis Holdford** ... complainant dismisses his suit ....

Page 310: **Willis Halford** guardian &c vs **George Apple** et al ... complainant dismisses his suit ....

Page 311: **Nelson Sadler** vs **Merlin Young** & others ... continued ....

Page 311: **Thomas D. Simpson** vs **Milton Draper** et al ... cause is ordered to be remanded to the rules for further steps to be taken then.

Page 311: **Edward B. Draper** Exr &c vs **Reuben R Rogers** et al. Came the parties by their Solicitors and on motion the judgement for confessed heretofore taken in this cause against Defendant **John Rogers** is set aside and said Defendant is permitted to answer at the present term ....

Page 311: **William Scanland** vs **Clayton Rogers** ... continued ....

Page 311: **Henry & Garret Sadler** vs **Abisha Cannon** et al ... on motion the judgt. for confessed heretofore taken in (Page 312) this cause is set aside as to **James M. Shepherd** guardian ad litem and the minors for which he is such guardian ... cause is continued ....

Page 312: **Richard P. Brooks** vs **William C Burke** ... two terms have lapsed since any order was made in this cause. It is therefore ... dismissed ....

Page 312: **Richard P. Brooks** vs **Henry Sadler** et al ... two terms have lapsed since any order was made in this cause. It is therefore ... dismissed ....

Page 312: **Silas C Cornwell** & son vs **Richardson** & **Reeves** ... complainants have leave to file their amended and supplemental bill ....

Page 312: **Martha Wright** vs **Ridley Roberts** et al ... (Page 313) this court had no jurisdiction of this cause wherefore the chancellor is pleased to order said bill to be dismissed ... complainants pay the costs for which execution may issue jointly against **James A. Spurlock** and **James A. Manier** security for complainants ....

Page 312: **James Tinsley** vs **Thomas H Butler** Exr of **Bailey Butler** Decd and **William Hawkins** & Thos Butler. O.B. And Thomas H. Butler Exr &c vs James Tinsley. Cross Bill ... upon the interlocutory decree and report of the Clerk ... it appeared from the report that the Defendant Tinsley had collected of the note upon **Franklin W Butler** the sum of $50 the complainant Thomas H Butler Executor is entitled to. It is decreed that the Defendant Tinsley pay the same accordingly and also the costs of this suit for which executions issue and it further appeared that William Hawkins was a joint security with complainant and Defendant **Thos H Butler's** testator and has paid no part of Franklin W Butler's liabilities ... further decreed ... that James Tinsley recover of said William Hawkins $168.60 1/2 it being one half of one third of the liabilities paid by said Tinsley & Thos H Butler for the said Franklin (Page 314) W. It is further Decreed by the court that Thomas H Butler Executor of Bailey Butler Decd recover of said William Hawkins $168.60 1/2 ....

Page 314: **Samuel Turney** vs **Samuel E. Stone, Thomas Johnson Jefferson Johnson, George M McWhirter William H Botts, Thomas L Bransford Joel W. Settle** & others ... upon interlocutory decree heretofore pronounced and the report of the commissioner ... sold the tract of land in the pleadings at the court house door in Gainesborough 6 March 1848 when George M. McWhirter purchased the same for $400 ....

Page 315: **Nathan J Goss** & **James A. Davis** vs **James Guffy** ... the land in the pleadings was sold pursuant to a decree heretofore pronounced when Nathan J Goss became the purchaser at the price of $51 ....

Page 315: **David Griffith** Admr of **James P Griffith** vs **Mary Josephine Griffith** and **Mariah Clay Griffith** ... it appeared ... James P Griffith departed this life intestate seized of lands in the pleadings mentioned and that the defendants are his heirs at law and that the personal assets which were of said deceased at the time of his death are insufficient to pay the debts due ... that the clerk of this court sell the undivided interest of the defendants in the lands ... (Page 316) to be sold subject to the dower of the widow of said decd ....

Page 316: **Samuel E. Hare** and **Watson M Cooke** vs **Polly Henry** et al. Decree ... on 6 March 1848 after advertising as required by decree ... the land directed to be sold ... where Samuel E. Hare became the purchaser of the same ... at the price of $70.00 for which he executed his note with **James T. Quarles** his security ... that the title of said Polly Henry to the following described lands to-wit: containing 53 acres Beginning at a stake on the bank of **Roaring River** 30 poles below the beginning corner of **Michael Henry** tract and running thence south 23º West 7 1/2 poles-thence South 1º East 26 poles-thence south 3º West 27 poles-thence South 7 1/2 East 12 poles thence South 50º West 14 1/2 poles thence South 78º West 32 poles-thence South 73º West 29 poles to the line of **Robert Young** Decd thence South with said line (Page 317) 52 poles to a stake-said Young's corner-thence East 53 poles to a stake-thence North 40º East 135 poles to a stake thence North 53 º West 77 poles to the Beginning, including the dwelling house formerly occupied by Michael Henry Decd be divested as to the said Polly Henry and vested in Samuel E. Hare his heirs assigns for and during the life of said Polly Henry ....

Page 317: **David Griffith** Admr &c vs **Mary L Griffith** and **Mariah C. Griffith.** In this cause it appearing to the satisfaction of the court that both of the Defendants are minors under the age of 21 years and have no regular guardian. On motion **William R. Kenner(?)** is appointed guardian ad litem ....

Page 317: **George M McWhirter** vs **Jackson T. Wood** and **John Richmond** ... upon the interlocutory decree herein pronounced at last term and the report of **James T. Quarles** commissioner appointed to sell the lands attached in this cause ... said commissioner on 6 March 1848 at the court house door in Gainesboro ... (Page 318) at public auction ... when George M McWhirter became the purchaser ... at the price of $1000 for which said purchaser executed note with **Kinnard & Bransford** his security and a lien also being retained ... for the purchase money ... It is ordered ... that the title of Jackson L.(?) Wood and **John M Richmond** in and to the lands in the pleadings ... is hereby divested as to them and vested in said George M McWhirter his heirs and assigns forever ... that a writ of habere facias possessinun issue to put said purchaser in possession of said lands ....

Page 318: **Susan Cason** vs **Edward M Cason** & **Mounce Gore**. Decree ... it appeared ... that the allegations in the Bill were not sustained by the proof in the cause ... complainants bill be dismissed ... that Defendant Mounce Gore proceed to exc– [sic] the last will and testament of **James Cason** Decd (Page 319) so far as the same is not revoked by the deed executed by said testator to Edward M Cason ....

Page 319: **Amon Haile** vs **Sam E. Hare** et al. Came the complainant by his solicitor and dismissed his suit ....

Page 319: **Reece C. Stewart** & **Henry W. Sadler** vs **Matthew C. McKinly** ... came the complainants and dismiss their suit ....

Page 319: **William Mansell** vs **Wm H Barnes** & **Sam Mansell** ... continued till next term ... ordered that the cause be opened for proof ... until January rules 1849 ....

Page 320: **James T. Hughes** vs **Christopher Shaw** et al. And **David G Shepherd** & Co vs Christopher Shaw et al. And **James M. Shepherd** Admr vs Christopher Shaw et al. ... upon interlocutory decree and report of the Clerk and Master ... that on 19 February 1848 he sold the lands in the pleadings mentioned at public sale in **Granville** when **William C Hogin** became the purchaser ... at the price of $500 for which he executed his note with James M. Shepherd security and a lien was also retained upon the land for the purchase price ....

Page 320: **John H.ughes** Admr of **Letty Roberts** Decd. Exparte Decree ... (Page 321) upon report of the Master from which it appeared that on 19 February 1848 after giving notice as required by interlocutory decree he at **Granville** proceeded to sell the slaves in the pleadings mentioned at public sale on a credit of six months ... **John K Sadler** became the purchaser of negro girl **Jane** at the price of $126 which he executed his note with **James M. Shepherd** security and James M. Shepherd became the purchaser of the negro girl **Polly** at the price of $352 which he executed his note with **David G Shepherd** and **William B Holmes** security ....

Page 321: **Matilda Shaw, Jane Shaw, Burckey Shaw Rebecca C Shaw** & **Martha Shaw** ... upon the interlocutory decree and report of the Clerk & Master ... that on 19 February 1849 he sold the lands in the petition described at **Granville** at public sale ... on a credit of twelve months ... (Page 322) **James M. Shepherd** became the purchaser ... at the price of $50 the minimum value offered thereon for which he executed his note with **David G Shepherd** and **William B Holmes** his security and a lien was retained ... for the purchase money ....

Page 322: **Samuel E. Hare** et al vs **Wm Scanland** et al ... cause be continued ....

Page 322: **Lewis R. Vance** vs **Herald D Marchbanks** & **Thos C Marchbanks.** Decree. (Page 323) ... upon the report of the Clerk & Master ... defendants are entitled for consideration paid for said land and interest and valuable improvements $285.15 ... that there is due from defendants for rents and interest thereon $214.31 ... that complainant pay to defendants $70.84 & that a lien be retained upon the land in dispute ... the Defendants pray an appeal to the Supreme Court ... to be held at **Nashville** on the first Monday in December next which ... is granted ....

Page 323: **David Griffith** Admr &c vs **Hiram Crabtree** et al ... in the presence of Solicitors on both sides where by consent it is decreed ... (Page 324) that the Clerk & Master take and state an account of the indebtedness of the Estate of complainants intestate in doing which the Master will charge complainant with any waste of said estate that he may have committed also with all loss said estate may have sustained by the negligence of complainant ....

Page 324: **Mary W Ross** vs **Alfred W Ross** & others ... an attachment had issued to the Sheriff of Jackson County in this cause directing said Sheriff to attach such property of Defendant as might be found ... one gray horse, two cows & calves, one heifer, seven head of hogs, one burru [*sic*] & one feather bed ... that Sheriff proceed to sell all of said property on twelve months credit at public sale ... however if Defendant will enter into hands with good and sufficient security in double the value of said property ... Sheriff may release property to Defendant.

Page 325: **Mary H Brooks** vs **Richard P. Brooks.** Decree ... upon report of the Clerk and Master ... the following persons are indebted to Richard P. Brooks to wit. **Barret Kernal** $392–**Joseph Cowan** $1.37 1/2 **Prudence Thompson** $1.25–**Burton Thornton** $3.06–**Claiborne Jones** $3.00 **Stephen Vitatoe** $11.00 **Thomas Haile** & **Elias Jones** $11.77 **John Burke** $2.00 **Ann Chism** $1.25–**James Taylor** 20 cts **Richard Welch** $1.37 1/2 **James T. Quarles** $3.50 **Pleasant Cherry** $50.00 **Wm Elkins** & **Thos D Simpson** $16.00 **Jason Meddors** 40 bbls [*sic*] corn– **Wm Price** $1.00 **Calloway Sizemore** & **S. S. Gray** $28.83 **Josiah Price** $3.30 **Jas H Richmond** for rent ascertained–Do Do. $10.00 **James W. Burke** $5.77–(blank) **Dudney** $?0.?3 **Henry Taylor** $15.68 **John G Jones** $1.25–**Barret Kernal** $26.44 **R F Richmond** $3.12 1/2 **Dennis McCauley** $4.50 **H. McCarver** $2.78 **David M Rector** $15.37 1/2 **Josiah Price** $2.00 **Wm H Botts** $40 **David M Rector** $4.90 **John Jones** $75.00 Do. Do $100.00 **Abner** & **Wm Chaffin** $100.00 Do Do $50.00 Do Do $60.00 **Pinckney McCarver** $16.50 County claim $66.00 **Barret Lee** $30.00 Do Do 15 Bbls corn **A M**

Flynn $18.00 **Daniel Cummings** note $4.87 **Pinckney McCarver** 16 1/2 Bbls of corn **Peter Smith** 30 Do. **Josiah Price** 36 Do. **George Jenkins** $7.00 **N M Cox** $1.62 1/2 **W G Darwin** $50.00 **E L Burke** $3.99 **George W Burton** $1.00 **B. S. Patton** & **Merlin Young** $10.25 **Jas H Richmond** $575.00 **N M Cox** $2.00 **F Patterson** & **Jas W Burke** $2.56 **Wm Hawkins** $10.00 **Benj Chaffin** $11.70 **H D Osborne Peter Huffines** & **Solomon Price** $18.75–**Daniel Keith** $13.50 **Joseph Davenport** $5.50 **Wm Putty** $10.53 **Danl Osborne** $17.00 **Alex Cuppage** $8.83 **Merlin Young** $33.00 **James W. Burke** & **John G Burke** $60.00 **Solomon Price** amt. uncertain **Pleasant F. Cornwell** 60 barrels corn Do Do & $3.75 and $155.00 in Bank Bills on the Farmers & Merchants Bank (Page 326) at **Memphis** ... it is suggested there are other outstanding debts due and unpaid to said Richard P. Brooks ... Master to make report to the next term ... that Richard P. Brooks is seized of the following tracts of land in addition to those decreed upon at last term to-wit: 55 acres beginning at a stake on the Bank of **War Trace Creek** and running with the meanders of said Creek N 84º. E. 16 po. S. 53º E. 31 1/2 po. to a stone on the Bank thence N. 62º. E 20 poles to a large Spanish oak–thence with the meanders of an old road N. 23º E. 35 poles–N. 15 E 41 poles to a stake in the road with three beech & one sugar tree pointers–thence N. 45º W. 17 1/2 poles to a beech–thence N. 58 1/2 W 37 poles to the top of a ridge to a stake with two buckeyes, elm & hackberry pointers–thence with the meanders of the top of the ridge N. 1º. W. 16 poles–thence N. 23 W 26 1/2 poles to a white oak–thence N. 35 W. 20 pol. to a hickory thence N 37 W 38 poles to a honey locust, sugar tree & hackberry thence South to the beginning. And ... one twenty (illegible) acre tract that **Abraham Lee** purchased of **Wm Brooks** one hundred acre tract purchased by Abraham Lee of **William Ray**. Also one 27 acre tract purchased by Abraham Lee from **Wm Scanland** all of said lands lying on **Bullers** [*sic*] **Creek** and adjoining each other they being the same which Richard P. Brooks purchased of the Clerk & Master of this court on 11 June 1844 under a decree pronounced in the case of **Daniel Lee** Admr &c vs Abraham Lee Decd ... (Page 327) one other tract containing 50 acres more or less Beginning at a Black locust the South East corner of **Nelson Sadler's** 75 acre tract and running West to the extreme height of the first high hill to a stake. then southwardly with the extreme length of said ridge to said Richard P. Brooks corner on the river bluff thence up the river with it various meanders to the Beginning. It is decreed that all of said lands be divested out of Richard P. Brooks and vested in Mary H Brooks ....

Page 327: **William Mansell** vs **Samuel Mansell** and **William H. Barnes** ... upon appeal by complainant from the decission [*sic*] of the Clerk disallowing the exceptions to the depositions of **John B. Pointer** and **John West** ... complainant tenders his Bill of exceptions ... Court adjourned ... /S/ **Bromfield Ridley**

Page 328: **January Term 1849** ... Chancellor not being present the Clerk & Master ordered the sheriff to open court ... and kept open until 4 O'clock P.M. when the chancellor not having arrived court was ... adjourned. /S/ **G. M. McWhirter** C & M

Page 329: **25 July 1849**. Wednesday ... the Chancellor not having arrived ... the sheriff to open court which was kept open until 4 O'clock P.M after which Court was adjourned until tomorrow morning 9 o'clock.

Page 329: Thursday morning 9 O'clock. 1849. The Chancellor having arrived and taken his seat upon the bench court was opened ... that the office of the Clerk & Master of this Court is vacant. **William H. Botts** who was heretofore in vacation appointed Clerk & Master of the Chancery Court at Gainesboro ... William H. Botts then presented to the Chancellor the following three Bonds ... **Russell M Kinnaird**, **Thomas L Bransford**, **Samuel E. Stone Joel W. Settle James T. Quarles** and **Watson M. Cooke** all of Jackson County are held and firmly bound unto **Neill S. Brown** Governor of the State of Tennessee ... in the penal sum of ten thousand dollars ... (Page 330) this 26 July 1849 whereas said William H. Botts has this day been appointed by the Honorable **Bromfield L Ridley** Chancellor ... for the term of six years ... (Page 331) (Oath of office given.)

Page 332: **Hicklins Heirs** vs Hicklin's Admrs & others ... continued ....

Page 332: **David H. Draper** Admr. vs **Abraham Lee's** Creditors ... continued until next term ... and on motion it appearing to the court from the affidavit of **Cebert Pate** that he heretofore filed with the Clerk & Master of this court a certain note for $9.50 with a credit of $3. & that the same has been mislaid. Ordered that he be made a Defendant to said Bill ....

Page 332: **Samuel E. Hare** & **Watson M. Cooke** vs **Nathan Montgomery**, **Benjamin Monroe** & **George M McWhirter** ... it appeared to the Court that the Defendants Montgomery and Monroe were partners in the practice of medicine and that Monroe is indebted to complainants & to his co-Defendant Montgomery ... (Page 333) that the receiver and Defendant McWhirter pay to Montgomery the amounts by them reported to be collected out of the partnership effects ....

Page 333: **Perry Mahany** vs **Edwin F. McKinney** & others ... continued ....

Page 333: **Nelson Sadler** vs **Merlin Young** & others ... continued ....

Page 333: **William Mansell** vs **Samuel Mansell** & **William H. Barnes** ... (Page 334) on 9 February 1841 Samuel Mansell sold to complainant a title to the lands in the pleadings .... on 3 January 1843 but before said bond was registered defendant Barnes purchased the same land from Samuel who was then in possession ... ordered that said deed from Samuel to his co-defendant Barnes be cancelled and the title of Mansel and Barnes to said lands bounded as follows Lying in Jackson County 1st Tract Beginning at ... the south boundary line of a tract called **Alexander's** old tract running thence South 80 poles to a stake and black oak and post oak pointers Thence West 100 poles to a black thence North 80 poles to a hickory thence East 100 poles to the Beginning. 2nd Tract containing 100 acres by survey bearing date 13 December 1836 but in consequence of an interference of an old survey of **Micajah Moore's** it is supposed to contain 80 acres ... bounded as follows Beginning at ... the West boundary line of a 50 acre tract which is above described running thence North with said West boundary passing the North West corner at 80 poles in all 140 poles to ... the South boundary line of **John Barnes** 100 acre tract thence West 12 poles to the South West corner of said tract Thence North with the West boundary line of said survey 20 poles to ... said Barne's fence Thence West 90 poles to a black oak, Thence 160 poles to a stake in **Michael Moore's** field Thence East 102 poles to the beginning be divested as to Defendants Mansell & William H Barnes (Page 335) and vested in William Mansell ... Barnes prays an appeal to the Supreme Court of Tennessee to be held at Nashville on the first Monday in December next which ... is granted ... and **Elijah Car** his security ....

Page 335: **Thomas D. Simpson** vs **Milton Draper** & other ... continued ....

Page 335: **Edward B. Draper** Exr &c vs **Reuben R. Rogers** & others ... continued ....

Page 335: **Samuel Martin** vs **Thomas Henderson** & **William Henderson** ... (Page 336) it appears William Henderson is indebted to complainant in the sum of $53 and that defendant Thomas fraudulently and without consideration conveyed the lands in the pleadings to his son William Henderson and that one of the tracts has heretofore sold at Sheriff's sale and bought by complainant and that the other tract ought to be sold in satisfaction of complainants debt ... it is decreed by the court that the Clerk & Master ... sell said 50 acre tract ....

Page 336: **Mary H. Brooks** vs **Richard P. Brooks** ... continued ....

Page 336: **William Scanland** vs **Clayton Rogers** et al ... continued ....

Page 337: **Henry & Garrott Sadler** Trustees &c vs **Abisha Cannon** et al ... the Clerk & Master take and state an account of the services and expenses of said Henry & Garrott Sadler as trustees in the management of said Trust estate for the Defendants also the value thereof ....

Page 337: **David Griffith** vs **Campbell Price** et al ... continued ....

Page 337: **James A. Manear** vs **Richard Carter** & **Henry Carter** ... Defendants Henry Carter and Richard Carter are both non residents and that Richard Carter is indebted to complainant as stated in his bill and an attachment has issued against a certain tract or parcel of land described in said Bill the legal title of which is fraudulently and wrongfully in Henry Carter and that said land rightfully belongs to Richard Carter and should be put to the payment of his debts and the same has been properly attached ... (Page 338) that the title to the said land be divested out of Henry Carter and his heirs forever and the same be vested in Richard Carter and his heirs forever and that said land be condemned and sold ....

Page 338: **Absalom Johnson** vs **Henry Carter.** Came the parties by their solicitors and on motion & affidavit of **Benjamin B. Washburn** Defendants Solicitor this cause is continued ... leave is given defendant to retake the depositions of **Thomas L. Bransford**, **James A. Manear** and **John Clemmons** ....

Page 338: **Thomas W. Wooton** et [sic] **William Cullum** vs **Joseph Eaton** & al. Attachment. Came the complainants by their solicitors and dismiss their suit ....

Page 338: **John Sommers** & wife **Margaret** vs **Stephen Dill, Solomon Dill, Elijah Dill, Elizabeth Sutton, Polly Rutlege** [sic]**, Archibald Dill, Roland C. Dill, Stephen Dill Jr Solomon Dill Jr Dorcas Williams** the wife of **Emanuel Williams Anar Medlen** the wife of **Samuel Medlin** & **Milly Loftis** (Page 339) ... it appearing to the court that **Geo. M. McWhirter** former clerk of this court has collected the proceeds of the sales of the lands in the pleadings ... it also appearing ... Solomon Dill Stephen Dill, Elizabeth Sutton, Elijah Dill, Elizabeth Sutton & Polly Rutlege (both widows) and Margaret Sommers wife of complainant John Sommers are the only children living of **Archibald Dill Sr.** decd and his lawful heirs and are entitled each to one eighth of the proceeds of said land and that Archibald Dill Roland C. Dill, Stephen Dill jr Dorcas Williams wife of Emanuel Williams, **Ann Medlin**, wife of Samuel Medlin and Solomon Dill jr are children of **Arthur Dill** decd a son of said Archibald Dill decd and as such collectively entitled to one eighth of the proceeds of said land and that Milly Loftis a widow and daughter of Archibald Dill decd. a son of Archibald Dill Sr. decd and as such entitled to one eight of the proceeds ....

Page 339: **Mary W. Ross** vs **Alfred W. Ross** & others. Attachment Bill ... it appearing to the court that this cause has been irregularly set for hearing. It is ordered by the court that said cause be remanded to the rules for further steps to be taken therein. And that an alias copy and subpoenas be issued to Sheriff of Smith County as to all the Defendants who are not now before this court.

Page 339: **S. C. Cornwell** & Son vs **John Richardson** & **John Reeves** ... (Page 340) in presence of the parties & solicitors on both sides where it is agreed by the parties that Richardson pay to the complainants $61.67 and the cost of the cause ....

Page 340: **Ridley Roberts** vs **John K. Sadler** et al. O B. Came the parties by their solicitors and it appearing ... this cause is irregularly set for hearing it is ordered that the same be remanded to the rules for further steps to be taken therein.

Page 340: **Matthew C. McKinly** vs **Napoleon B. Pillow**. Injunction Bill. Came the complainant by solicitor and dismisses his suit ....

Page 340: **John H.** & **Allen Young** vs **John Rogers** et al. Injunction Bill. Came the parties by their solicitors and on motion and it appearing to the court that this cause is irregularly set for hearing it is ordered that the same be remanded to the rules for further steps to be taken ....

Page 341: **Edward M. Cason** vs **Nathaniel M. Cox** & wife ... in 1842 complainant was appointed Trustee for the Defendant **Eliza Cox** to take the control of a negro girl named **Mary** and to hold the same to the use of said Eliza ... complainant has been at some expense with said negro as trustee ... complainant is anxious to be relieved from further trouble & expense as said trustee to which defendants consent ... **William H. Botts** the Clerk & Master of this court be appointed Trustee in the stead of complainant ....

Page 341: **Polly Henry** vs **Samuel E. Hare** & **Watson M. Cooke.** Injunction Bill ... motion to dismiss the injunction granted in this cause (Page 342) ....

Page 342: **John W. Carr** Admr &c & the heirs of **W. H. Car** decd vs **Elijah Carr** & **Archibald M. Lindsey.** Decree ... it appeared to the court that **William H. Car** in his lifetime sold to Defendant Lindsey the land in the pleadings for $450 and said money has not been paid and the Defendant Lindsey is non resident it further appearing that Defendant Elijah Carr is the holder of the first of the notes for the purchase of said land ... the Clerk of this court proceed to sell the lands in the pleadings to the highest bidder at the court house door in Gainesboro ....

Page 342: **Nancy Nettles** vs **Zebulon Nettles** & **William Gore**. Inj. Bill. In this case **Samuel E. Hare** (Page 343) ... presented to the court his Bill & asked leave of the court to file the same as a cross bill ....

Page 343: **Garrett Sadler** vs **Merlin Young** & others ... it appeared to the court that Defendant Young had transferred two negroes together with other property to Defendant **Goodall** for the use and benefit of his co defendants who were his securities while clerk of the circuit Court of Jackson County ... It is therefore ordered by the court ... proceed to sell to the highest bidder on a credit till the 3rd Monday in January next the two negroes, to wit **Jordan** & **Simon** ....

Page 343: **Calaway Sizemore** & **William Gray Guardians** &c vs **Thomas H. Butler**, **Milton E. Burke**, **Angelina Burke**, **Elizabeth Burke**, **John M. Burke**. (Page 344) In this case complainants having exhibited their Bill in open court with a proper affidavit praying for relief in the premises and also for writs of Injunction ... ordered by the Court that **John G. Burke** a resident of Jackson County be appointed Guardian ad litem for the minor defendants Milton E. Burke, Angelina Burke, Elizabeth Burke, John M Burke and **(blank) Burke** (who are all) non residents of this state ... ordered ... that publication be made for three successive weeks in the Sparta Times a newspaper published in the town of **Sparta Tenn** commanding said nonresidents to appear at the next Chancery Court ... for (Jackson County) ....

Page 344: **Elizabeth Ridley** vs **Benjamin F. Ridley**. Decree ... it appeared to the court that Defendant and complainant had intermarried in Jackson County in the Spring of 1848 that complainant was of good character but that Defendant had been guilty of adultery and of personal abuse of complainant and it (Page 345) further appeared to the court that complainant had been a citizen of Jackson County more than one whole year next preceding this application. It is therefore ordered and decreed by the Court that complainant be divorced from the defendant ... that she be allowed to keep the charge of her infant daughter until it shall arrive at the age of three years and until which time the Defendant is enjoined and restrained from interfering or meddling ....

Page 345: **Nelson Sadler** vs **Thompson Cason**. Decree ... the attachment in this cause be discharged ....

Page 345: **John Hughs** Admr. of the estate of **Letty Roberts** decd vs The Creditors of Letty Roberts ... ordered that the Clerk & Master take the necessary steps to make the Creditors of said Letty Roberts decd defendant to this Bill.

Page 346: **Edward Anderson** vs **Lewis R. Vance** ... leave is given defendant till the September rules to file his answer ....

Page 346: **David Herbert** vs **John Lee** & others ... leave given to Defendants **Lee & McBroom** to take the Deposition of their codefendant **William Q. Hughs** ....

Page 346: **Nancy B. Ammonett**, **Virginia Amonett**, **Tennessee G. Amonett**, **Benjamin F. Amonett**, by their next friend & **Martha P. Amonett Luke T. Armstrong** & **Josiah H. Langford** vs **Thomas L. Bransford**. Decree ... it appeared to the Court that **William Amonett** departed this life intestate in Jackson County, his place of residence, about March 1849 That previous to his death he and defendant were merchants in copartnership and that one **David Biggerstaff** conveyed to them for the consideration of $5000.00 which was to be paid out of the partnership effects a tract of land in Jackson County on the North side of **Cumberland River** in District No 6 bounded as follows Beginning at ... (Page 347) the forks of **Proctors Creek** running up **Little Proctor** with its various meanders North 50º West twelve poles to an elm and hickory, thence North 14º West 36 poles to a sycamore and hickory, thence North 24º West 16 poles to a sycamore thence North 28º East 20 poles to a beech, thence North 24º West 24 poles to a beech thence north 70º West 15 poles to a beech, thence North 30º West to a beech thence North 20º W. 24 poles to a stake thence North 12º East 6 poles to a stake, thence North 30º West 44 poles to a stake thence North 7º West 8 poles to ... the bank of the creek in **Savage's** line thence West 142 poles to three beeches, thence north 146 poles to a beech stump at the mouth of the first hollow above **Martins Spring** branch on the north fork of Proctors Creek, thence North 55º west 14 poles to ... near the brink of a bluff thence north 50º West 63 poles to three young poplars, thence North 51º East four poles to a white walnut thence North 39º West 40 poles to a poplar near **Carter's** fence, thence North 82º West 84 poles to two beeches, thence south 30 poles to a poplar & ash thence West 12 poles to a beech, thence south 12º West 32 poles to a beech and poplar thence south 75º West 34 poles to ... Savage's line of a 25 acre survey, then south 47 poles to a stake in Savage's field, thence West 18 poles to a stake in the same the corner of Savage's 65 acre survey thence South 152 poles to a forked black walnut near Savage's fence, thence South 74º East 77 poles to a sugar tree, thence South 75º East 12 poles to the corner of **Browns** 100 acre survey thence East with the north boundary line of said 100 acre survey 80 poles to a stake, thence South 20º West 80 poles to ... the south bank of Proctor's Creek, thence down said creek immediately at the brink of the bluff South 72º East 15 poles to a stake thence East 19 poles, thence South 50º East 24 poles, thence South 80º East 32 poles, thence East 20 poles, thence South 80º East (Page 348) 32 poles, then east 20 poles, then South 80º East 28 poles then South 28º East 28 poles then South 43º East 28 poles, then East 28 poles [*sic*] then South 83º East 36 poles then south 70º East 40 poles then North 24º East 20 poles then South 85º East 31 poles to the beginning containing by estimation 600 acres ... it was agreed upon by and between said **Amonett & Bransford** that at the termination of their partnership Amonett was to take the land for the consideration of $4500.00 but before Bransford executed a deed of conveyance for the same which he contracted to do Amonett departed this life. It also appeared that Amonett & Bransford at the time of the death of Amonett were the joint owners of the following negro slaves to wit, **Susan** age 17 years, **Polly** aged about 15 years, Polly's child a boy aged about 6 months, **Elizabeth** aged about 14 years, **Martha** aged about 18 months **Sandy** aged about 16 years **Jenkins** aged about 16 years, **John** aged about 15 years, **James** aged about 15 years, **David** aged about 14 years, **Charles** aged about 14 years, **Jack** aged about 14 years, **Spencer** aged about 13 years Charles aged about 12 years, **Jim** aged about 10 years, **Craton** aged about 13 years & **Jasper** aged about 13 years. And the complainant Nancy B. Amonett, Virginia Amonett, Tennessee G. Amonett, Benjamin F. Amonett are the heirs and distributees and that Martha P. Amonett is the widow of said William Amonett ... decreed ... that the title of Thomas L. Bransford to the above described land be divested and vested in the Nancy Amonett, Virginia Amonett, Tennessee G. Amonett & Benjamin F. Amonett ... Martha P. Amonett is entitled to her dower in the same. It is therefore decreed that one third part of said land be allotted to her for her dower ... (Page 349) It is further decreed that **Nancy Andrews**, **Samuel B. M. Fowler** and **William C. Walker** be appointed to divide said negroes equally according to their value between Thomas L. Bransford and the widow and distributees of said William Amonett decd ....

Page 349: Court adjourned until the regular term. /S/ **Bromfield Ridley**.

Page 350: **January Term 1850**. 30 January 1850. Chancery district composed of Jackson County in the 4th Chancery division at 10 A.M. the chancellor not having arrived ... adjourned until court in course. /S/ **William H Botts**

Page 351: **10 July 1850** ... The Chancellor not having arrived said court was by the Clerk &

Master adjourned until 10 A M tomorrow morning. /S/ **William H Botts**.

Page 351: **11 July 1850**, Thursday. The Chancellor having arrived ... proceeded to the dispatch of business.

Page 351: **David H. Draper** Admr &c vs **Abraham Lee's** Creditors. Bill for Settlement of Insol^t Estate ... cause continued ....

Page 351: **Samuel E. Hare** vs **John Scanland** & others. Att. Bill ... considered by the court that defendants ... recover of the complainants the costs not heretofore adjudged in this cause and that execution issue.

Page 352: **Nelson Sadler** vs **Merlin Young** & **John Scanland**. Attachment Bill. Came the complainant by his solicitor and dismisses his suit ....

Page 352: **Mary White** vs **Raulston Ray** & **William Draper**. O. B. ... agreed that Defendants have till the first rule day to file their answer in this cause ....

Page 352: **Edward Anderson** vs **Lewis R. Vance**. O. B. ... continued ... and leave is given defendant to take the deposition of **J. Pucket** of **DeKalb County Tenn** ....

Page 352: **Merlin Young** vs **Samuel E. Hare**. O. B. ... leave given defendant (Page 353) until November Term of (Jackson County) Circuit Court to file his answer ....

Page 353: **Samuel Cox** & wife **Sally** vs **Charles W. Anderson** & **Nancy Anderson**. I & A Bill ... on motion of Defendants leave granted them to amend their answers ....

Page 353: **Winburn W. Goodpasture, Andrew McClain** & **Holland Denton Esqrs** ... placed upon the roll & that they be admitted as practicing attorneys at this bar.

Page 353: **John Hughs** & others vs **Dixon Brown** et al ... ordered ... that the negro and all other personal property conveyed by defendant Dixon Brown to his co-defendant in trust for the use of complainant ... that **William H Botts** be appointed receiver upon the Complainant entering into bond ... (Page 354) ....

Page 354: **Perry Mahany** vs **Edwin F. McKinney** & others. I.B. It appearing to the court that the complainant in this suit has departed this life and has no personal representative. It is ordered that this suit be abated.

Page 354: **William Scanland** vs **Clayton Rogers** et al. I. Bill ... this day suggested and proven in open court that the Complainant in this suit has departed this life and that **Benjamin Scanland** is his executor ... filed here in court his letters testatomentary [*sic*] ... cause revived in the name of said Benjamin Scanland Exr &c.

Page 354: **Bank of Tennessee** vs **Montraville Masters**. Final Decree ... upon agreement of the parties upon both sides ... matters in said Bill has been settled and adjusted by the parties and that the Bill is to be dismissed ....

Page 355. Thursday **July 11th 1850**. **Samuel Martin** vs **Thomas and William Henderson** ... This cause ... made herein at the July Term of this Court 1849 from which it appeared that said clerk pursuant to sd. decree had sold the land in the bill mentioned when complainant became the purchaser at the price of $25.00 ....

Page 355: **Nancy Nettles** by her next friend **W R Kenner** vs **Zebulon Nettles** & others. Bill & Decree. **Samuel E. Hare** vs Nancy Nettles & others. Cross Bill ... it appears that the said Nancy is entitled as one of the distributees of **John and Anna Stafford** decd. to a fund now in the hands of **William Gore** as administrator of John & Anna Stafford & that defendants Nancy & Zebulon are indebted to the Complainant Hare in the sum of $162.00 and no more ... (Page 356).

Page 356: **William W. Ray** vs **William Cray William Draper**, **Raulston Ray**, **Cornelius Carver** & others. Inj Bill ... the parties by their Solicitors and the complainant dismisses his suit ....

Page 356: **James Daws** vs **James Draper.** Inj Bill ... the complainant by his solicitor ... dismisses his suit ... (Page 357).

Page 357: **William Lambert** vs **James Pharis** and **James Vinson** ... the parties by their solicitors ... agreed that Defendants have till the first rule day to file their answers ... Court adjourned till tomorrow morning 7 o'clock.

Page 357: Friday morning **July 12, 1850**. Court met pursuant to adjournment. **B. L. Ridley** presiding.

Page 357: **Samuel S. Butler** and others. Exparte Decree ... the matters in the petition be referred to the Clerk & Master to report to the present term 1st Whether it would be obviously to the interest of the minors mentioned in the petition that their guardian should purchase the land in the petition mentioned for them and if so the value of said land.

Page 358: **Samuel S. Butler** & others. Exparte Decree ... this cause came on again to be heard ... upon the report of the Clerk & Master ... it would be manifestly to the advantage of the minors mentioned ... that their Guardian **George M. McWhirter** should purchase for them the land mentioned ... said land is worth at least $800 ....

Page 358: **Mary H. Brooks** vs **Samuel E. Hare.** O. Bill ... cause is remanded to the rules for further steps to be taken ... leave given Defendant to file his cross bill ....

Page 358: **David Griffith** Administrator vs **Campbell Price** & others ... upon the application of complainant to renew the decree heretofore rendered in this cause for an account ... extended to October rules (Page 359) 1850 ...

Page 359: **Thomas D. Simpson** vs **Milton Draper** et al. Original & Amended Bill. And Milton Draper vs Thomas D. Simpson et al. Cross Bill ... upon the original & amended Bill of complt Simpson and the answers of Defts and the cross Bill of complt Draper and the answer of Simpson and pro confesso as to **Young & Johnson** & Replication and proof in the causes ... it appears that Thomas D. Simpson purchased from the defendant **David Johnson** on 8 January 1846 the land in the pleadings ... took a deed from said Johnson with full covenants that said Simpson gave one hundred and fifty dollars $75 of which was paid by Simpson and a note give to Johnson for $75 ... Simpson took possession of the land and made improvements upon the same ... the note for $75 was transferred by Johnson to Draper after the same was due ... Draper sued Simpson upon the note and recovered a judgement for the amount . . .that at the time Johnson sold the land to Simpson that the President & directors of the Bank of Tennessee had at the time of the sale ... by Johnson to Simpson a judgement in the Circuit Court (Page 360) of Jackson County against Johnson for $181.19 1/2 which was their lien upon the land and said

Bank of Tennessee afterwards had said land sold in satisfaction of judgement at which sale **Merlin Young** became the purchaser ... at the sum of one dollar ... Simpson had actual knowledge of the lien upon the land at the time he purchased the same from Johnson ... after the said sale ... by the Sheriff and the purchase of the same by Young to wit on 30 March 1847 Draper paid the bid of the Young so made for said land to him, and paid Young the further sum of $9 for his interest so acquired in said land, and took from Young his transfer in writing of his interest in said land and also an order to the Sheriff of Jackson County to make to deft Draper a deed for said land ... Draper after the sale of the land by the Bank purchased from the Bank the balance of their judgement against deft Johnson and after his purchase of the interest of Young in the land ... he bid the balance of the judgement upon the land and thereupon ... on 5 April 1847 he took from **Holland Denton** Sheriff of Jackson County a deed ... (it is) decreed that the sale of the land by David Johnson to Thomas D. Simpson and the deed for the same is fraudulent & void as against defendant Milton Draper and the deed from Johnson to Simpson be delivered up & cancelled ... that ... (Page 361) Milton Draper ... in virtue of his purchase of the interest of Merlin Young in the land and his purchase of the Bank judgement and the bidding of the same upon the land and the taking of the Sheriff's deed for the same vested in Milton Draper a good & valid title to the land ... (Page 362) Clerk & Master to report to the next term of court.

Page 362: **Stephen Price** vs **Edward Price**. Int. Order. This cause is continued by consent and remanded to the rules with leave to take proof on both sides ....

Page 362: **Garrott Sadler** vs **Merlin Young** & others ... Clerk and Master ordered to take ... an account of the amount which has been paid by the securities of Merlin Young as Clerk of the (Jackson County) Circuit Court and report to the next term ....

Page 362: **Edward M Cason** vs **Nathaniel M. Cox** and **Eliza Cox**. Decree ... upon report of the Clerk & Master (Page 363) ... Edward M Cason vs Nathaniel M Cox & wife ... the complainant agreed to charge defendants nothing for his services as Trustee of the defendants would charge him nothing for the time he had the negro woman in his possession which is agreed to by defts. The master also reports that from the evidence of **John L. Goodall Esq. G. M. McWhirter** complts Solicitor is entitled to $20 for his services in this cause ....

Page 363: **Nancy Jennings** vs **James Postons**. Decree ... it appears ... that all the equity set up in the bill is fully met and denied by the answer ... bill dismissed ....

Page 364: **Edward B. Draper** Exr &c of **B. M. Draper** vs **Reuben Rogers** et al ... upon an appeal from the decision of the Clerk & Master upon the complainants exceptions to the deposition of **Mary S Taylor** and **Silas C. Cornwell** ... exception to Taylor's deposition is ... allowed & exception to Cornwell's deposition is ... disallowed ... cause continued ... and ... an injunction granted enjoining the collection & payment of the note of $300 due 19 October 1848 on **Fletcher** and **Dillard** & **Youngs** ... that said injunction be so far dissolved as to allow the Clerk & Master to collect said note and hold the sum subject to further order ... (Page 365) ....

Page 365: **John W. Car** Admr of **Wm H. Car** &c vs **Elijah Car** & **Archibald Lindsey** ... Clerk and Master according to the directions of the interlocutory decree on 1 October 1849...sold the land in the pleadings...for cash...Elijah Car became the purchaser at...$120.00...that **Samuel Turney** the solicitor be paid $2 for services....

Page 365: **James Boyd** vs **William R. Vance** et al. Decree ... James B.oyd is one of the lawful (Page 366) heirs of **John Boyd** deceased and as such has $48.31 due him from the sale of personal property of said deceased and the sum of $12 was due him for rent of lands received by the administrator ... sum was due 1 October 1838 and payment then demanded by said Boyd of the Administrator. And it further appertaining [sic] that **William R. Vance** was the lawful administrator of said Boyd decd and **John Hughs** & **William Q Hughs** defts to this bill were his securities ... Vance refused payment of said distribution share until this time ....

Page 366: **Stephen Price** vs **Edwin Price** ... complainant have leave for the commissioners **William Plumlee** and **Thomas D. Cassetty** to amend their certificates to the depositions ....

Page 366: **James A. Manear** vs **Henry Carter** & **Richard Carter** ... (Page 367) on 1 October 1849 after advertising as required by decree ... land ordered to be sold at the Court House door in Gainesboro for cash in hand when **James A. Spurlock** became the purchaser of the same ... at the price of $120.00 ....

Page 367: **Thomas L. Draper** vs **Young & Hare** in presence of Solicitors on both sides it appeared to the Court that **Merlin Young** was Clerk of the Circuit Court of Jackson County ad as such was entitled to costs against Complainant ... The clerk (of Chancery Court) may make his report from the testimony on file ....

Page 368: **Absalom Johnson** vs **Henry Carter.** Decree ... to the satisfaction of the court ... Henry Carter is indebted to Absalom Johnson in the sum of $100.00 by note executed by his agent **Dale Carter** for medical service rendered said Henry Carter due and payable on 1 Feb 1847 and that a certain negro boy named **Bill** has been attached to satisfy said debt and that said boy has been replevied [sic] and that **John Lee** & **William Q. Hughs** are the securities of said Henry Carter ... ordered that Absalom Johnson recover of Henry Carter $100 with interest from 1 February 1847 ... that said boy Bill (Page 369) be given up and sold ... (Bond given and signed by Absom [sic] Johnson and **James A. Spurlock**.)

Page 369: **James B. Buchanan** vs **Ridley Roberts Thomas J. Roberts James M. Shepherd** Admr of **Letty Roberts** decd **Saml Turney William Cullom** & **William W. Goodall Sheriff** of Jackson County Tenn. ... at the March Term of the Circuit Court of Jackson County 1842 complainant recovered a judgement against the said Ridley Roberts for $500 & costs of suit which with interest is still due ... at the March Term of the said (Page 370) Circuit Court 1849 ... Ridley Roberts recovered a judgement against ... James M. Shepherd Administrator for $1,070.10 ... on the same day Ridley Roberts made a transfer of said judgement in the words and figures following to wit: I hereby transfer to Samuel Turney and William Cullom my attorneys the amount of the judgement the amount of judgement of $900.00 besides interest that I recovered against James M. Shepherd Administrator of Letty Roberts decd at March Term in the Jackson Circuit Court 1849 ... they are to transfer the balance to Thomas J. Roberts to whom it belongs this 7 March 1849 ... said transfer was made without any consideration as to Thomas J. Roberts and there appearing to be no fraud in said transfer as to the said Cullom & Turney ... (Page 371) ....

Page 371: **Hicklins Heirs** vs Hicklins Admr. ... it appeared to the court that **Samuel Olive** the Brother of the half blood of **Perry R. Hickland** deceased departed this life in the state of Alabama in 1836 leaving a son and daughter his distributees ... that his said son had also departed this life and that **Elizabeth Fitz** formerly **Elizabeth Olive** is his only heir and distributee. It is therefore ordered and decree that **G. M. McWhirter** former clerk & master ... pay to said **Henry B. Fitz** & wife the distributive share of said Samuel Olive in the estate of **Perry Hicklin** decd ....

Page 372: **Catron C. Hogin** vs **William C. Hogin.** Decree ... complainant and defendant intermarried in Jackson County in January 1847–that they have been residents of this state more than two years previous to the exhibiting the bill in this cause ... that before and after his marriage with complainant defendant was afflicted with luise veneri[11] in such manner as rendered it highly improper for complainant to live and cohabit with him as his wife ... that Complainant has in her possession in property and money the sum of $400 and that defendant has some of the property and money but it not appearing to the court that defendant had defrauded complainant in the premises ... it is ordered that the bonds of matrimony ... be dissolved ... And it appearing that Complainant and defendant have a son aged between two and three years ... that complainant be allowed to keep said child **Anthony Wayne Hogin** until he shall arrive at the age of ten years ... (Page 373) but nothing herein shall prevent defendant from visiting and seeing such child ... It is further decreed ... that the name of complainant be changed from Catron C. Hogin to that of **Catron C. Sadler**.

Page 373: **James T. Hughs** vs **Pinckney McCarver** et al ... remanded to the rules for further steps to be taken ... leave is given defendants **Kinnaird & Bransford** to file their Cross Bill ...

Page 373: **John D. Lusk** vs **James A. Spurlock** & **Josiah Spurlock**. Came the parties by their solicitors and on motion of defendant James A. Spurlock and for sufficient reasons ... ordered that the judgement to pro confesso & taken against them be set aside ... leave given to file his answer which is here tendered ....

Page 374: **David Herbert** vs **John Lee** & others ... dismissed ....

Page 374: **Kinnaird & Bransford** vs **Benjamin B. Washburn John Price** Admrs of **Charley N & James Price** decd & **Solomon Price** ... Charles N Price & **James W. Price** departed this life intestate and Benjamin B. Washburn and John Price are their administrators. It further appearing Solomon Price is the father of Charles N & James Price decd and is their legal distributee ... Solomon Price is indebted to complainants and he is insolvent ... Clerk & Master ordered to take & state an account of the indebtedness ....

Page 375: **Polly Henry** vs **Samuel E. Hare** & others. Decree ... bill dismissed. Court adjourned until tomorrow morning 7 o'clock. /S/ **Bromfield Ridley**
Page 375: Saturday morning **July 13, 1850. Bromfield Ridley** presiding.

Page 375: **Nancy Jennings** vs **James Poston**. Decree ... upon agreement and compromised of the parties, which is as follows The contract of 9 March 1846 so far as it obliges defendant and to keep and maintain complainant is rescinded and instead defendant is to pay to complainant $400 and complainant and his security **Toliver** (Page 376) **Kirkpatrick** are to pay all the costs of this suit and the defendant is released from any and all obligation to complaint except the said $400 ... the bond of defendant **Merlin Young** & **S.W. Cassetty** for the support and maintenance of complainant be given up ....

Page 376: **Edward Vaughn** vs **Lawson Draper**. Ordered ... **Sarah Richardson** be appointed guardian ad litem for all the minor heirs of **William Richardson** decd and that she answer said [sic] bill in behalf of said minor heirs on or before the next term of this court ....

Page 376: **Matthew C. McKindly** vs **William Woodrum** & **James Drennum** Exrs &c ... (Page 377) it appearing to the satisfaction of the court that **Matthew C. McKinly** [sic] filed his bill to enjoin the collection of a note for $100.31 1/4 by **James Drennan** and W<u>m</u> Woodrum as

---

[11] This term, although hard to decipher, means the person was diagnosed as having pubic lice.

executors of **Jacob Woodrum** decd ... that the injunction heretofore granted be dissolved ....

Page 377: **Joseph C. Fletcher** vs **Alexander Dillard, Allen Young, John H. Young** & **Archibald Scruggs**. In this case the death of **A Scruggs** one of the defendants is suggested & admitted and the cause continued until next term at the rules.

Page 377: **Volney S. Stephenson** vs **Alexander Dillard, John H. Young, Allen Young** & **Archibald Scruggs**. In this case the death of **A Scruggs** one of the defendants is suggested & admitted and the cause continued ... to the next term.

Page 377: **Nancy Nettles** by next friend vs **Zebulon N. Nettles** & **William Gore** ... (Page 378) that complainant is a legatee of **John Stafford** deceased and a distri-butee of the estate of **Anna Stafford** decd and that defendant William Gore is administrator with the will annexed of said John Stafford decd and administrator of the estate of Anna Stafford decd but ... has not yet made settlements with the county court it is not ascertained to what amount ... that Zebulon N. Nettles is the husband of complainant and an improvident man and very much addicted to intoxication and that it would be unsafe to entreat him with the legacy and distri-butive share of complainant ... that said administrator pay the cost of the original bill in this case out of the legacy & distributee of complainant and $25 to complain-ant's solicitor **James T. Quarles** and that he retain in his hands an amount sufficient to pay off a note executed to said administrator with **Harriett Nettles** his security for property purchased at the administration sale ... and he pay the residue to which complainant is entitled as legatee and distributee ... to **William R. Kenner** who is appointed trustee at her request for her separate use ....

Page 378: **Calaway Sizemore** & **William Gray** Guardian &c vs **Thomas Butler, Milton E. Burke, Angelina Burke Elizabeth Burke John M Burke Sarah Burke** & **John G Burke** ... (Page 379) complainant Sizemore is guardian of **Rufus Gaines** & **Margery Gaines** and Complt Gray is Guardian of **William C. Gaines** ... said minors are the only heirs and distributees of **James H Gaines** decd–that James H. Gaines on 18 July 1842 recovered in the Circuit Court of Jackson County against **Henry F Burke** amounting to $125.92 1/2 besides cost of suit and by said judgement the undivided interest of Henry F. Burke in the lands of his father **John Burke** decd was ordered to be sold for their satisfaction which was not done ... and yet unpaid ... that on 4 January 1845 the lands of John Burke decd were sold under decree of the Circuit Court of Jackson County for distribution Henry F Burke being a party to that decree & a distributee ... it further appeared Henry F Burke departed this life in **Missouri** insolvent and Milton E. Burke Angelina Burke Elizabeth Burke, John M Burke and Sarah Burke are his only heirs at law are minors, non residents that publication and judgement has bee made & taken against them and defendant John G. Burke is their Guardian ad litem and has answered for them ... that deft **Thos H Butler** is now Clerk of the Circuit Court of Jackson County and has in his hands the distributive share of said Henry F Burke ... (Page 380) and pay over to complainants the share ... that a fee of $20 be allowed **Hall & Washburn** Complain-ant's solicitor for their services in this case.

Page 380: **John D. Lusk** vs **James A. Spurlock** & **Josiah Spurlock**...complainant given leave to amend his Bill...if the same is done before the first rule day at his own cost.

Page 380: **James B. Buchanan** vs **Ridley Roberts** & others ... complainant prays for an appeal to the next term of the Supreme Court of the State of Tennessee to be held at **Nashville** on the first Monday in December next which is granted ....

Page 380: **Hare & Cooke** vs **Monroe Montgomery** & others. Bill. And **Nathan Montgomery** vs

Ben Monroe & others. Cross Bill ... (Page 381) that **William Davidson** the receiver report the amount of the partnership debts of Montgomery & Monroe ....

Page 381: **Mary H Brooks** vs **Richard P. Brooks**. On motion it is ordered that the order heretofore pronounced in this cause directing the Clerk & Master to report herein be revived ... to next term.

Page 381: **John Hughs** Admr &c vs **Letty Roberts** Creditors ... continued until next term. That the creditors of said estate have three months to make themselves defendants to this Bill ....

Page 381: **Tandy K. Witcher** vs **Joseph Moss**. Attachment & A. Bill. The complainant by leave of the court filed and amended bills in this case. This entry should have appeared on the minutes of Thursday last but is made now for them.

Page 382: **Nancy B Ammonett** et al vs **Tho L Bransford**. In this case it appearing to the Court that Nancy B **Martha P** [sic] **Ammonett** has intermarried with one **James Ammonett** since the division of the slaves by the commissioners ... ordered that this cause be revived in the name of James Ammonett & others vs Tho L Bransford and ... cause be continued until next term ....

Page 382: **John Lee** Admr &c vs **Thomas Huddleston.** This cause being prematurely set for hearing. It is ordered that it be remanded to the rules for further steps to be taken therein.

Page 382: **Jefferson & Thomas Johnson** vs **George M. McWhirter** et al. O Bill ... upon demurrer to complainants bill ... decreed that the demurrer be allowed and defendants have leave to file their answers on or before the next rule day.

Page 382: **Henry W. Kirby** vs **Absalom Johnson** ... upon the demurrer to complainants bill ... said demurrer be disallowed and defendant have leave to file his answer on or before the second rule day and complt have leave to file his (Page 383) bill or cross Bill in the suit of Absalom Johnson vs **David Johnson** et al.

Page 383: **William P. Witcher** vs The President & Directors of the Bank of Tennessee . . . demurrer be disallowed and defendants have leave till second rule day to file their answer ....

Page 383: **Edward P. Pate** & others vs **Cebert Pate** & others ... in the presence of Solicitors on both sides it appeared ... **Willeroy Pate** decd was possessed of the lands in the pleadings mentioned at the time of his death that **Sabe Pate** a son of Willeroy has also departed this life that both of said estates are settled up and closed ... complainants and defendants are the heirs at law of said deceased person excepted complainant **Oliver Young** who purchased the interest of Defendant Cebert in said land ... that said Sebert Pate had purchased the interest of **Sampson W. Pate** and has a title bond for same. It is ordered ... that the matters in complainants bill be referred to the Clerk & Master to take proof and report to the next term whither [sic] said land is susceptible of partition amongst complainants and defendants having regard in said report to the legally acquired interest of Defendant Cebert ... (Page 384) ... that some of the complainants had before the filing of this bill empowered **William W. Goodall** and **Andrew McClellan** to sell said land ... that said power of attorneys not being acted on before the filing of the bill in this cause are revoked ... that complainant **Cyrela Pate** had subscribed her name to a deed purporting to convey her interest in said lands to defendant Cebert said deed not being witnessed ... said complainant Cyrela and defendant both have leave to take proof touching the manner said signature was procured whether fraudulently by deceit or otherwise ....

Page 384: **Garrott Sadler** vs **Merlin Young** & others ... upon report of the Clerk & Master of the sale of part of the property in the pleadings ... the following property which is embraced in the trust deed to deft **Goodall** from deft Young has come to his hands, to wit, a negro man named **Jordan** a negro boy named **Simon**, 1 China press, 1 Secretary, 1 Likeness, 2 bed quilts 3 small tables, 2 clocks, 1 bureau, 1 Jackson press (Page 385) 2 feather beds and 2 pillows 1 rocking chair, 1 trunnel [sic] bed stead, 2 large bedsteads, 1 sugar chest, 6 Windsor chairs, 2 split bottomed chairs, 1 dining table, 1 crib ... exposed the same to public sale ... at the court house door in Gainesboro on a credit until the 3rd Monday in January 1850 when the same was bid off and purchased as follows, The negro man Jordan by Garrott Sadler $485.00 the negro boy Simon by **John M. Gipson** $169.25 The China press by **R. C. Kirkpatrick** $26 The Secretary by **William Davidson** $13. The likeness by **G. M. McWhirter** $1.05. Two bed quilts by R. C. Kirkpatrick $1.10 One small table by **L. C. Hall** $4.10 one clock by **James A. Spurlock** $5.10 one clock & dining table by **Stephen McCormic** [sic] $1.60 one bureau by **B B Washburn** $15.25. The Jackson press by L C Hall $7.40 one feather bed by **Joel W. Settle** $9.25 one feather bed 2 pillows and one trunnel bed stead by **Colunor(?) White** $9.50 two large bed steads by **Tho H Butler** $5.10 one sugar chest and one crib by **Joseph E Baldwin** $2.05 6 Windsor chairs by **John Williams** $3.10 2 split bottomed chairs by **Richard Price** $.20 cts 1 small table by **Sampson W. Cassetty** $1.85 amounting in the whole to $762.85 ... (Page 386) ....

Page 386: **Henry Sadler** and **Garrett Sadler** vs **Abisha Cannon Sally Cannon James M. Shepherd** Guardian ad litem of **Jane Cannon, Martin V. Cannon.** Henry H. Cannon Lewis F. Cannon & Abisha Cannon Minors and children of said Abisha Cannon ... upon report of the clerk & master and defendants exceptions ... taken together the sum of $85.12 it being the amount paid by Complt Garrott to **James Wlliamson** for accompanying him to **Georgia** on business of his trust is well taken ... And ... from said report that there has come to the hands of Complainants as Trustees a fund of $4262.56 and complainant Garrott has disbursed as per vouchers filed the sum of $4234.47 and he is entitled to $278.79 1/2 it being the amount expended by him in travelling expense ... (Page 387) he has bestowed ... when taken together the sum of $5647.52 1/2 which shows an excess over and above the trust ... Complt. Henry is entitled to the sum of $8.06 travelling expense incurred by him and $45.67 for time & attention bestowed by him in and about said trust–and the further sum of $29.40 for articles furnished Abisha & wife ... it would be a reasonable fee to be paid **James T. Quarles** Esq defts Solicitor in this cause and ... that James M. Shepherd Guardian ad litem for said minors ought to be allowed the sum of $14.50 for his time & expenses incurred by him in attending to this suit ... Complainant Garrott Sadler recover of the defendants except the defendant Shepherd the sum of $1384.76 1/2 it being the amount showed in his favor from the master's report the same being corrected as before stated ... that Henry Sadler recover of said defendants with the exception of defendant Shepherd $83.13 ... (Page 388) decreed that Complainants as Trustees ... proceed to sell the negro boy **Calvin** and the negro girl **Amanda** and her child they being part of the trust property in their hands at public sale ... report to next term ....

Page 388: **Matilda Shaw, Jane Shaw Burcky Shaw Rebecca C. Shaw** & **Martha Taylor** formerly **Martha Shaw**. Exparte. It appearing ... that $20 is a reasonable fee to **James T. Quarles** Solicitor of petitioners who are minors except Petitioner Martha. ... that the clerk pay him said sum out of the funds in his hands arising from the sale of the lands of said petitioners for the purpose of division among them, the report of which sale was confirmed at July Term 1848 and on motion of Martha Shaw widow of **George W. C. Shaw** from whom the land descended to the other petitioners. It is ordered the Clerk & Master pay to her 1/3 part of ... (Page 389) the proceeds of said sale after paying all costs and expenses ....

Page 389: **Ridley Roberts** vs **John K. Sadler** et al. Final Decree ... the equity in complainants

Bill has been fully met and devised ... the complainant prays an appeal to the next term of the Supreme Court to be held at **Nashville** on the first Monday in december next which to him is granted ....

Page 389: **James Newby** vs **Temperance Stone** et al. Int. Decree ... (Page 390) the perishable property named in the Complainants bill levied upon by the Sheriff under the attachment in this cause is now in the custody of said Sheriff ... the Sheriff of Jackson County proceed to sell said property ....

Page 390: **John Butler** vs **Susan Butler, William Butler, Bailey Butler, William Sargeant** & **Mary** his wife **William Kendall** & **Sarah** his wife **Doctor Head** & **Siothy** his wife **Thomas Butler** & **Erwin F. Langford.** ... it appeared to the Court that **Welcome Butler** departed this life in May 1849 that the parties to this suit are his widow & heirs at law–& E. F. Langford that on 22 January 1838 he made and published his last will and testament thereby bequeathing all his property real and personal to (Page 391) Defendant Susan - that on 23 January 1841 he purchased the tract of land mentioned in the pleadings ... that Defendant Susan sold the land mentioned to defendant Langford without title thereto and ... that the land is not susceptible of division and that it is manifestly for the interest of the parties to this suit that the same be sold for distribution Whereupon the Court was pleased to order adjudge and decree the sale of the land mentioned in the pleadings by defendant Susan Butler to deft. Ervin F. Langford ... and because it does not appear what amount of assets of the estate of said Welcome Butler came to the hands of deft Susan as the executrix of his estate and what amount of the debts ... have been paid ... It is ordered that the Clerk & Master of this Court take and state an account ... (Page 392) It is also decreed that the children of **Peggy Head** mentioned in the answer be made parties to this suit and the Clerk of this court be appointed guardian ad litem for them that he file his answer at next term.

Page 392: **John H. Young** & **Allen Young** vs **Shelby Pharris** & others ... it appears the complainants have had a trial of the same matters in Jackson Circuit Court where they might have made the proper defence and it not appearing that they were prevented by accident fraud or the conduct of the defendants and all the equity in complainants bill being met ... and the allegation not being sustained by the proof ... bill be dismissed with cost and that the deft Shelby Parris recover of the Complainant John H. Young Allen Young & **William Q. Hughs** the security in the prosecution bond the costs of this suit ....

Page 393: **Mary W. Ross** by her next friend **David R. Halliburton** vs **Alfred W. Ross** & others ... the complainant by her solicitor says she desires to prosecute this suit no further ... that said Mary W. Ross is a married woman and she sued by her next friend **David R Halliburton** Whereupon the Court doth aver adjudge and decree that Defendant Alfred W Ross recover the costs of this suit ....

Page 393: **Martha Taylor** formerly **Martha Shaw** & others. Exparte. **John Hughes** attorney in fact for **George W. Taylor** and wife Martha Taylor, and **Daniel Hogin** guardian of **Mary Jane Shaw, Burckey Shaw** and **Rebecca Shaw** which upon examination appears ... to be in accordance with the statutes of this State ... that **George W. McWhirter** former Clerk and Master of this court pay out to said attorney the shares of said persons ... Court adjourned ... /S/ **Bromfield Ridley**

Page 394: **15 January 1851** ... the chancellor not having arrived ... ordered the sheriff ... to adjourn ... /S/ **William H Botts** C & M.

Page 395: **February Term Special 1851**. 5 February 1851 and the time appointed by the chancellor to hold a special Term of the Chancer Court ... County of Jackson 4th Chancery division ... chancellor not having arrived ... adjourn said court until tomorrow morning 10 o'clock. /S/ **William H Botts** Clerk & Master.

Page 395: Thursday morning 6 February 1851 the chancellor having arrived and taken his seat ...

Page 395: **Mary White** vs **William Draper** et al ... continued ....

Page 395: **Mahaly Jackson** vs **Elias Jackson**. Attachment Bill. Came the complainant by her sollicitor and on motion and for reasons appearing from the affidavit of complainant it is ordered by the court that the following property be attached to wit 1 single tree one pair drawing chaines 1 pair haimes one shovel plough (Page 396) one bull tongue plough one pair of stubords(?) & one spinning wheel and when so attached that the same be delivered over to complainant.

Page 396: **David R Johnson** vs **John Burrus**. Attachment Bill. The death of complainant David R Johnson was this day suggested ... and admitted by the defendant ... this cause set aside (and) revived in the name of **Benjamin C. White** administrator of David R Johnson ....

Page 396: **Benjamin Scanland** Executor &c vs **Clayton Rogers** and others. Attachment Bill. The death of **William Brooks** one of the defendants in this cause was this day suggested ... and admitted by defendants sollicitor ... this cause be revived in the name of **James H Lee** Administrator of William Brooks deceased ... continued till next term.

Page 396: **Mary H. Brooks** vs **Sam E. Hare**. O.B. And Sam E. Hare vs Mary H Brooks & **Richard P. Brooks** ... (Page 397) this cause is irregularly on the hearing docket ... ordered ... the same be remanded to the Rules for further steps to be taken ....

Page 397: **Sam Cox** & wife vs **Nancy Anderson** et al. Attachment Bill ... cause is continued until further order of the court.

Page 397: **James T. Hughs** vs **Pinkney McCarver** & others. Injunction & Attachment Bill. And **Thomas L Bransford** et al vs James T. Hughs. Cross Bill ... this cause is irregularly on the hearing docket it is ordered that it be remanded to the Rules for further steps to be taken.

Page 397: **Matthew C. McKinley** vs **Drennan** & **Woodrum.** Injunction Bill ... the complainant saith he will prosecute his suit no further ... bill be dismissed ....

Page 398: **John H.ughs** Administrator &c vs **Letty Roberts** Creditors. Original Bill ... cause is continued by order until next Term ....

Page 398: **Joseph C. Fletcher** vs **Alexander Dillard** and others. Injunction & attcht [sic] ... equity in complainants bill was fully met by the answers of defendants ... chancellor is therefore content to dismiss the complainants bill ....

Page 398: **Edward B. Draper** Executor &c vs **Reubin R Rogers** & others. Attachment Bill ... this cause is continued ....

Page 398: **Edward Vaughn** vs **Lawson Draper** et al. O.B. It appearing to the Court that this cause was prematurely set for hearing it is ordered that the same be remanded to the Rules.

Page 399: **Joseph C. Fletcher** vs **Alexander Dillard John H. Young** & **Allen Young** ... said defendants as partners in trade and complainant as an individual acting for himself on 19 October 1846 purchased of **John Rogers** a tract of land lying in Jackson County Dist No 13 supposed to contain about 500 acres more or less & bounded as follows Beginning on a dead poplar in the field thence South 77 poles to a beech, thence West 160 poles to stake, thence North 119 poles to a sugar tree, then West 12 poles to a stake, thence South 100 poles to a stake thence East 38 poles to **Riley McDaniel's** South east corner, thence North 74 poles to a stake, thence East 26 poles to a hickory, thence North 86 poles to a sugartree thence West 50 poles to a lynn [sic], thence North 22 poles to a Chestnut stump, thence East 86 poles to a hickory thence North 10 poles to a beech, thence East 98 poles to a sugar tree, thence South 64 poles to an Oak thence East 154 poles to three lynns near a branch thence South 74 poles to a beech, thence West 7 poles to a beech thence South 94 poles to a hickory thence West 108 poles to the beginning upon the following terms viz Dillard & the Youngs one half of said tract as partners and the complainant Joseph C. Fletcher the other half as an individual ... that said Joseph C. paid and secured to be paid one half the purchase money ... it further appearing ... that through inadvertence or want of legal knowledge the land was conveyed by said Rogers to Alex^r Dillard, Allen Young John H. Young & complainant Joseph C. Fletcher as joint and equal purchasers ... (Page 400) the title be divested out of Alexander Dillard, Allen Young & John H. Young to the extent of 1/4 of the entire tract ... and vested in said Joseph C. Fletcher ... that the complt. & his security **James B. Wallace** pay the cost of this suit for which execution may issue.

Page 400: **John D. Lusk** vs **James A. Spurlock** & others. Attachment Bill. On motion of complainant this cause is remanded to the rules ... if done before the first day of March next.

Page 400: **David H. Draper** Admr &c vs The creditors of **Abraham Lee** decd. O. Bill. ... from the report of the clerk and master that since the account was taken in this cause he has collected of the assets of said estate $100 ... report to next term.

Page 401: **Samuel E. Hare** & **Watson M. Cooke** vs **Nathan Montgomery Benjamin Monroe** & others. Bill. And Nathan Montgomery vs Benjamin Monroe **Sam E. Hare** & **G M McWhirter**. Cross Bill ... complainant in the cross bill and Benjamin Monroe were partners in the practice of medicine in Jackson county ... there are unsettled partnership accounts between them ... clerk and master ordered to take account and report to the next term ... and take the testimony of **Martha McWhirter**.

Page 401: **Thomas** & **Jefferson Johnson** vs **George M. McWhirter** & others. Bill ... this cause is improperly set for hearing ... ordered that the same be remanded to the Rules and on motion of defendant McWhirter ... ordered that the Bill be taken for confesses against defendant **Botts** and the same be opened for proof ....

Page 401: **Mary H Brooks** vs **Richard P. Brooks**. ... cause is continued until next Term (Page 402) ... Court adjourned until tomorrow morning 8 o'clock.

Page 402: Friday morning 7 February 1851, **Bromfield L. Ridley** presiding.

Page 402: **Edward B. Draper** Exr &c vs **Reubin R Rogers** and others. On motion of Defendants by their sollicitor ordered by the court that the clerk and master loan the funds in his hands received upon the note of **Fletcher** & **Dillard** and others taking note with good security payable at the next Term of this court ....

Page 402: **Thomas J.ohnson** et al vs **George M McWhirter** & others. ... it appears that the complainants are in possession of the land in dispute and are insolvent that they are the tenants of defendant McWhirter. It is ordered by the court that the complainants give security to be approved by the clerk and master for the rents of the land for the year 1851 and in default thereof ....

Page 403: **Thomas D. Simpson** vs **David Johnson** and others. Bill. And **Milton Draper** vs Thomas D. Simpson et al. Cross Bill ... continued until next Term ....

Page 403: **John Butler** vs **Susan Butler** et al ... upon the interlocutory decree pronounced at the last Term of this court ... upon argument and exceptions thereto ... that **E L Gardenhire** be allowed $85 out of the proceeds of the sale of the land and **W W Goodpasture** be allowed $15 out of the same ... (Page 404) clerk instructed to make further report to the next term of this court ....

Page 404: **William Carter** vs **Elizabeth Carter** ... continued ....

Page 404: **John L Mahany** et al vs **Thomas L Bransford** et al. Injunction Bill ... complainants say they will prosecute their suit no further ... bill dismissed ....

Page 404: **Zebulon Nettles** & wife vs **John Stafford** et al ... leave granted to amend the bill by making **Matthew Frost** and wife **Harriet Frost** assignees of complainants ....

Page 405: **Nathan Pharis Guardian** &c vs **Joseph Eaton** & **Dicy Eaton**. Attachment Bill. ... complainant by his sollicitor suggests ... the marriage of defendant Dicy Eaton to **Edward Vaughn** a citizen of **Davidson County Tennessee** which marriage being sufficiently proved ... that a scire facias issue as to said Edward Vaughn to show cause if any he has why said suit should not be revived against him and his wife **Dicy Vaughn** ....

Page 405: **Sarah Hall** by her next friend &c vs **Adam Hall**. Decree ... complainant and defendant were intermarried in 1829 at which time there was a subsisting contract for the settlement of the property of complainant &c upon her that on the 13th day of October 1845 a written deed was executed by defendant to **Andrew McClenan** of Jackson County setting upon him for the use of complainant certain property therein named and certain other negro property as described in bills of sale ... that Andrew McClenan the trustee has departed this life and it is necessary to have another appointed in his stead. It is therefore decreed that **James Young** be appointed trustee of the complainant ....

Page 405: **Edward Anderson** vs **Lewis R. Vance**. Decree ... (Page 406) it appears to the court that on 27 November 1847 the complainant loaned to the defendant $500 and took as security a deed for the following described land. Beginning on a bank marked L. R. V. and E. A. on the west side of the **Buffalow Valley** at a wet weather spring near an old tobacco barn running east to the top point of the ridge dividing the boord(?) tree hollow and a branch running through the plantation where **Thomas McCullough** west [sic] with said ridge to L R Vance's east line, then south to the north boundary line of a tract called the **Morr** [sic] tract, then East to the corner of said line, then South and round to **Bartlett's** line, then with his line to his corner in **Smith County** line to a tree marked by Bartlett & Vance for a conditional corner, then East to the beginning containing by estimation 300 acres lying in Jackson County and on the same day said complainant executed his bond binding him to recovery on payment of said money & which was to be repaid on 25 December 1848 ... that said money has not been paid ... Complt is entitled to have said land sold (said deed being a Mortgage) for the satisfaction of said sum of

$500 and interest ... proceed to sell said land to the highest bidder for cash & report to the next term ....

Page 407: **John Lee** Admr of **Mark Harper** decd vs **Thomas Huddleston**... the complainants intestate was the first endorser of a bill of exchange for **Lawson Clark** for $1,500.00...the defendant was the second endorser and Clark mortgaged to them a tract of land and seven hogsheads of tobacco to indemnify them as his endorser that the tobacco was freighted by **Daniel Huddleston** and sold (for) $194 (that) was paid to...Thomas Huddleston...that the complainants had paid off the bill of exchange and is entitled to the trust fund but ... it does not appear how much if any has been paid by the complainants as admr...ordered that the Clerk & Master state an account between the parties...and report the same next term ....

Page 407: **Merlin Young** vs **Samuel E. Hare** ... Clerk & Master take and state an account of all matters accounts and dealings of the parties ... and report the same to the next term ... (Page 408) ....

Page 408: **Samuel P. Butler** et al. Exparte-Report ... **George M. McWhirter** Guardian of the minor heirs of **Bailey Butler** decd reports to the court ... he has purchased the lands in the petition from **Mary Anderson** at the price of $800 taking a deed, warranty of title &c in the names of the heirs. /S/ G M McWhirter

Page 408: **Samuel S. Butler** & others. Exparte-Decree ... upon report of **George M. McWhirter** guardian of **Samuel I. Butler**, **Mary Anderson**, **Susan Hampton**, **John S. Butler**, **Bailey Butler** & **Martha Butler** minor heirs of Bailey Butler decd ... said guardian had purchased from Mary Anderson the tract of land mentioned in the petition in this cause at the price of $800 which was paid for out of the funds in his hands belonging to said wards ... (Page 409) ....

Page 409: **Tandy K. Witcher** vs **James J. Pursell** & **Joseph Moss** ... James J. Pursell is indebted to the complt in the sum of $113 ... said defendant is a non resident and insolvent and ... Joseph Moss is indebted to his co defendant in the sum of $103 due by note which is due and has not been transferred and has been attached by complainant in this case ....

Page 409: **John Hughs** & others vs **Dixon Brown** et al ... upon the report of the Clerk & Master who is receiver for this case ... (Page 410) ... certain of the property specified in said deed had been attached and by said Master with the assent of Plaintiffs left in possession of Mrs **Mary Brown** ... decreed ... that the master ... proceed to sell all of said property ... the Master will take and state an account and report to next term ... The Clerk will also report whether said Dixon Brown has assigned to **Samuel M. Fite** any amount of the balance of the proceeds ....

Page 410: **James Neely** vs **Temperance Stone** & others. Int. Decree ... (Page 411) Temperance Stone is indebted to the Complt in the sum of $91.90 ... said Temperance Stone is a non resident of ...Tennessee and she has not personal property within the jurisdiction of this court ... and further appearing ... that defendant Temperance Stone's right of dower in the land described in Complts Bill has been attached And that her Dower in said land has not been allotted to her. It is therefore ordered ... that the Sheriff of Jackson County summon five free holders unconnected to the parties either by affinity or consanguinity & entirely disinterested and that they allot & assign to said Temperance Stone one third part of said land including the mansion house as her dower ....

Page 411: **William P. Witcher** vs The President & Directors of the Bank of Tennessee ... at the last term of court demurred to the bill which demurrer was over ruled and the deft ordered to answer that no answer being filed the bill was taken for confessed and set for hearing... that on 18 February 1845 a note was made payable in Bank by **Daniel K. Witcher** to **Joseph Eaton** for $162.00 endorsed by said Eaton and purporting to be endorsed by complainant and that complain-ant's name was endorsed thereon without his knowledge or consent and that the same was not his act (Page 412) or deed and never came to his knowledge until after a judgement was rendered against him in 1849 in the Circuit Court of Jackson County ... the Court is of the opinion that complainant is entitled to relief ... and the defendant prays and obtains an appeal to the next term of the Supreme Court to be held at **Nashville** the first Monday in December next and it is granted ....

Page 412: **Samuel E. Hare** & **Watson M. Cooke** vs **Benjamin Monroe**, **Nathan Montgomery** & **George M. McWhirter**. Bill. And Nathan Montgomery vs Benjamin Monroe, Samuel E. Hare & George McWhirter. Cross Bill ... (Page 413) upon the report of the clerk & master which is unexcepted to ... it appears there is a balance due Nathan Montgomery the complainant in the Cross Bill by the Defendant Benjamin Monroe in the sum of $563.69 in and about their partnership in the practice of medicine ... Monroe pay to Montgomery ... $563.69 ... That the original Bill in this cause be dismissed and that Samuel E. Hare & Watson M. Cooke pay the cost of said Original Bill and recover the same over against defendant Monroe ....

Page 413: **James B. Buchanan** vs **Ridley Roberts Thomas J. Roberts William Cullom Samuel Turney James M. Shepherd** Admr of **Letty Roberts** & **W W Goodall** Sheriff of Jackson County. Decree ... it appearing to the Court that on 21 March 1842 in the Circuit Court of Jackson County complainant recovered a judgement for $500 and cost of suit against Ridley Roberts that fifa were repeated by issued [*sic*] and returned nulla bona, that on 7 March 1849 Ridley Roberts recovered a judgement for $1072. 10/100 in the Circuit Court of Jackson County against James M. Shepherd Admr of Letty Roberts decd. That on the same day he assigned said judgements to Cullom & Turney in Trust after paying themselves their fees in the suit in which said judgement was recovered to transfer the balance to Thomas J. Roberts that by an interlocutory decree of the Supreme Court made in this (Page 414) case at the December Term 1850 defts Cullom & Turney are entitled to a reasonable compensation for their services in said suit ... that the estate of the Letty Roberts is insolvent and that **John H.ughs** the present Admr. of said Letty (said Shepherd the former Admr having resigned) has filed his bill in this court for a pro rata distribution of said estate ... (Page 415) a certified copy of the final decree of the Supreme Court shall be filed in this cause ....

Page 415: **Stephen Price** vs **Edwin Price** ... there being exceptions taken by plaintiff in this cause since last term which were allowed when by agreement of the Solicitors on both sides this cause is ordered to be continued ....

Page 415: **Henry & Garrett Sadler** et al. Exparte Decree ... the Clerk and master take proof and report to the present term whether it would be manifestly to the advantage and interest of Plaintiff **Abisha Cannon** and wife that the exchange mentioned in the petition should be effected and if there is any difference in the value of the negro and land and how much if any (Page 416) ....

Page 416: **William Davidson** Admr of **Richard Davidson** & others. Exparte Decree ... that Richard Davidson departed this life in Jackson County in 1849 intestate that William Davidson was appointed and qualified as his adminstrater–that the other plaintiffs are his widow and his heirs at law ... that at the time of his death said intestate was possessed of the land described in the petition and exhibits that the widow of said decd is entitled to dower therein–that there are outstanding claims against said estate which there are no assets to pay ... decreed by the Court that said **Sarah Davidson** be endowed of said lands that a writ of dower issue properly directed to assign the same after which the Clerk & Master shall proceed to sell the balance of said land and also the reversion of said dower to the highest bidder ....

Page 416: **Edward P. Pate** et al vs **Cebert Pate** et al. Decree ... (Page 417) the court is of opinion that the title to the land in the pleadings is in dispute and this not being the proper forum in which to determine said controversy ... direct that an action of ejectment be instituted in a court of law to settle the question of title ... continued till next term.

Page 417: **Eliza Putty** vs **John A. Putty.** Decree ... that heretofore in the county of Jackson plaintiff and defendant had intermarried–that defendant has been guilty of adultery and that he has also been guilty of personal violence towards plaintiff ... a copy of this Bill had been placed in the hands of the Sheriff more than three months previous to the January Term 1851 of this court directing said Sheriff to summon said defendant to appear and defend this suit which said process has been returned by said Sheriff "Not found in my county" ... decreed by the Court that the bonds of matrimony ... be dissolved ....

Page 417: **Garrett Sadler** vs **Merlin Young** et al...complainants exceptions are not well taken ... ordered the same be disallowed ... that defendant Merlin Young was formerly Clerk of the Circuit Court of Jackson county and the other defend-ants except **McWhirter** and **Hogin** and Daniel K Witcher were his securities...also **Simon Hogin** and **Daniel K. Witcher** who are since dead were his securities and that defendants McWhirter & **Rawlins Hogin** are the personal representatives of said Simon Hogin and Daniel K. Witcher decd. And it further appearing that Merlin Young became insolvent and that his securities have paid the several amounts mentioned in the Masters report ... that Young on 25 may 1847 executed the deed in the pleadings mentioned to his co defendant **Goodall** and the court being of opinion that said deed was executed to shield said securitys from loss ... (Page 419) it further appearing the Clerk has in his hands a fund arising from the sale of said property of $762.85 ... Master proceed to pay out to said securities the amounts mentioned in said report ... And complainant obtained an appeal to the next term of the Supreme Court to be held at **Nashville** on the first Monday in December next ....

Page 419: **Thomas L Draper** vs **Merlin Young** & **Sam E. Hare.** Decree ... upon report of the Clerk ... complainant Thomas L Draper was at the time of the execution of the note enjoined in this cause indebt-ed to defendant Young in the sum of $40.09 and no more ... ordered ... that Samuel E. Hare recover of complainant Thomas L Draper and **James Draper** his security in the injunction bond ... (Page 420) $40.09 with interest from 24 September 1845 ....

Page 420: **Garret Sadler Henry Sadler Abisha Cannon Sally Cannon** and **James M. Shepherd.** Exparte Decree ... upon report of the Clerk ... it would be manifestly to the advantage of complainants Abisha Cannon wife and children that the negro man named in the petition should be exchanged by Henry and Garret Sadler Trustees of said Abisha and wife to complainant James M. Shepherd for the land mentioned in said petition there being no difference in the value of each ... (Page 421) also as to said Abisha Cannon & Sally Cannon his wife and as to **Jane Cannon Martin V. Cannon William H H Cannon Lewis F. Cannon** and Abisha Cannon children of the said Abisha and Sally Cannon (the title to said negro be divested) and vested in said James M. Shepherd ... And that the title to the following described tract of land situated in Jackson County and bound as follows to wit. Beginning on **Martins Creek** above the mouth of **Lick Branch** of said creek at a beach red oak & ash on the east bank of said creek it being the south west corner of a 24 acre tract of land conveyed to **Z. B. Thaxton** by **James Roberts** bearing date 8 November 1811 & Registered in the registers office of Jackson

County 3 March 1812 Book B Page 110 Running thence east passing a dogwood poplar & lynn corner of 100 acre tract at 40 poles to a stake southeast corner of said 100 acre tract. thence north 124 1/2 poles to a stake the north east corner of 100 acre tract thence west 120 1/2 poles to a white oak and iron wood the north east corner of 100 acre tract and northeast [*sic*] corner of a 24 acre tract thence west 25º South 46 poles to a hickory and iron wood on the bluff of the creek above Roberts mill thence with the meanders of the creek along the high water mark of Roberts mill pond to the beginning corner be divested as to the said James M. Shepherd and vested in the (Page 422) said Garret & Henry Sadler to be held by them in trust for the use and benefit of Abisha Cannon and wife Sally Cannon and their children ....

Page 422: **Henry & Garrott Sadler** vs **Abisha Cannon** et al. Decree ... that the order of the Court at last term to pay the amount recovered by Complainants had not been complied with and therefore in pursuance to the provisions of said order Complainants on 30 December 1850 ... sold at public sale to the highest bidder the following negroes to wit **Amanda** & her infant child purchased by **William Matlock** $900.00 ... negro boy **Calvin** was sold to **David G. Shepherd** $807.00 said sale being on six months credit ... (Page 423) ....

Page 423: **Benjamin B. Washburn** vs **John Price** ... it appeared ... that complainant and defendant were the administrators of **James Price** decd and of **Charles N. Price** decd it further appeared that James & Charles N. Price decd were the joint owners of a lot of hogs and that defendant had converted them to his own use disregarding his official obligation to sell and account for them as Administrator of said estates ... that said defendant had replevied(?) said hogs and executed bond to that effect with **John Leach** his security ... (Page 424) that said defendant had surrendered the horse belonging to said estate and claimed by him which has been sold by pltf ... it is therefore ordered and decreed by the court that pltf as administrator of said estates recover of defendant and John Leach ... $43.75 which when collected is to be equally divided between said estates ....

Page 424: **Nancy B. Ammonett, Virginia Ammonett Tennessee G. Amonett, Benjamin F. Ammonett, James Ammonett** & **Martha P. Ammonett** vs **Thomas L. Bransford** ... upon report of the jury summoned & sworn to allot to Complt Martha P. Ammonett her Dower in the land described in a decree in this cause pronounced at July Term 1849 which report is unexcepted to and is as follows to wit, We the undersigned being unconnected with the parties either by affinity or consanguinity and entirely disinterested ... and duly sworn by **William P. Witcher** one of the lawful deputies [*sic*] Sheriff of Jackson County as a jury to allot and set off to Martha P Ammonett her dower out of the real estate of **William Ammonett** her deceased husband ... (Page 425) the following described land with the erections and improvements thereon ... land in Jackson County on the waters of **Proctor's Creek** containing by survey 183 acres and bounded as follows, viz, Beginning at a sycamore in the bed of said creek running North 15º 28 poles to a stake thence South 75º East 12 poles to a stake thence North 5º E. 60 poles to a black walnut, thence North 25º West 42 poles to a hickory, thence North 5º West 39 poles to a hickory, thence North 3º East 28 poles to a hickory Thence North 10º East 30 poles to a white oak thence North 70º West 25 poles to a white oak, Thence North 80º West 30 poles to a hickory, Thence South 30º West 63 poles to an ash, Thence South 48º West 22 poles to a small elm, Thence South 18º East 28 poles to ... **Savage's** line Thence East 18 poles with sd line to a stake Savage's corner, Thence South 20º West 80 poles to a beech on the South bank of Proctor's Creek, thence down said creek with its various meanders to the beginning Which in our opinion constitutes one third of the land quality & quantity ... signed 27 December 1849 by **S B M Fowler, Bennett Stone, William Gearhart, Varney Andrews** and **J. A. Stone** ... And it appearing to the Court that James Ammonett who was made a party plaintiff to this suit at last term has been duly notified of that fact ... (Page 426) ... also upon report of the Commissioners appointed to divide the negroes belonging to the late firm of Ammonett & Bransford between the distributees and widow of William Ammonett and said Thomas L. Bransford ... (that) on 2 November 1849 at **Kinderhook** near **Celina** ... in the presence of Martha P. Ammonett & **Luke T. Armstrong** next friend of said distributees who are minors & Thomas L. Bransford divided the negroes between the parties as follows. To said Widow & distributees they allot **Sandy** of the value of $600. **Susan** & child of the value $650. **Jack** of the value of $550. **Dave** of the value of $550. **Charles** of the value of $550. **Elizabeth** of the value of $500. **Crayton** of the value of $500. **Jim** of the value of $400. in all $4300.00. To Thomas L. Bransford they allot **Jenkins** of the value of $600. **Jim** of the value of $600. **John** of the value of $600. **Polly** & child of the value of $600. **Jasper** of the value of $500. **Spencer** of the value of $500. **Daniel** of the value of $400. **Charles(?)** of the value of $400. in all $4200.00 ... (Page 427) ... which is respectfully submitted 8 July 1850. /S/ **W. C. Walker** and Varney Andrews ....

Page 427: **William Lambert** & wife vs **James Pharris** et al. Decree ... it appearing ... that **William Pharis** departed this life in 1836 leaving property real and personal and one infant child **Elizabeth** who has married complainant William Lambert ... that **James Vinson** & (Page 428) James Pharis the defts were executors of the last will & testament of William Pharis decd. ... that **Elizabeth Lambert** the Complt is a minor and sole legatee of said estate and is entitled to an account ... Clerk to take and state an account ... and report to next term ....

Page 428: **William Lambert** et al vs **James Vinson** & **James Pharis** ... complainants security for prosection of this suit **Robert G. Hughs** has heretofore given him notice in writing that he ... moved to be released from any further liability as his security ... ordered (he) be released ... (Page 429) ....

Page 429: **Kinnaird** & **Bransford** vs **B B Washburn** Admr &c ... continued ....

Page 429: **Volney S. Stephenson** vs **John H. Young** et al ... complainant failing to appear and prosecute this suit ... the same be dismissed and ...Defendant recover against Complainant & **Henry B. McDonald** his securities for prosecution costs ....

Page 429: **Absolom Johnson** vs **Henry W. Kirby**. Came the parties by their solicitors and on motion ... cause is continued ....

Page 429: **Henry W. Kirby** vs **Absolom Johnson**. Came the parties by their solicitors and complt dismisses his suit. Ordered that deft recover against him & **Francis M. Goolsby** his security all costs herein ....

Page 430: **Absolom Johnson** vs **Benjamin Scanland** & others. Came the parties by their Solicitors and complt dismisses his suit. Ordered that defts recover against the complt & **James Draper** his security ....

Page 430: **Absolom Johnson** vs **David Johnson**. Came the complainant by his solicitor and dismissed his suit. Ordered that defendant recover against him & **James Draper** his security the costs herein & that execution issue.

Page 430: ... adjourn to the next regular term. /S/ **Bromfield Ridley**.

Name/Place Index

Abbott	14	
Abisha	45	
Alexander's	76	
Allen		
Geo. D.	15	
George D.	5, 12	
Hugh P.	5	
Margaret	34	
Sampson	49	
Ammonett		
James	87, 96	
Martha P.	87	
Nancy B.	79, 87	
William	96, 97	
Amonet		
William	17	
Amonett	80	
Martha P.	79	
Nancy B.	80	
Virginia	79	
William	50, 80	
Anderson		
Charles W.	81	
Edward	67, 79, 81, 92	
Mary	93	
Nancy	34, 53, 58, 90	
Peter	57	
Andrews		
Nancy	10, 80	
Varney	96	
Apple		
David	43, 45	
George	64, 71, 72	
Ridley	71	
Armstrong		
Landon	60	
Luke T.	79, 97	
M.L.	10	
Micajah L.	10, 14	
Armstrong and Howard	14	
Atterberry		
George W.	37, 38	
Backinstoe?		
J. G.	27	
Baker		
Sarah	6, 11	
Thomas	8	
Baldwin		
Joseph E	88	
Ballew		
John H.	16	
Bank of Tennessee	81	
Barnes		
John	56, 61, 71, 77	
William H.	57, 76	
Wm. H.	74	
Bartlett	92	
Beagley		
Isham	46	
Benson		
Richard	51, 53	
Biggerstaff		
Aaron	25, 37, 38, 43, 55, 60	
Benjamin	37	
David	14, 23, 79	
Bill		
Lyman E.	23, 26, 31, 34, 35, 42	
Billingsley		
William	6	
Birdwell	42	
Bland		
Elizabeth	13	
Matthew	13	
Matthew M.	10, 28	
Sally	29	
Blankenship		
Jacob G.	17	
Bohanan		
Henry	65	
Botts	66, 91	
William H.	73, 76, 78, 80, 81, 89, 90	
Wm H	75	
Bowman		
Letha Jane	69	
Boyd		
James	83	
John	83	
Bradley		
John	41	
Bransford	73, 80, 85, 97	
see Kinnaird & Bransford	29, 47, 51	
see Kinnaird and Bransford	27	
see Kinnard & Bransford	51	
Tho L	87	
Thomas L	90	
Thomas L.	7, 11, 12, 13, 17, 26, 27, 31, 33, 37, 38, 39, 49, 59, 61, 64, 66, 73, 76, 77, 79, 80, 92, 96, 97	
Brock		
James	65	
Brooks		
Albert W. W.	69	
John	70	
Mary H.	69, 70, 75, 76, 77, 82, 87, 90, 91	
Matthew	70	
R. P.	27	
Richard P.	5, 6, 7, 40, 42, 43, 48, 51, 69, 70, 72, 75, 77, 87	
Richd P.	32	
William	65, 90	
Wm	75	
Brooks Bend	32	
Brown		
Benjamin	9	
Devore	25	
Dixon	32, 81, 93	
Mary, Mrs.	93	
Robert O. & Reas___	50	
Browns	80	
Buchanan	49, 62	
James B.	84, 86, 94	
Jane	62, 65, 66	
John	60	
John A.	62	
William	44, 46, 60, 62	
Wm	60	
Buck		
Isaac	27	
Buffalow Valley	92	
Bugg		
George S.	16, 26	
Bullers Creek	75	
Burk		
Isaac	17	
Burke		
Angelina	79, 86	
E L	75	
Elizabeth	79	
Henry F.	13, 28, 32, 35, 40, 47, 86	
James W.	70, 75	

Jas W 75
John 32, 43, 47, 75, 86
John G 75
John G. 32, 36, 43, 79
Milton E. 79, 86
William C. 26, 40, 42, 43, 48, 59, 72
Wm. C. 32, 49, 59
Burns
   John M. 69
Burris 11
   John 10
Burrus
   John 90
Burton
   Charles F. 53, 57
   George W 75
   Robert 31
   Robert G. 32, 40
   Stephen D. 55, 56
   Thomas 32
Butler
   Bailey 10, 47, 50, 68, 72, 93
   Franklin W. 37, 68, 72
   John 89, 92
   John S. 93
   Martha 37
   Polly 37
   S. S. 37
   Samuel I 93
   Samuel P. 93
   Samuel S. 82, 93
   Tho H 88
   Thomas 86, 89
   Thomas H. 59, 68, 72, 79
   Thos 72
   Thos H 86
   Welcome 10, 24, 89
   Wilenne 14
Butler Jr.
   Bailey 11
Button
   Whitfield 56, 61
Cage
   Leroy H. 17
Cameron
   Mark 9, 10
Campbell
   William B. 26
   Wm. B. 60
Caney Fork 13
Cannon 44
   Abisha 10, 43, 64, 72, 77, 88, 94, 95, 96
   Bird 10, 23, 28, 35, 38, 43, 45
   Bird S. 32
   Jane 88, 95
   Lucinda 32, 35, 38
   Martin V. 65
Canter
   James 15, 34
   Levi 32, 53
   William 32
   Wilson C. 15, 34, 40, 45
   Zachariah 15, 32
Car
   Elijah 9, 77
   Eliza 57
   John W. 83
   W. H. 78
   William H. 78
   Wm H. 83
Carlin
   Hugh W. 23, 26, 28, 31, 35
Carlisle
   James 41
Carr
   Elijah 17, 27, 78
   John W. 78
Carter
   Dale 54, 84
   Elizabeth 92
   Enoch 6, 12, 15, 17
   Enock 10
   Henry 46, 61, 63, 77, 84
   James 46, 47, 56, 64
   Levi 25
   Richard 77
   Thackston 16, 59
   Thaxton 8, 59
   Wilson C. 25
Carter's 80
Carver
   Aletha 71
   Cornelius 14, 23, 71, 82
   Hiram C. 71
   John 49
   Joseph 42, 49
Cason 51
   E. M. 54
   Edward M. 53, 78, 83
   James 54, 74
   Susan 74
   Thompson 32, 51, 79
Cassetty
   Alexander 65
   S. W. 27, 85
   Sampson W. 8, 17, 34, 49, 88
   Thomas 15
   Thomas D. 8, 17, 27, 64, 84
Catlet
   A. M. 44
   John 44
Chaffin
   Abner 75
   Benj 75
Chapman
   A. J. 27
   Amos J. 5, 17, 46
   Benjamin 13
   John 13
Cheek
   Cook vs Cheek 16
   Henry 34, 42, 48
   Nicholas 5, 6, 9, 11, 15
Cherry
   Pleasant 75
Chism 52
   Ann 75
   Ann Frances 5
   James 5
   nancy Trigg 5
   Nancy Trigg 9
   Priscilla Frances 9
   Priscilla Francis 5
   Robert F.? 24
   Robert K.? 10
   Robert N.? 25
Chisms Heirs 5, 11
Chisms Heirs and Widow..........................6
Christian
   Cornwell 54
   Polly 54
Clark 93
   James 45
   Larson 27
   lawson 53
   Lawson 17, 55, 57, 59, 71, 93
   see Williams & Clark..................25
Clarke
   Lawson 53
   Peter 25
Clemens
   Christopher 44, 49
   John 36, 49
   Thos. L. 30
Clements
   Thomas L. 5, 9, 25
   Thos. L. 25

Clemmons
   Christopher 13, 36, 42
   John   13, 77
Clemons
   Christopher 23, 29, 33, 34, 35, 44, 50
   John   29, 36
Clinton
   George W.   57
Collier   71
Conger
   John   59, 63
Congo
   John   58, 59
Cook   62, 70
   Watson M. 26, 31, 62
Cook vs Cheek   16
Cooke 54, 56, 65, 72, 86
   Richard F. 5, 6, 9, 11, 15, 17, 27
   see Hare & Cooke 45, 51, 54
   Watson M. 5, 38, 42, 46, 60, 64, 68, 69, 73, 76, 78, 91, 94
   Wilson M.   34
Coons
   Nathaniel   54
Coonskin Branch   7
Copeland
   Josiah 30, 31, 33, 37, 39, 44, 50
Cornwell
   Mary   31, 36, 38
   S. C.   78
   Silas C. 14, 23, 40, 43, 48, 72, 83
Costillo   58
Cowan
   Ira's children   66
   Joseph   75
   Matthew   8, 9
Cox
   A. M.   54
   Ann   47, 51, 53
   Eliza   78
   N M   75
   Nathaniel M. 56, 62, 78, 83
   Peter G.   54
   Peter J.   25
   Sam   90
   Samuel   81
Crabtree
   Hiram   42, 65, 74
Crawford
   Isaac   24
   James   44
Cray

   William   82
Crenshaw
   John   41
Cross   33
Crowder
   Henry   17, 55
Crowell
   Hezekiah   13
Cullom
   William   84, 94
Cullum
   A.   22
   Alva   26
   William   77
Cumberland river 61, 70, 79
Cumberland River 24, 27, 32, 70
Cummings
   Daniel   75
   John   31
Cuppage
   Alex   75
Darwin
   G. C.   59
   George C. Jr.   59
   W G   75
   William G. 32, 36, 43, 70
Davenport
   Joseph   75
Davidson
   Sarah   95
   William 39, 51, 56, 66, 87, 88, 94
Davis   65
   James A.   57, 73
   Mary   50
Daws
   James   82
Dean
   Hezekiah   8
Denton
   Erasmus   37
   H.   69
   Holland 56, 62, 81, 83
DeWhitt
   Samuel   55
Dill
   Archibald   62, 78
   Archibald Senr.   63
   Archibald Sr.   78
   Arthur   78
   Elijah   78
   Roland C.   68, 78
   Solomon   62
   Stephen   78

Dillard   83, 91
   Alex'r   91
   Alexander 59, 63, 64, 67, 86, 90, 91
   J. L.   25
Dixon
   Johnath   32
   Saml   44
Dod
   Abba   44
Doll_ll
   Reuben H.   55
Dowell
   John   55, 62
Draper   43, 83
   B. M.   83
   Brice M. 9, 10, 14, 17, 19, 20, 21, 22, 26, 30, 35, 38, 39
   David H. 56, 76, 81, 91
   Edward B. 14, 18, 19, 20, 21, 22, 70, 72, 77, 83, 90, 91
   James 14, 18, 19, 20, 21, 22, 51, 53, 58, 82, 97
   Lawrence   14
   Lawson   85, 90
   Lawson H. 19, 20, 21, 22
   Milton 14, 20, 21, 22, 51, 71, 72, 77, 82, 83, 92
   Sarah 14, 18, 19, 21
   Thomas 14, 18, 20, 22
   Thomas L. 18, 19, 20, 21, 22, 84, 95
   William   81, 82, 90
Drennan   90
   James   85
Drennum
   James   85
Dry branch   29
Dudney
   Patrick N.   28, 43
   Sidney S.   28
   _____   75
Duffy
   Francis   58
Duke
   Matthew 13, 25, 32, 35
   Matthue   15
   Micajah   25, 32, 45
   Richard   34
Dunn
   Hezekiah   9
Eakel
   John   24

Eakle
   Christian 47
   Henry 28, 29, 53
   Henry Jr. 33
   John 14, 16, 33, 47
Eaton 45
   Dicy 92
   Joseph 7, 17, 27, 45, 48, 77, 94
Elkins
   Wm 75
Ellison
   Joseph 45
Enocs
   Samuel 9
Erwin
   Andrew 64
   Benjamin 64
   Benjamin Sr. 71
   Dice 57
   Elizabeth 57
   Margaret 57, 71
Evans
   Obadiah 18, 19, 20, 21, 22
   Obediah 14
Farrar
   Garland 8
Farris
   Nathan 56
Ferrell
   Isaac E. 9, 25
   Jefferson 12, 25
Fite
   Samuel M. 41, 60, 93
Fitz
   Elizabeth 84
   Henry B. 84
Fitzgerald
   Joseph B. 39
Fletcher 83, 91
   Joseph C. 86, 90, 91
   Lewis 46, 51, 53
Flynn
   A. M. 75
Fose
   William 5, 6
Fowler 10
   S B M 96
   Samuel B. M. 10, 14, 26, 27, 37, 80
Fraim
   William 54, 58
Franklin
   Owen 43

Frazier
   J. G. 71
Frost
   Harriet 92
   Matthew 92
Gailbreath
   Isabella 47, 49
   T. J. 49
   Thomas J. 49
   William A. 17, 49
Gaines
   James H. 86
   Rufus 86
Galder
   James T. 10
Gales
   John N. 14
Gardenhire
   E L 92
Garrett
   Green 56
Garrison
   Henry 57
Gates 29, 42, 56
   John N. 10, 15, 23, 24, 25, 26, 27, 31, 50, 52, 56, 61
Gaw
   Thomas 69
Gearhart
   William 96
Gentry
   Thomas 23, 26, 31, 34, 35, 42, 65
Georgia 88
Gipson
   John M. 11, 88
   Randal M. 51, 52
   William 6, 17, 27, 30, 34, 42, 51, 52, 53, 64
Glenn
   Jemima 48
   Patsy 48
Golder
   James T. 52
Goldes
   James T. 24, 25
Goodall 22, 79, 88, 95
   John L. 26, 83
   see Nelson & Goodall 38
   W W 94
   William W. 58, 84, 87
Goodpasture
   W W 92
   Winburn W. 81

Goolsby
   Francis M. 97
Gore 51, 54
   Mounce 5, 7, 17, 24, 27, 38, 40, 43, 47, 53, 65, 69, 74
   William 79, 82, 86
Goss 65
   Nathan J. 55, 57, 62, 73
Gr_shill
   Robert 50
Graham 43, 66
   Jared H. 65
   John 68
Graves
   Alva 32
   Alvey 39, 40, 42, 48
   Beverly 40, 42, 48
Gray
   S. S. 75
   William 69, 79, 86
Green
   Joseph 40, 43
Greene
   Joseph 27
Griffith
   David 12, 26, 31, 33, 39, 42, 73, 74, 77, 82
   John 33, 37
   Mary L. 73
   Nancy 64
Griffiths
   John 30
Guffy
   James 55, 57, 65, 73
   V. James 62
Gully
   James 33
Gwinn 61
Hail
   Dudley B. 59
   Nicholas 65
Haile
   Amon 74
   John B. 7
   Nicholas 7
   Thomas 49, 75
Hale
   Amon 30, 51
   Dudley B. 59
   Joshua P. 17
   Locke 33
Halford
   Willis 64, 72

Hall 68, 86	William 68, 72	Rebecca 44, 60, 62, 65
John A. 55, 57	Wm 75	Richard 66
L. C. 88	Hays	Rollins 8, 9, 23, 27
Lyttleton E.(?) 46	Samuel R. 10	Sally 44
Sarah 92	Head	Sarah 53
William A. 65	Doctor 89	Simon 17, 38, 66, 95
Halliburton	Peggy 89	William 65
David R. 89	Heady	William C. 66, 74
Hamilton	John W. 47	Hogins Heirs 46, 52
A.C. 12	Heare 67	Holdford
Adam C. 9, 64	Henderson	Willis 71, 72
Adonis C. 5	Kinman W. 57	Holford
Hampton	Nancy 10	Willis 71
Susan 93	Rebecca S. 57	Holladay
Hardcastle	Thomas 77, 81	Henrietta 14
Alex. 50	William 77	Stephen 14, 18, 19, 21, 22
Alexander 45, 48, 56	Henry	Holliday
Hardin	James 69	Henrietta 18
Alexander 33	Michael 5, 12, 60, 65	Holliman
Hare 67, 70, 84, 86	Polly 54, 60, 65, 69, 73, 78, 85	Elizabeth 25, 40
Achilles 17, 68, 70	Henson	James G. 37
Sam E. 7, 46, 48, 51, 74, 90, 91, 95	William 26, 31, 42	Margaret 25
Saml E. 51, 56	Herbert	Mark 35
Samuel E. 26, 31, 34, 38, 42, 45, 46, 47, 54, 55, 58, 60, 62, 64, 67, 69, 71, 73, 74, 76, 78, 79, 81, 82, 85, 91, 93, 94	Daniel 12	William P. 25, 40
	David 8, 9, 24, 29, 45, 47, 50, 53, 58, 63, 79, 85	Hollimon
	Hickland	James 48
Z. 27	Perry R. 84	Mark 48
Hare & Cook 62	Hicklin 41, 46, 50	William P. 45
Hare & Cooke 45, 51, 54, 56, 65, 72	A.M. 12	Holloman
Hare & Jackson 58	Alvira 12	James G. 46
Harper	Avery M. 5, 9, 37	Margaret 32
M. 57	Avra M. 9	William P. 32
Mark 53, 57, 93	Hugh 12	William W.ade 32
Harris	Perry 37, 43, 84	Holloman's 28
Sterling 32, 58	Thomas 37, 60	Holmes
Harrison	Hicklins Heirs 55, 60, 63, 65, 71, 76, 84	Benjamin D. 24, 31
Reubin 44	Hinson	William B. 59, 74
Squire L. 58	William 39	Homes
Hart 27	Hogin 34, 95	Benjamin D. 26
Hawes	Anthony 44	Hood
Daniel 53	Anthony Wayne 85	Brison 17, 26
Daniel W. 46	Catron C. 84	Bryson 15
Danl W. 51	Daniel 61, 65, 89	Hoodenphyle
Hawkins	E. 60	A. J. 62
Cleveland Winchester 11	Edward 44, 60, 62	Howard
Dice 11	Isaac 30, 35, 41, 46, 51, 60, 62, 66	Harman 23, 29
Elizabeth Jane 11	James 44, 66	Harmon 33, 34, 35, 36, 42, 44, 49, 50
James A.lexander 11, 12, 13	M. C. 60	Harrison 13
Jane 12	Matthew C. 44, 46, 49, 52, 60, 62, 65	Thomas 23
John 11	Rawlings 55, 61, 65, 66, 67	Huddleston 20
Nelson 11, 13	Rawlins 53, 55, 95	Daniel 93
		John L. H. 65

Tho. 57	Jenkins	Kinnaird and Bransford............27
Thomas 14, 18, 20, 21, 22, 23, 53, 57, 87, 93	George 75	Kinnard 73
Hudelston	Jennings	Kinslow
Thomas 53	Nancy 83, 85	Bird C. 55, 56
Hudson	Jennings Creek 30, 33, 37, 44	Kirby
William 47, 54	Jewett	Henry W. 87, 97
Huff	John W. 37	William 49
Leonard 8	Johnson 82	William H. 51
Huffines	Absalom 39, 51, 77, 84, 87	Kirkpatrick
Peter 75	Absolom 97	Francis 44
Hughes 9	Absom 84	L. F. R. 27
Abraham 33	David 33, 39, 47, 82, 83, 87, 92, 97	R. C. 88
Harrison J. 32, 34	David R 90	Toliver 85
James F. 59	Jefferson 66, 87	Tollivar 5, 8, 17
James L. 33, 53	Samuel 44	Lambert
James T. 41, 42, 46, 51, 59, 64, 68, 74	Thomas 9, 73, 91	William 82, 97
John 8, 23, 27, 28, 42, 66, 74, 89	William 6, 10, 12, 15, 17	Lancaster
Robert G.? 17	Jones	Avery K. 8
William H. 6	A. 47, 53	Avra F.? 11
William L. 40	Alfred 58	Avra K. 12
William Q. 6, 25, 31, 32	Claiborne 75	Thomas A. 58
Hughs	Elias 75	Langford
James T. 34, 38, 46, 48, 58, 62, 68, 85, 90	Henry 70	E. F. 89
John 38, 66, 79, 81, 84, 87, 93	James C. 26, 39	E. L. 24
John J. P. 68	John 75	Ervin F. 89
Robert G. 97	John G. 75	Erwin F. 61, 89
William Q. 84, 89	Martin 47	Josiah H. 79
William Q.(?) 79	Jordan 79	Stephen 15, 23
Hunter	Judd	Leach
Squire 10, 12	Nathan 57	John 65, 96
Hurricane Branch 7, 29	Keith	Lee
Hutchinson	Daniel 75	A. 71
James 17	James 45, 51, 54, 55	Abner 61
Thomas D. 17	Kendall	Abraham 45, 46, 63, 72, 75, 76, 81, 91
Indian Creek 13, 70	Bailey B. 14	Abram 56
Irvin	William 38, 89	Barret 75
Andrew 71	Kenner	Curry 13
Jackson 58, 67	W R 82	Daniel 32, 33, 40, 45, 52, 63, 71, 72, 75
Eli 6	William R. 17, 73, 86	Danl 46
Mahaly 90	Kentucky	James H 90
N. G. 27, 35, 43	Monroe County 52	John 79, 84, 85, 87, 93
Nathaniel G. 5, 37, 49, 56, 62	Kernal	Leonard
Nathaniel S. 17	Barret 75	Solomon 40
Jackson & Williams 35	Kernel	Solomon L. 39, 42
Jarod 13	Patrick 39	Solomon S. 32
Joseph 13	Kinnaird 85, 97	Lick Branch 95
William 23, 26, 28, 31, 35	George 33	Lindsey
Jarvis	Russel M. 8, 11, 12, 13, 17, 26, 31, 33, 49, 59	Archibald 83
Argyle R. 56, 61	Russell M. 7, 37, 38, 76	Archibald M. 78
Jems 61	Kinnaird & Bransford 12, 29, 37, 39, 46, 47, 51, 85	Lock
		J. W. 27

James W. 7, 17, 36
John 65
William 10
Locke
  James W. 28, 31, 38, 43
  William 10
Loftis
  James M. 68
  Milly 63, 78
Louisiana
  New Orleans 30, 31, 33
Love
  John 45
  John M. 47, 58
Lowe
  Green B. 25
Lucinda
  Lucinda 44
Lusk
  John D. 85, 86, 91
Lynn
  Asa 27, 31, 34, 40, 43, 50, 55
  Joel 7, 31, 39, 44, 50, 56
Maddusk
  Silas 12
Maddux
  Carven 27
  Craven 17
  Cravin 25
  Silas F. 25
  Siles F. 9
Mahanay
  Perry 7, 36, 41, 52, 65, 72
Mahaney
  Perry 7, 47
Mahany
  John L. 92
  Perry 56, 76, 81
Majors
  David 50
Manear
  James 56
  James A. 77, 84
Manier
  Allen 49, 52
  Benjamin 54
  James 45, 48, 50, 56
  James A. 72
Mansel 76
Mansell
  David 9
  Jesse 9
  Sam 74

Saml. 65
Samuel 9
William 65, 74, 76
Marchbanks
  Burton 17, 27
  H. D. 27
  Harold D. 59
  Hearld D. 68
  Herald D. 17, 46, 64, 65, 74
  Thomas 59
  Thos C 74
Marsh
  Shelby B. 43
Marshall
  James 54, 55
Martin 52, 71
  David W. 30
  George 10, 24, 25
  Mary L. 25
  Samuel 77, 81
Martins Creek 95
  Shaws Branch 29
Martins Spring 80
Masters
  Montraville 81
Matlock
  William 96
Mattocks
  Adderson 9
Maxey
  Rice 34
Mayfield
  Z. H. 24
McBroom 24, 29, 79
  James 8, 9, 24, 29, 45, 47, 50, 53, 58, 63
McBroom Jr.
  James 12
McCalgin 16
  Wilson 10
McCarver
  H. 75
  Harrison 17
  Pinckney 10, 12, 14, 16, 24, 27, 33, 75, 85
  Pinkney 90
McCauley
  John 44
  McCauley 75
McCauleys
  John 44
McCaulley
  John 44

McClain 22
  Andrew 81
  William 26
McClellan
  A. 48
  Andrew 32, 40, 42, 43, 48, 87
  Jesse 28
McClellen
  Jesse 5
McClellin 43
McClenan
  Andrew 92
McClendan
  Jesse 9, 15
McClenden
  Jesse 70
McClendon
  G. W. 25
  Jesse 25, 30, 70
McClenon
  Andrew 92
McColgin
  Wilson 24
  Wilson T. 50, 52
McConnell
  Richard 48
McCormack
  John 26
McCormic
  Stephen 88
McCullough
  Thomas 92
McDaniel
  H. L. 27
  Henry L. 17
  Riley 91
McDonald
  H. B. 63, 64, 67
  Henry B. 59, 64, 97
McGee 11
McGipson
  George 54
  Levi 55
  Randall 53
  Tobias 53
McKindly
  Matthew C. 85
McKineley
  Matthew C. 32
Mckinley
  Matthew C. 26
McKinley
  Eliza 15, 17, 26, 31

James 31, 41
Matthew 17, 40
Matthew C. 15, 31, 90
Robert 40
Sarah 17, 41
McKinly
   Eliza 38
   James 38
   Matthew C. 66, 74, 78, 85
McKinney
   E. F. 52
   Edwin F. 7, 36, 41, 47, 52, 56, 65, 72, 76, 81
McKinny 36
MClellan
   Andrew 40
McNichol
   A. B. 53, 58
   Alexander 47
   Mary A. 53
McNichols 58
McWhirter 11, 66, 95
   G. M. 15, 22, 24, 27, 34, 45, 50, 51, 76, 83, 84, 88, 91, 93
   Geo M. 55
   Geo. M. 10, 12, 54, 78
   George M. 9, 11, 26, 36, 54, 56, 61, 66, 67, 73, 76, 82, 87, 91, 93, 94
   George W. 89
   Martha 91
   see Montgomery & McWhirter 39
McWhorter
   Geo. M. 6
   George M. 5
Meddors
   Jason 75
Medlen
   Anar 78
   Aner 63
Medlin
   Samuel 78
Middleton
   Sady 6
Miller 48
Minnis
   John A. 5
Minor
   Hiram 51
Missouri 36, 86
Monroe
   Ben 87

Ben. 51
Benj. 62, 72
Benjamin 39, 45, 46, 56, 70, 76, 91, 94
Montgomery
   Alexander 5, 7, 17, 20
   Alexander H. 65
   Monroe 86
   Nathan 38, 46, 49, 51, 59, 64, 70, 76, 91, 94
Montgomery & McWhirter 39
Moore
   Elizabeth 31, 32, 40
   Micajah 77
   Michael 65, 77
   Richard 31, 40
Morel
   William 44
Moreland
   William 15
Morgan
   Daniel 41
Morr 92
Morrele
   William 33
Morrell 44
   Reece & Morrell 17
   William 30, 37
Morrow
   Mark H. 8
Moss
   Joseph 87, 93
Mullins
   Willis 13, 15, 25, 35
Murphey
   Levi 56
Murry
   Thomas 6, 51, 59
Myers 39
   John 30, 33, 37, 39
Nance
   Lewis R. 53, 59
   William R. 53
Neely
   James 93
Negroes
   Aletha 39, 40, 42
   Alvira 12
   Amanda 48, 88, 96
   Anderson 7
   Ann 45
   Anna 69
   Barbara 40

Barbary 31
Benjamin 61
Bill 84
Booker 23
Calvin 88, 96
Charles 22, 26, 69, 80, 97
Charlotte 61
Cinda 26
Craton 80
Crayton 97
Cynthia 40
Dan 23
Daniel 97
Dave 97
David 80
Dick 27, 38, 41
Eliza 26
Elizabeth 80, 97
George 69
Hal 37, 43
Hall 37
Hampton 61
Handy 27
Hannah 61
Harriet 7
Harriett 7, 27
Jack 69, 80, 97
James 29, 80
Jane 66, 74
Jasper 80, 97
Jenkins 80, 97
Jim 27, 69, 80, 97
Jin 29
John 80, 97
Jordan 88
Laura 69
Lina 29
Lou 26
Margaret 40
Maria 7
Marion 69
Martha 69, 80
Martin 69
Mary 21, 29, 78
Old Handy 16
Polly 66, 74, 80, 97
Rachel 7, 69
Randal 7
Reuben 26
Ridley 69
Sally 27
Sandy 80, 97
Sarah Ann 29

Simon	88	
Spencer	80, 97	
Sucky	48	
Sukey	12	
Susan	80, 97	
Tom	69	
Turner	12	
Wade	40	
Willie	7	
Winney	61, 63	
(F?)armer	29	
Nelson	22	
William E.	46	
Nelson & Goodall	38	
Nequs?		
James E.	14	
Nettles		
Harriett	86	
Hiram J.	12	
Nancy	79, 82, 86	
Zebulon	79, 82, 92	
Zebulon N.	86	
Nevins		
James	25, 37, 38, 60	
Newby		
James	89	
Nichol		
David H.	23	
Nickens		
William B.	40	
Wm. B.	43	
Nickins	40	
Norris		
William	65	
Nunly		
Nelson	37	
Nunnelly	60	
Olive		
Elizabeth	84	
Joseph	37, 60	
Samuel	55, 84	
Olly(?)	47	
Osborne		
Danl	75	
H D	75	
Parish	60	
James	37	
Polly	37	
Parris		
Shelby	89	
Pate		
Cebert	76, 87	
Cyrela	87	
E.P.	18	
Edward	18, 22, 23	
Edward P.	14, 18, 20, 21, 95	
Lucy	14	
Overton	64	
Sabe	87	
Sebert	87	
Willeroy	87	
Patterson		
E. M.	35	
F	75	
Robert	10, 14	
William	35	
William C.	14	
Patton		
B. S.	75	
David	9	
Paul		
Nancy	57	
Pennington		
Boon	33	
Perkins		
Joseph S.	8	
Nancy	8	
Petty	66	
Pharis	43	
Elizabeth	97	
James	82, 97	
Nathan	48, 50, 51, 92	
Pharris	7	
James	97	
Nancy	32	
Nathan	7	
Shelby	89	
Pillow		
Napoleon B.	78	
Plumlee		
Denton	10	
William	84	
Pointer		
John B.	54, 65, 76	
Polk		
James K.	5	
Poston		
Andrew	64	
James	85	
William	30, 42	
Postons		
James	83	
Presley		
Arena H.	13	
Elizabeth	13	
Sanders	13	
Price		
Campbell	77, 82	
Campbell B.	39	
Charles N.	64	
James	85, 96	
John	85, 96	
Josiah	75	
Michael	47	
Nancy	39	
Nathan	12, 39	
Nathan, heirs of	26	
Reuben	55	
Richard	88	
Solomon	75, 85	
Stephen	83, 84, 94	
Wm	75	
Proctor's Creek	80, 96	
Proctor's Creek	79	
Pucket		
J.	81	
Pursel		
Alfred	33	
Pursell		
James J.	93	
Putty		
Eliza	95	
William	11, 17, 27	
Wm	75	
Quarles		
James G.	5, 6	
James T.	7, 26, 49, 67, 73, 75, 76, 86, 88	
Jas. F.	27	
Raccoon Branch	7	
Ramsey		
Daniel	70	
John	70	
Ray		
Raulston	81, 82	
William	75	
William W.	82	
Rector		
David M.	75	
Sarah	15, 17, 26	
Reece & Morrell	17	
Reeves	72	
John	78	
Rich		
Joel	11	
John M.	67	
Richardson	72	
Joel	67	
John	78	

Sarah 85
William 85
William B. 26
Richie
   David 26
Richmond 33, 67
   Henry 6, 16, 45, 46, 48, 49, 59
   James H. 47, 53
   Jas H 75
   Jas H. 75
   John 49, 59, 73
   John M. 10, 16, 24, 27, 61, 67, 73
   John W. 31, 45, 59
   Joseph 45
   R. F. 75
   Robert 27, 59
   Sophia 34, 45
Richmonds Heirs 50, 53
Ridley
   B. L. 42, 43, 46, 54, 59, 82
   Bronfield 6
   Brownfield 5, 9, 12, 14, 17, 26, 34, 46, 50, 52, 54, 56, 59, 61, 62, 65, 67, 71, 76, 80, 85, 89, 91, 97
   Brownfield L. 6, 9, 16, 25, 30, 34, 36, 40, 50, 52, 56, 57, 61, 65, 67, 71, 76
   Elizabeth 79
Right
   John 33
Rison
   Richard 46
Ritter
   Henry 33
Roaring river 69, 73
Roberts 9, 96
   James 16, 27, 95
   Jefferson 65
   Letty 15, 23, 27, 35, 37, 46, 66, 74, 79, 84, 87, 90, 94
   Ridley 8, 9, 10, 16, 25, 56, 58, 68, 72, 78, 84, 86, 88, 94
   Thomas J. 84
   Zadock B. 58, 62
   Zadok N. B. 65
Robertson
   Phillip 33
Rocky Branch 69
Rodgers
   John 31
Rogers 20
   Clayton 65, 72, 77, 81, 90

John 14, 18, 19, 20, 21, 22, 38, 70, 72, 78
Jonathan 34
Matthew 57
Reuben 83
Reuben R. 72, 77
Reubin R 90, 91
Rogers 91
Roland
   John 12
Ross
   Alfred W. 15, 89
   Mary W. 75, 78, 89
Rucker
   George 44
   Lucy 44
Rutledge
   Polly 62
Rutlege
   Polly 78
Saddler
   Henry 43
Sadler
   Catron C. 85
   Garret 10, 23, 28, 35, 38, 43, 45, 96
   Garrett 79, 95
   Garrott 83, 88
   Henry 23, 32, 64, 72, 77, 88, 94, 95, 96
   Henry W. 28, 74
   Hiram 34
   John K. 74, 78, 88
   Lee 56
   Nelson 39, 55, 63, 65, 70, 72, 75, 76, 79, 81
Sadler's 27
Sanders
   Elisha Jr. 55
   Francis 46
Sargeant
   William 89
Savage's 80
Savage's line 96
Scanland 63
   Benjamin 64, 65, 81, 90, 97
   John 27, 30, 35, 39, 41, 46, 47, 50, 51, 52, 55, 58, 60, 62, 66, 67, 81
   William 10, 34, 51, 62, 65, 67, 69, 72, 77, 81
   Wm 58, 67, 74, 75
Scarlett

Angeline 58
John 57
Moses 57
Scruggs
   A 86
   Archibald 86
Settle 69
   Jane 6, 7, 24
   Joel 6, 7, 9
   Joel L. 6, 7
   Joel L., Heirs of 25, 26
   Joel W. 12, 73, 76, 88
   Joel, Heirs of 24
   L. B. 39
   LaFayette 6, 7
   Leroy B. 13, 28, 31, 32, 44, 47, 50
   Sewell 6, 7
   Sidney 7
   Sydney 6
   Tecumse 7
   Tecumseh 6
   Tipton 6, 7
Settle, Heirs of
   Joel L. 11
Settle's Heirs
   Settle's 6
Settle's Heirs 6
Shadden
   William 9
Shaden
   William 6
Sharr
   Christopher 8, 9, 11, 12, 42
Shaw
   Burckey 55, 74
   Cassy 12
   Christopher 23, 27, 31, 34, 38, 42, 55, 58, 59, 62, 68, 74
   G. W. C. 27
   George C. 23
   George W. C. 8, 28, 67, 88
   Jane 74
   Martha 8, 9, 10, 23, 27, 34, 65, 66, 88, 89
   Mary Jane 89
   Matilda 74
   Rebecca 8, 89
   Rebecca C. 55
   Saml 68
   Samuel 8, 23, 24, 28, 68
   Widow 16
Shaw(?)
   Christopher 42

Shepherd 28, 35
   Augustin 9, 11
   Augustine 5
   Augustus 5
   D. G. 53, 55
   David G. 5, 8, 23, 28, 55, 74, 96
   James 24
   James M. 5, 8, 55, 58, 62, 65, 68, 72, 74, 84, 88, 94, 95, 96
   Jesse George 8
   John 6
   Martin B. 8
   Mary L. 8
   Nancy 8
   Sarah 8
   Sarah Baker 5, 11
   Thomas 8
Simon 79
Simpson 82
   Thomas D. 71, 72, 77, 82, 83, 92
   Thos D 75
Sizemore
   Calaway 41, 79, 86
   Calloway 75
   Caloway 41
Sloan
   John A. 23
Smith 9, 69
   Col. 34
   J. W., Col. 28
   Peter 75
   Thomas 25, 46, 51, 65
Smyrna Meeting House 27
Sommers
   John 62, 68, 78
   Margaret 78
Sophia 45
Spivey
   Joseph 55
Spring Branch 34
Spurlock
   James A. 57, 67, 72, 84, 85, 86, 88, 91
Stafford
   Anna 86
   jOHN 82
   John 17, 86, 92
   Joseph 69
Stamps
   John 69
Stanton
   Champ 9, 47
Stephenson

Volney S. 86, 97
Stewart
   Hugh 9
   Reece C. 27, 74
Stone
   Bennett 96
   J. A. 96
   J. N. 27
   Joshua R. 6, 17
   S. E. 27
   Sam E. 32
   Samuel E. 10, 13, 17, 28, 35, 40, 45, 47, 49, 66, 73, 76
   Temperance 33, 89, 93
   William 57
Stone and Settle 10
Stone?
   John A. 14
Stypes
   Rebecca 54
Sullivan
   Samuel 27
Sutton
   Elizabeth 78
   Elizabeth Dill 62
Swearingen
   Miranda 17
   William 17
Sweat
   Robert 48
Taylor
   Absalom 65
   Elvis 61, 65, 66
   George W. 89
   Henry 75
   James 75
   Martha 88, 89
   Mary S. 83
Tennessee 5
   Bagdad 25
   Carthage 31
   Celina 24, 70, 97
   Cumberland River 6, 7
   Davidson County 47, 92
   DeKalb County 81
   Doe Creek 8
   Granville 6, 24, 25, 31, 40, 43, 53, 64, 66, 74
   Highland 25, 43
   Horse Point Branch................13
   Kinderhook 97
   Macon County 49
   Marion County 66

   Martin's Creek 6
   Memphis 75
   Nashville 5, 64, 71, 74, 86, 89, 94, 95
   Putnam County 16, 17, 25, 29, 30, 34
   Roaring River 13
   Smith County 17, 47, 92
   Sparta 41, 49, 67, 79
   White Plains 24
Terry
   Carr 17, 27
   Elijah 9
Thaxton
   Z. B. 95
Thompson
   Prudence 75
Thornton
   Burton 75
Tinsley
   James 59, 68, 72
Tolbert 36
   John H. 41
Toney
   Elijah 11
   William 55, 57
Trapp
   John 9
Tucker
   Henry L. 9, 12
Turkey Creek 38
Turney
   Saml. 71, 84
   Samuel 5, 29, 41, 55, 60, 66, 73, 83, 84
   Turney 94
Ursery
   Lucy 11, 47
Vaden
   Saml T. 47
   Samuel L. 58
   Samuel T. 45
Van Hooser 36
Vance
   L R 92
   Lewis N. 46
   Lewis R. 33, 38, 41, 46, 51, 59, 63, 64, 65, 67, 68, 74, 81, 92
   William R. 83
VanHooser
   John 51
Vaughn
   Edward 85, 90, 92

Vinson
    James   82, 97
Vitatoe
    Stephen   75
Walker
    Elizabeth   60
    Joseph H.   40
    Joseph J. 7, 27, 31, 34, 43, 50, 55, 58
    Joseph L.   7
    W. C.   97
    William C.   80
Wallace
    James B.   91
Walters Road   16
War Trace Creek 70, 75
Washburn   68, 86
    B B   88
    Benjamin B. 46, 77, 85, 96
Wassom
    Andrew   64, 71
Watson
    Stewart   29
Webb
    George W.   32, 34
Welch
    George   56, 61, 71
    Jesse   56
    John R.   33
    Richard   75
    William P.   56
West
    John   65, 76
White
    Benjamin C.   90
    Colunor(?)   88
    George   70
    Joshua   57
    Mary   81, 90
    Robert 28, 31, 36, 38, 43
Whitley   69
    Anderson   7
    Andrew   7
Williams
    Benj. E.   27
    Benjamin E. 17, 35, 37, 43, 49
    Dorcas   63, 78
    Emanuel   63, 78
    John 5, 9, 15, 25, 28, 30, 88
    Joseph R.   25
    Thomas L.   30, 32
Williams & Clark   25
Williamson
    James   44, 88
Wilson   16
    E.J.   17
    James S.   25
    John   25
    John A.   10
    Saml   50
    Saml. T.   52
    Samuel T. 10, 24, 25, 52
    Thomas G.   54
    Thomas M.   47
    William H. 10, 24, 25, 50, 52
Witcher
    Daniel K.   94, 95
    Tandy K.   87, 93
    William P. 87, 93, 96
Wood   14
    Jackson   16
    Jackson T. 61, 67, 73
    William   61, 67
Woodfolk
    William W.   37
Woodrum   90
    Jacob   85
    William   85
Woods
    Jackson   10
Wooton
    Thomas W.   77
Wossom
    Andrew   57, 64
    Andrew Jr.   57
Wright
    Martha   66, 68, 72
Young 19, 22, 82, 83, 84
    Allen   86
    Betsy   14
    Elizabeth   35
    I.   49
    James 9, 10, 14, 15, 17, 18, 19, 20, 21, 22, 26, 30, 33, 35, 37, 38, 39, 44, 57, 59, 92
    John H. 78, 89, 91, 97
    Marlin   65
    Merlin 7, 11, 14, 17, 24, 26, 27, 29, 30, 35, 43, 50, 55, 63, 72, 75, 76, 79, 81, 83, 84, 85, 88, 93, 95
    Oliver   87
    Robert   69, 73
___ford
    Isaac   34
___ver
    William R.   27

Made in the USA
Coppell, TX
22 June 2020